NOT ON ANY MAP

Essays on Postcoloniality and
Cultural Nationalism

Edited by Stuart Murray

'It is not down in any map; true places never are.'
(Herman Melville, *Moby Dick*: Chapter 12)

UNIVERSITY
of
EXETER
PRESS

First published in 1997 by
University of Exeter Press
Reed Hall, Streatham Drive
Exeter, Devon EX4 4QR
UK

British Library Cataloguing in Publication Data
A catalogue record of this book is
available from the British Library

ISBN 0 85989 468 1

Typeset in 11/12pt Monotype Bembo
by Kestrel Data, Exeter

Printed and bound in Great Britain by
T. J. International Ltd.

For Valérie

Contents

Acknowledgements

The idea for this collection began over a series of discussions with Kate Bowles in 1993, and I am very grateful to Kate for all her help and assistance in its planning. I would also want to thank Richard Maltby, who supported the project from its inception and was a constant source of encouragement. Jim Livesey and John Nash read over parts of the manuscript and I appreciate their comments and support. Others who helped, at differing times and in differing ways, include Shirley Chew, David Dabydeen, Emily Hedges, Neil Hegarty, Roger Little and Amanda Piesse. The Arts and Social Sciences Benefactions Fund at Trinity College Dublin provided financial support which was very much appreciated. Lastly, I would like to thank Simon Baker, Richard Willis and Genevieve Davey at the University of Exeter Press for their tolerance, guidance and encouragement.

Dublin, 1997

The cover illustration is a map of the Pacific Ocean by Pieter Goos (*c.* 1660), and is reproduced by kind permission of Jonathan Potter Ltd, London.

Notes on Contributors

Graham Barwell is a senior lecturer in the Department of English at the University of Wollongong, Australia. His publications in the study of electronic texts include a report on the success of electronic scholarly publishing for a working group of the Australian Vice-Chancellors Committee. As joint electronic editor for the Academy Electronic Editions Project, Australian Academy of the Humanities, he is currently preparing a prototype electronic edition of Marcus Clarke's *His Natural Life*.

Kate Bowles lectures in screen studies in the Department of English at the University of Wollongong, Australia. She is completing a thesis on the representation of suburbia in Australian film and television.

Wilson Harris started his career as a surveyor, for twenty years leading many survey parties into the Guyanese interior for mapping and geomorphological purposes, and becoming Senior Surveyor to the Guyanese Government. Resident in England since 1959, he has been visiting Professor at universities in the West Indies, Canada, England, the United States and Australia, and recipient of honorary degrees and awards which include the 1992 *Premio Mondello dei Cinque Continenti*. Among his more than twenty novels are *The Guyana Quartet* (1960–63; reprinted as one volume in 1985), *The Carnival Trilogy* (1985–90; reprinted as one volume in 1993, *Resurrection at Sorrow Hill* (1993) and *Jonestown* (1996). His essays and critical writings include *Tradition, the Writer and Society* (1967), *The Womb of Space: The Cross-Cultural Imagination* (1983), and *The Radical Imagination* (1992).

Paul Hyland is a poet and travel writer whose most recent works about Portugal were two programmes for BBC Radio 3: *Crick in the Neck* (1994) and *Once-and-Future Portugal* (1994). He is co-author of the *Babel Guide* to the *Fiction of Portugal, Brazil and Africa* in English translation (1995). His last published travel books are *Indian Balm* (1994; paperback, 1995) and *Backwards Out of the Big World, a Portuguese Journey* (1996). His most recent book of poems is *Kicking Sawdust* (1995).

Declan Kiberd is Professor of Anglo-Irish Literature in the Department of English at University College, Dublin. One of the most prolific commentators on Irish writing, he has published a number of studies, in both English and Irish, on Irish literature as well as other postcolonial literatures. His books include *Synge and the Irish Language* (1979; 2nd edition 1993), *Anglo-Irish Attitudes* (1984), the Penguin Annotated Student's Edition of *Ulysses* (1992), *Idir Dhá Chaultúr* (1993) and *Inventing Ireland: Literature of the Modern Nation* (1995).

Sarah Lawson Welsh is a lecturer in English and Postcolonial Literature at the University College of Ripon and York St. John in the UK. She works on issues of postcolonial theory, cultural nationalism, language politics (particularly Creole lingusitics) and oral poetics, with a specific emphasis on the black diaspora in the United Kingdom. She is the co-editor of *The Routledge Reader in Caribbean Literature* (1996).

Máire ní Fhlathúin lectures in the Department of English at the University of Nottingham in the UK. She works on issues of colonial and postcolonial literature and theory, particularly Anglo-Indian fiction. She has contributed an essay on Salman Rushdie in *Authorship: From Plato to the Postmodern: A Reader* (1995), edited by Sean Burke.

Powhiri Rika-Heke claims Ngati Hine, Ngapuhi, Te Rarawa, Ngati Kahu and Te Aupouri descent. Currently working at the University of Osnabrück in Germany, on study leave from the University of Waikato, New Zealand, she has been a social worker in the Department of Social Welfare in New Zealand and from 1988–89 was the Private Secretary for the Minister for Women's Affairs in the New Zealand Government. Having worked as a policy analyst and educational adviser on issues of race and education in New Zealand, she has studied and published material on Aboriginal Australia and Native Canada. She has also published creative work and studies of Maori genealogy.

Dominic Thomas is an Assistant Professor of French and Francophone Literature at the University of Notre Dame, South Bend, Indiana, USA. He obtained his Ph.D. from Yale University with a dissertation titled 'New Writings for New Times: Nationalism in Congolese Literature,' He is currently working on a book on Francophone sub-Saharan African Theatre.

Ravi S. Vasudevan works at the Centre for the Study of Developing Societies in Delhi, India. He was previously a Fellow at the Nehru Memorial Museum and Library, and is a member of the guest faculties of the Film and Television Institute of India and the Department of Film Studies at Jadavpur University. He has published articles on Indian nationalism and cinema in a variety of journals, including the *Indian Economic and Social History Review, Screen* and *Third Text*. He is currently completing a book on representations of society and nation in the Indian cinema of the 1940s and 1950s.

Mark Williams is a senior lecturer in the Department of English at Canterbury University, Christchurch, New Zealand. He has written extensively on New Zealand and other twentieth-century writing. He was co-editor of the journal *Landfall* (1986–1992) and editor of *The Caxton Press Anthology: New Zealand Poetry, 1972–1986* (1987) and *The Source of the Song: New Zealand Writers on Catholicism* (1996). He is co-editor of *Dirty Silence: Language and Literature in New Zealand* (1991), *In the Same Room: Conversation with New Zealand Writers* (1992), *The Radical Imagination: Lectures and Talks by Wilson Harris* (1992) and *Opening the Book: New Essays on New Zealand Writing* (1995). His study of recent New Zealand fiction, *Leaving the Highway: Six Contemporary New Zealand Novelists*, appeared in 1990, and his critical study, *Patrick White*, appeared in 1993.

Introduction

Stuart Murray

I

This book is about the ideology and the practice of cultural nationalism in postcolonial contexts. It has a number of purposes. Firstly it offers a wide-ranging analysis of the effects of nationalism in the former colonies of the world and the old colonial centres. The essays in this collection come from a variety of disciplines, and each of them is rooted firmly in the local conditions it seeks to articulate: the specifics and complexities of the organization of settler and bicultural nationalisms in New Zealand are a long way from the debates surrounding the issues of immigration from ex-British colonies into the United Kingdom. Likewise, the essays make use of a number of theoretical approaches. But they do so in the belief that there is much to be gained from the subsequent juxtaposition of these localities; that, when we choose to put these postcolonial contexts together, we will be able to approach some wider conclusions as to the nature of nationalism and post-coloniality more generally.

The discursive method of the collection points to its second objective: to illuminate the ever increasing complexity displayed by the modern manifestations of the national and the postcolonial. That complexity can only be addressed by multidisciplined studies which recognize the necessity to move beyond traditional methodological boundaries. As these essays show, the nature of the modern postcolonial world order involves the latest innovations in technology, contemporary displays of State power, the reworking and understanding of history and myth, as well as the various aesthetics that have evolved as forms of representation of these disparate cultures. If we are to understand this most current of issues, we need to chart its varying forms in all their multiplicities.[1]

The diversity of the essays in this collection aims to fulfill a deliberate function. With such a massive amount of potential material suggested by the terms of the subtitle, it seemed important to incorporate as many views as possible. This extends not only to the various geographies covered by the essays, but also their form and authors. Wilson Harris, Paul Hyland and Powhiri Rika-Heke are primarily creative writers, and the juxtaposition of these pieces with the other, more traditionally critical studies attempts to register the relevance of different voices—personal, creative, critical—on the subject of the postcolonial nation.

The term 'postcolonial' itself seems, at times, to encompass material and methods that are extremely diverse, with a potential to obscure the use of the word in a constructive manner. In reality, this is because the discipline of postcolonial studies has gone out of its way to keep the label full of the complexities and ambivalence that define the nature of culture contact and the subsequent histories of areas of the world reacting to the shared heritage of European colonization. As used here, postcoloniality represents an appropriate category of conceptualization that aims to embrace the many forms of experience that colonization produced. As an umbrella term, it includes analyses of the processes by which decolonizing literatures 'write back' to the colonial centre, sociological and anthropological accounts of the ways cultures developed following culture contact, and historiographical interrogations of the very ways in which history is written. These are just some of the forms the postcolonial takes, and the flexibility of the term allows for the reading of these multiple effects in conjunction with each other. That much said, it is important to stress that postcoloniality is not simply a celebration of plurality or eclecticism. What all of these diverse methods have in common is that they are a response to the physical fact of colonization and its subsequent material manifestations. Much contemporary post-colonial theory comes from movements that were expressly anti-colonial in focus, and while it is not the case that post-coloniality is purely oppositional, this base in cultural praxis is vital to the workings of the discipline.

Because of its multiple outlook, postcolonial criticism has been particularly successful in bridging (and breaking down) the divides that exist between differing methods of cultural analysis. The recognition that the writing of the history of culture contact has

been the privilege of the colonizer has led to important conclusions about questions of power in the construction of history.
The very creation of historical narratives becomes one of the
myriad forms taken by colonization. History and Literature merge
in textuality, enabling the study of the various devices by which
they try to 'normalize' their accounts of events. Similarly, an issue
such as slavery sees the contextualization of economics within
analyses of race. In this way, postcoloniality sees sociology become
a form of textual analysis and literary studies a kind of geography.
But, at all times, the discipline is concerned to map or chart (the
exploration metaphor is itself a deliberate appropriation of a
language of colonization) the various forms of lived experience in
postcolonial culture. Hence the adaptation of this collection's title
from Herman Melville's *Moby Dick*. Itself part and parcel of the
writing of the Pacific into the American consciousness of
the nineteenth century, the novel points towards the necessary
recognition of the forms of lived experience that have yet to be
mapped.

These multiple methods and experiences inform the other key
term in the book's subtitle, namely that of 'cultural nationalism'.
In a strict sociological sense, nationalism is usually defined by
central factors that point to the way a community seeks to achieve
coherence within a nation state. These factors include the notion
of citizenship, the payment of taxes and often the necessity of
military service, among others. They are the core practices of a
national community. By using the phrase 'cultural nationalism'
this book seeks to widen the scope to include not only socio-
political manifestations, but also such factors as the images of the
nation in the media, or the myths of the national that exist in the
popular imagination. These examples of the national may seem
less tangible than the classic sociological criteria, but even a cursory
examination of any nation reveals that much of the power of
nationalism is bound up in activities that lack strict definitions.
The notion of patriotism is explicitly amorphous, an appeal to the
emotions. It is exactly these kind of displays of the national that
the methodology of postcoloniality can explore. As I will discuss
later, the two terms 'nation' and 'culture', although yoked together
here, have an equally strong history of opposition, and in the
contemporary world can appear as rivals in any discussion of
collective identity. 'Cultural nationalism' is then a phrase like
'postcoloniality', one that needs to be interrogated even as it is
used.

3

II

The modern world order is a postcolonial order. Empires of all kinds have dissolved over the last fifty years, not simply the last manifestations of the many European colonial empires, but also the coalitions founded on shared political ideologies and financial dependence. The fragmentation of these blocs is matched by the increasing move towards either new nation states or area communities, often based on economic ties that seek to redraw old relationships. While not all of these instances are the direct result of colonialism, the methods of postcoloniality—concentration on exile, separatism, self-assertion, struggle—are useful in charting the new languages of location. As old boundaries vanish, new ones emerge, and are contested. The current focus on issues of immigration in so many former imperial powers displays the extent to which the very idea of 'the border' is one that is fixed in our minds, and that these borders are sites of cultural contest, positions which remind us that the legacies of colonialism permeate our modern experience. From tourism to the marketing of novels, the manifestation of culture reminds us that the imperial division between a secure, stable 'us' and an inferior, unstable, exploitable 'them' no longer applies.

This postcolonial order is one characterized by fluidity and hybridity, a cultural criss-crossing, what has been referred to as the 'in-between'.[2] The colonial age depended on at least the appearance of distance: a belief that Europe was the central repository of knowledge, and therefore power, and that colonies existed to supply what Europe needed, whether that be the material goods of the Tropics or an object for the various cultural and social ideologies the imperial powers exported[3]. In truth, the colonial relationship was multi-faced and complex. The colony was not simply the receptacle of imperial rule in terms of force, it was also the Other by which a newly modernizing Europe sought to define itself.[4] But the surface manifestation was that of a simple divide, the colonizer and the colonized. The postcolonial world both borrows and destroys the essentialized nature of this duality in a complicated system of inheritance. In the same way that people move between states and emigrants become immigrants, attitudes and knowledge become similarly elastic. The aesthetic codes that govern our appreciation of art are no longer the same as they were earlier this century. Our histories of colonialism, of slavery and the issues surrounding race and gender

4

have been redrawn in ways which would have been unthinkable even thirty years ago. The vocabulary of knowledge, and the forms in which it is couched, provide ever changing maps for where we are.

The idea and concept of the nation was one built into the foundations of European expansion from the eighteenth century onwards, forming the genesis of the colonial process. The voyages of exploration, the mapping of the blank areas of the world, coincided with the huge upheavals in society, politics and culture that saw the development of European modernity. As the modern nation state developed in Europe, it found in the spatial locations of exploration objects and peoples by which it could continue its consolidation. This dynamic became vital in determining questions of individual and social identities in postcolonial cultures because it posited what we might term an interrogative gaze on the non-European areas of the world. Explorations in Africa, Asia and the Pacific sought to record the cultures they encountered, and to use these cultures as a pole against which Europeans could practise self-definition. For their part, the indigenous populations who were the subjects of such 'discoveries' began to operate more and more within the world systems, the paradigms of military force, government and representation, of the Europeans.

As the period of exploration and culture contact quickly gave way to that of colonialism and the systematized processes of exploitation, the idea of the nation as a social and cultural unit worked to preserve the duality that the colonial centre required. This is the nation working in what Benedict Anderson in his classic formulation of nationalism terms a *limited* sphere, the European mind working in terms of a unity of knowledge. Not only could the cultures encountered be 'known', but these very processes of knowledge aided in the ordering of the developing nation back in Europe. No person in England wanted any of these newly encountered peoples to actually *become* English, but the discussion and classification of places and peoples encountered in the eighteenth and nineteenth centuries contributed towards the increasing solidification of English, and British, identities.[5]

As a result of this kind of limitation during the period of high colonialism, cultural interchange, in the form of trade, education policies, forms of government and legislation was not perceived as a process as such, but as a transfer between two bounded and separate areas, each with their own definitions supplied by the colonizer.[6] The knowledge that one was superior to the other was vital for the success of this colonial discourse. For this discourse to work, a new conception of the world was needed. The idea of the world that emerged during the period of colonization was of a space that can be systematized and systematically represented. It could be subject to law and it offered an almost unlimited amount of new possibilities. In the mid-nineteenth-century European mind, the only limit to these possibilities was a boundary defined by *proof*. The empirical nature of the universe, the evidence that could be gathered, was the key to understanding. It seemed that all manner of new relations based on trade, religion, morality, or definitions of the social were possible if the world could be thought of in such terms of homogeneity.

The voyages of expansion in the eighteenth century were embedded within a version of Enlightenment thought that was more plastic than the homogeneity and empiricism described above[7], but it is still easy to see how the journeys of exploration provided the space for the development of this ideology. The workings of Western expansion laid the base for the era of national colonialism that was to follow.[8] When Columbus approached Cuba in October 1492 to claim the 'Indies' for Spain, the Spain he had in mind was essentially that of the monarch, an idea of power that has little to do with a national community. By the time Wallis waded onto a Tahitian beach in June 1767, or Cook visited New Zealand in March 1770, culture contact, even as it displayed the kind of anthropological interest in other cultures that was very foreign to voyages before the eighteenth century, carried within it an outline of nationalism. In the nineteenth century the idea of the colonial and the national become fused into a complicated rhetoric of location. Such rhetoric developed to a point where, in 1902, J.A. Hobson—in a view that was typical of his era—could justify imperialism as the expansion of nationalism, and, as Edward Said notes, imply that '*expansion* was the more important of the two terms, since "nationality" was a fully formed, fixed quantity, whereas a century before it was still in the process of being *formed*, at home and abroad as well'.[9] Particularly during the nineteenth century, the colonial process worked to consolidate fully the idea of the European nation as given and immutable. In the words of John Stuart Mill, the foremost articulator of a mid-nineteenth-century utilitarian nationalism, 'That alone which causes any material interests to exist, which alone enables any body of human beings to exist as a society, is national character . . . A philosophy of laws and institutions, not founded on a philosophy of national character, is an absurdity.'[10]

The nation was in an evolving form, modifying the *natio* at home and operating as a unit of control and hegemony during a time of cultural expansion. It is easy to see the attractiveness of this concept to the European colonizers. Not only could a cultural distance be maintained, but the presence of an Other *unseen* by the majority of the European population offered the opportunity to solidify emerging identities *within* Europe. This version of nationalism was thus interwoven with the development of democracy in nineteenth-century Europe, and the emerging concept of 'the people'.[11]

In the hands of those Europeans actually involved in the colonizing process, such ideologies were necessarily revised by the specific local conditions they encountered. As Máire ní Fhlathúin shows in her study of the effects English writing on India had on Anglo-Indian identity, this discourse of colonialism resulted in the codification of much of the colonial world, but within a two-way process that operated on levels which corrupted the seeming stability of such codification. England abroad *could not be* the same as England at home, even though the rhetoric and icons might be identical. In terms of legislation and civil government, but also in terms of myth, it was natural to use the nation during colonial expansion, but when it was divorced from the territory it named, its representation and power became problematic.

If the unit of nation was one that came naturally to the European colonizing process, it is also understandable how that unit should be the one employed when the colonizing power, often beset by the increasing cost of maintaining colonies and facing growing resistance to its presence, sought to transfer colonial administration to a trained elite within the colony itself. Whether it involved the granting of colony status to New Zealand through the Treaty of Waitangi in 1840, or the new political identities shaped by so many new African states since 1950, this 'independence' was a situation fraught with the tensions of power. Much of the ambivalence over nationalism within postcolonial discourse has been created by this recognition that, despite the pre-colonial existence of the non-Western *natio* based on concepts of ethnic community, a predominantly *European* model of evolution has been employed whenever an ex-colony, often in a context of anti-colonial politics, has wished to assert its own identity. The fear has been that, in utilizing the model of the nation, the postcolonial culture will become locked into the European paradigm, capable of only repeating the structures and vocabulary of a nationalism founded during the colonial relationship.[12]

Yet it is true that this assertion of identity and of selfhood, one of the most important aspects to postcoloniality, has often been framed within the ideology and activity of the nation. As Mark Williams demonstrates in his analysis of the politics of differing New Zealand nationalisms, the national ideology may have far reaching consequences, continuing to dominate postcolonial articulation long after the process of decolonization appears to have been achieved. And, as is the case in Australia, the presence of a continued awareness of the national in governmental *policy* can bring a number of rewards (and debates) to the culture industry within the state. The recent critical and commercial success of Australian cinema has its roots in the governmental funding policies of the 1970s, a time when ideas of the national image on screen were hotly contested.[13] In his study of the versions of the national in contemporary Indian cinema, Ravi S. Vasudevan sees the films themselves combining complicated ideas of space, form and national narratives in a desire to cohere with a sense of national integrity. The nation found in the contemporary Indian cinema is not a simple reflection of society. Rather it is elliptical and fragmented, a mix of local politics and language, the inheritance of Hollywood, and ever-changing notions of group and individual identities. The desire for a bounded, linear and empirical version of selfhood that is so strong in many postcolonial societies finds in nationalism a set of useful ideological tools, yet the consequences of these ideological moves actually produce multiple and often contradictory images of the national self.

III

The nation that emerges out of the colonial process, whether that of the colonizer or the colonized, is no simplistic central totality. The processes of cultural exchange are too varied and hybrid to allow for any simple dualities, where a malevolent colonizer can be set against a wronged colonized. While we have to understand the manifestations of privilege and oppression, of opposition and struggle, we must do so within the context of the complexities of postcolonial epistemology. The hybrid nature of nationalism in the context of postcoloniality, the mix of different heritages, points to some fundamental tensions. The three main phases of nation building—Latin America in the nineteenth century, Europe after the 1918 Treaty of Versailles, and the post-1945 moves to self-determination in Asia, Africa and the Caribbean—are all due, in part, to the break-up of Empire.[14] The national unit is clearly set in opposition to the internationalism of the imperial process, yet the very concept of 'postcoloniality' also has clear internationalist ambitions. Postcoloniality stresses a common heritage of colonial oppression and subsequent decolonization, of the struggle for the right to produce, rather than consume, images of self and the local. Yet even while this can be seen to unite a myriad of cultures across the world, the idea of the national unit *needs* other similar units by which to define itself. The difficulties encountered in negotiations within the United Nations, particularly since the 1960s, show the stresses and strains of working with both a national and international model. The creation of the United Nations Conference on Trade and Development saw attempts by postcolonial nations to group together in order to move towards the shared goals of non-alignment in the cold war, the eradication of racism and colonialism, and modernization in economics and technology. Similarly, much of the debate about the role of the writer or artist in the newly independent African states of the 1950s and 1960s was conducted within the terms of 'Africanism', where the heritage of a shared colonial language and the growing availability of modern technological communications created a regional, as well as a national, dimension to the issues of cultural decolonization. Contemporary invocations of 'Arab' or 'Islamic' nationalism function in the same way.[15]

These fundamental tensions are explored in different ways by both Declan Kiberd and Sarah Lawson Welsh. The recent history of Ireland displays how an aggressive decolonizing nationalism may come to repeat the structures of the authority it overthrows. Using the classic model developed by Frantz Fanon, Kiberd shows how the achievement of Irish statehood led to the development of national narratives that were constricting and conservative in their proclamation of the national self. The further twist of Ireland's position *within Europe* has led (in the history of the European Union) to a particular confrontation between the rhetoric of decolonization, complete with its emphasis on struggle and liberation, and that of an integrated, possibly federal, Europe defined in terms of a classic liberal package of free trade and a lack of national boundaries. Sarah Lawson Welsh shows how the issues surrounding immigration complicate national articulation even more. The movement into Europe by people from the ex-colonies is one of the prime consequences of colonialism, and Lawson Welsh's analysis of the Caribbean communities in the United Kingdom show how the false consciousness of colonialism, the manufactured positions of colonizer and colonized, are challenged when the differing cultures inhabit the same nation space. Not only do the immigrant communities preserve many manifestations of their cultures (keeping the nation alive when it is within another), but their critique of the old colonial power forces a re-evaluation of the national narratives formed by the colonial process itself.

So, even as the new postcolonial nations and immigrant communities within the former centres of Empire seek to reclaim the right to articulate their own pasts, they move towards changes in the definitions of contemporary and future nationalisms. The need to write history is one that unites both postcoloniality and nationalism. The former wishes to correct the false image created by the warped logic of the colonial process. The latter seeks to provide mythologies to strengthen the sense of a collective self. Clearly, the two can, and do, combine. Yet, as these narratives are written, they are in a process of continual modification by new developments, particularly in global technology and economics. The advent of global trading areas and regional interest blocs, such as the European Union and the North American Free Trade Agreement (NAFTA), or the South Pacific Forum and the Association of South East Asian Nations (ASEAN), have necessitated the creation of regional identities. Such identities not only acknowledge the benefits of shared information and resources, but also display that the continuing complexities of the global market mean that geographical isolation is no defence from the workings of the international monetary system. A stock market crash in London, Tokyo or New York will influence the economies of every nation.[16]

Equally, developments in technology offer the potential for a radical critique of the classical workings of nationalism. In his study of contemporary Portugal, one of the first European nations to engage in colonization, Paul Hyland notes how the relationship between colonizer and colonized can become inverted when the modern culture of technology, combined with a shared language, replaces older forms of political and military dominance. Hyland finds Portugal, now one of the poorest of European countries, addicted to Brazilian soap operas and looking to its former colony to provide a regeneration of both language and image within the Portuguese diaspora. Technology is the vehicle for this kind of interchange, increasingly making it possible for media systems to cross national boundaries and offer what appears to be a common cultural language. Graham Barwell and Kate Bowles, concentrating on Canada and Australia, point to the ramifications of the juxtaposition of nationalism and the Internet, a site of particular conflict when confronting the difficult questions of law and censorship. In both of these cases, the idea of the border, that most sacred of national boundaries, is forced to come under interrogation. In the post-1945 period, over 100 new nations have been created, yet these issues indicate a fear on the part of some that a potential 'imperialism of technology' seems to offer a vision of hegemonic control greater than that manifested during the period of high colonialism.

These are the complexities of contemporary postcolonial praxis, yet it would be a mistake to see the national unit as being in real danger of being swept away completely by the growing international possibilities offered by increasing communication. Despite the utopian claims by some of its champions, the information superhighway does not offer access for all. In many cases postcolonial nations contain uneasy combinations of the technologically advanced and the heritage of sub-national and sub-societal cultures. The image of an Amazonian Amerindian with a camcorder may evoke possibilities of a bright new age of shared resources, but it points equally to the real cleavages that exist in cultures forced to map the super-modern and the pre-modern upon one another. In Powhiri Rika-Heke's discussion of the identity constructions of Maori within New Zealand (a situation sometimes referred to as 'Fourth World'), the definitions of an indigenous collective self create irruptive challenges to the settler nation state, and its own version of a postcolonial self. In every case, indigenous cultures within postcolonial settler societies find themselves excluded from the decision processes that are central to the state. Their subsequent declarations of nationhood as a non-Western nationalism based on genealogy and descent ties function not only as other sub-national units do in, say, the assertion of ethnicity, but point to the history of pre-contact and raise questions about the legal and moral legitimacy of the present national formation. This sense of the national is a long way from the genesis of the modern European nation state in the eighteenth century.[17]

IV

'It is nationalism which engenders nations', writes Ernest Gellner in his classic study *Nations and Nationalism*, 'not the other way round.'[18] The nation state as a unit is a product of modernity and the last 250 years, yet in its narratives and mythologies it projects itself back into history, creating accounts of origin and a sense of a 'timeless' occupation of the national space. Clearly, postcolonial nations, founded following a colonial heritage of one form or another, cannot simply duplicate these moves of nationalist ideology without difficulty. For the ex-dominions of the British Empire, such as Australia, South Africa, Canada or New Zealand, the account of settlement cannot stretch back into an unbroken past. Somewhere the nature of the rupture with the colonizing power must be confronted. Equally, as Dominic Thomas details in his study of identity formation in francophone nationalist Africa, the politically independent states of postcolonial Africa inherited borders that were colonial constructions following the 1885 Berlin Conference of European powers. These borders, mixing ethnic and linguistic groups, *created* national spaces where none existed before. In both these examples, of settler and non-settler versions of postcolonial cultures, the resulting nations and nationalisms display considerable variations on the model of nationalism as it evolved in Europe. Indeed, it has been suggested that the recent move away from a theoretical and intellectual celebration of nationalism within Europe might be in itself a reaction to the growing centrality of the ideology within emerging postcolonial culture.[19]

Certainly, postcoloniality has offered a powerful re-imagining of the nation. The differing *versions* of the national produced in postcolonial contexts disrupt the seeming stability and function of the inherited European concept. These take different forms. Singapore has emerged from its colonial past to remodel itself as a nation state that is fundamentally corporate, combining the national space and national institutions with an aggressive capitalism. The result is a considerable reworking of both the colonial past and the ideology of decolonization. It is somewhat ironic that Singapore, along with other South-East Asian nations, is now seen from within Europe as a threat to the prevailing capitalistic order, an order which, of course, owes much to the centrality of control inherited by European countries from their colonial pasts.

Elsewhere critical re-imaginings have been successful in promoting new theories of the nation with which we might re-read histories of the colonial era and come to new conceptualizations of the postcolonial present. The idea of the nation as a narrative, as a text that might unfold its secrets and complexities, has produced significant insights into the workings of the national.[20] It reminds us that 'the national' does not function on its own during its development, but is entwined within other categories—ideas of gender, of power, of social organization. So nations might be seen as social 'bodies', or as sites for ideological disputes.

One of the most significant aspects to emerge from this debate is the tension between ideas of the national and of the cultural, a tension that is even in the sub-title of this collection. Often nationalism's historical association with violence (with fascism as an extreme of this), as well as the rise in profile of issues of ethnicity and group affiliation, has resulted in communities choosing to highlight boundaries of culture in ways different to that of the classic definition of the nation. In actuality, though recent discussion of this fact has much to do with current ideas surrounding the word 'culture', this tension has always existed within the development of the social collective during the modern era. Communities, and minorities in particular, excluded from the prevailing image of the nation have often found in the notion of culture a method of self-assertion. Cultural practices and habits offer sometimes 'unofficial' versions of group and individual identity. The cultural does not come after national formation, like some sort of addition, but has been a continual presence in the narrative of national formation. With the demise of Empire and the increasing movement of both people and information across the globe, certain definitions of nationalism (particularly those laying a heavy emphasis on geography) have been placed under pressure. Cultural imagining may be based on event and habit, often the standard building blocks of nationalism. But it also includes key concepts such as desire, movement and the ability to transgress national boundaries, concepts which offer alternatives to the imagining of the national space. In the contemporary postcolonial present, the fluidity of the idea of the cultural, and the discussions of its trajectories, offers another point of departure in coming to terms with identity. To criticize such developments as being ahistorical because they do not tell us who ended up where and how is to run the risk of losing the new perceptions they do give us. It is also to fail to grasp the extent to which this kind of postcolonial critique challenges the normative boundaries of cultural interpretation.[21]

This book ends with just such a postcolonial re-imagining, this one taken from the fiction of Wilson Harris. Ever since the publication of his first novel *The Palace of the Peacock* in 1960, and particularly in his first four novels which constitute an interrogation and exploration of his home nation Guyana, Harris has produced versions of place that seek to come to terms with the multiplicities of the postcolonial situation.[22] For Harris the postcolonial nation cannot throw off its colonial history. Such history is too deeply imbedded within the cultural fabric to allow for an easy adversarial decolonizing. Instead, he seeks to portray the traces that these different histories, colonial and postcolonial, produce, and to articulate the ways in which this kind of vision challenges the various received wisdoms with which we divide societies and cultures. Nations are not fictions, though they contain elements which are clearly fictional. Harris' fiction here is the last of the angles used to address the status and resonances of the postcolonial and the national.

V

If, to continue using the metaphor of colonial expansion, this collection is an exploration of the issues surrounding postcolonial cultural nationalisms, its conclusions—the end of its journey—display the centrality of both the postcolonial and the national to the vital issue of identity formation. All of these essays illustrate that the processes of European expansion, the decolonizing responses to that expansion, and the new imperialisms created in the wake of these activities are central to the activities of contemporary modernity. This asserts that postcoloniality is not simply a question of geography. The workings of colonialism, particularly in the nineteenth century, influenced social development all over the world, not simply in territories which can be directly labelled colonies. The development of the nation as the dominant cultural unit of the contemporary world order took place in tandem with these colonial processes, and the link therefore between postcoloniality and nationalism is a key building block in the formation of the modern. This offers the possibility that other sites may benefit from the methodology of postcoloniality. As Declan Kiberd mentions at the end of his essay, the emergence of the nations of Eastern Europe from the Empire of the Soviet Union, and the dissolving of Yugoslavia, provide situations where the language of postcoloniality can be used, though this may result in the notion of the 'postcolonial' fracturing as it addresses different historical specificities. What *is* certain is that is is naive to imagine that the issues of postcoloniality *only* apply to cultures outside Europe. In the same way as European nationalism was modified and shaped to fit local contexts in the ex-colonies, the methods of the colonizing project were key vehicles for the languages of development within Europe from the eighteenth century onwards. It is vital to stress the differences in power relations and represen-tations between Europe and its colonies, but to boil the issue down to a Manichean opposition is to create a false polarity.

The essays here display the remarkable endurance of the idea of the nation. It is presented here in many differing forms—cultural policy, imaged geography, written text, legal censor, ambitious dream—and in each case ideas of nationalism have been modified, asserted and challenged. The sheer scale of the arguments and debates point to the centrality of the national idea, and serve to postpone the advent of any real 'post-national' era. Whether narrated idea or policed state, the national method of defining the collective is one of the most absorbing of contemporary mani-festations.

Notes

1. For a useful overview and introduction to the issues of postcoloniality see Bill Ashcroft, Gareth Griffiths and Helen Tiffin (eds), *The Post-Colonial Studies Reader* (London: Routledge, 1995) as well as Patrick Williams and Laura Chrisman (eds), *Colonial Discourse and Post-Colonial Theory: A Reader* (Hemel Hempstead: Harvester Wheatsheaf, 1993) and Padmini Mongia (ed.) *Contemporary Postcolonial Theory: A Reader* (London: Arnold, 1996). For a similar introduction to the issues surrounding nationalism, a good introduction is John Hutchinson and Anthony D. Smith (eds), *Nationalism* (Oxford: OUP, 1994).
2. Homi K. Bhabha, 'Introduction: Locations of Culture', *The Location of Culture* (London: Routledge, 1994), p. 2. For a more detailed explication of Bhabha's idea of the hybrid see 'Signs Taken for Wonders: Questions

of Ambivalence and Authority under a Tree outside Delhi, May 1817'
in the same volume, pp. 102–22.

3. Michel Foucault, 'Questions on Geography', *Power/Knowledge: Selected Interviews and Other Writings 1972–1977*, ed. Colin Gordon, (Brighton: Harvester, 1980).

4. There are many texts which illustrate the development of the modern European nation state and the ideology of nationalism. Some of the most useful are Liah Greenfeld, *Nationalism: Five Roads to Modernity* (Cambridge, Mass: Harvard University Press, 1992); Ernest Gellner, *Nations and Nationalism* (Oxford: Blackwell, 1983); Benedict Anderson, *Imagined Communities: Reflections on the Origins and Spread of Nationalism* (London: Verso and New Left Books, 1983). For accounts that take into consideration the expansion of European nationalism, non-European nationalisms, and the effect of postcolonial cultures on European thought, see Hugh Seton-Watson, *Nations and States: An Enquiry into the Origins of Nations and the Politics of Nationalism* (London: Methuen, 1977); Anthony Smith, *National Identity* (London: Penguin, 1991); V.G. Kiernan, *Imperialism and its Contradictions*, ed. Harvey J. Kaye, (London and New York: Routledge, 1995); Dorinda Outram, *The Enlightenment* (Cambridge: CUP, 1995); G.S. Rousseau and Roy Porter (eds.), *Exoticism in the Enlightenment* (Manchester and New York: Manchester University Press, 1990).

5. For an excellent account of the formation of the British nation in the eighteenth and early nineteenth century see Linda Colley, *Britons: Forging the Nation 1707–1837* (New Haven: Yale University Press, 1992).

6. There are clear difficulties with any definition of what might constitute the period of 'high colonialism'. Eric Hobsbawn dates the age of Empire between 1875 and 1914 (*The Age of Empire, 1875–1914*, London: Weidenfeld and Nicolson, 1987), referring largely to British history, but Patrick Brantlinger in *Rule of Darkness: British Literature and Imperialism, 1830–1914* (Ithaca and London: Cornell University Press, 1988) argues for an analysis that considers the earlier nineteenth century. Edward Said, in *Culture and Imperialism* (London: Chatto & Windus, 1993), points to the time lags that occur in the manifestations of British and French colonial expansion, with the full force of the latter appearing at the very end of the nineteenth century, after that of the British. But the point of 'high colonialism' for parts of Latin America, and for the Irish, would clearly be much earlier.

7. There was a substantial tradition of anti-colonial thought during the eighteenth-century Enlightenment, particularly in France. See Marcel Merle, *L'Anticolonialisme Européen de Las Casas à Karl Marx* (Paris: Colin, 1969). For an account of how this developed in the nineteenth century see Charles Robert Ageron, *L'Anticolonialisme en France de 1871 à 1914* (Paris: Presses Universitaires de France, 1973).

16

8. For the development of European ideas following culture contact, see Peter Hulme, *Colonial Encounters: Europe and the Native Caribbean, 1492–1797* (London and New York: Methuen, 1986); Stephen Greenblatt, *Marvellous Possessions: The Wonder of the New World* (Oxford: Clarendon, 1991); Bernard Smith, *European Vision and the South Pacific, 1768–1850* (Oxford: Clarendon, 1960).

9. Said, p. 99.

10. John Stuart Mill, *Essays on Bentham and Coleridge* ed. F.R. Leavis (Cambridge: CUP, 1980) p. 73. See also Mill's 'Of Nationality, as Connected with Representative Government' and 'Of the Government of Dependencies by a Free State' in *On Liberty and Other Essays* ed. John Gray (Oxford: OUP, 1991) pp. 427–34 and pp. 447–67.

11. A useful guide to the key issues of the national and citizenship in Europe is provided in Rogers Brubaker, *Citizenship and Nationhood in France and Germany* (Cambridge, Mass.: Harvard University Press, 1992). For a study of the ways in which postcolonial cultures supplied forms and structures that were then built into a developing European modernity see Paul Rabinow, *French Modern: Norms and Forms of the Social Environment* (Cambridge, Mass.: M.I.T. Press, 1989).

12. See Aijaz Ahmad, *In Theory: Classes, Nations, Literatures* (London and New York: Verso, 1992) pp. 95–122.

13. See Graeme Turner, *National Fictions: Literature, Film and the Construction of Australian Narrative* (Sydney and London: Allen & Unwin, 1986) and Graeme Turner (ed), *Nation, Culture, Text: Australian Culture and Media Studies* (London: Routledge, 1993). For a cultural analysis of Australian identity formation see Richard White, *Inventing Australia: Images and Identity, 1688–1980* (Sydney: Allen & Unwin, 1981).

14. Useful introductory texts on the issues of specific postcolonial nationalisms are Ndabiningi Sithole, *African Nationalism* (Cape Town: OUP, 1959); James Coleman *Nationalism and Development in Africa*, ed. Richard L. Sklar (Berkeley: University of California Press, 1994); Partha Chatterjee *Nationalist Thought and the Colonial World* (London: Zed, 1986) and his *The Nation and its Fragments: Colonial and Postcolonial Histories* (Princeton: Princeton University Press, 1993); Anil Seal, *The Emergence of Indian Nationalism: Competition and Collaboration in the Later Nineteenth Century* (London: CUP, 1971), Horace B. Davies, *Towards a Marxist Theory of Nationalism* (New York and London: Monthly Review, 1978) pp. 165–246, S. Neil MacFarlane, *Superpower Rivalry and 3rd World Radicalism* (London and Sydney: Croom Helm, 1985) pp. 42–130; R.L. Johnston *et al* (eds), *Nationalism, Self-Determination and Political Geography* (London and Sydney: Croom Helm, 1988).

15. See Wole Soyinka, *Art, Dialogue and Outrage: Essays on Literature and Culture* (London: Methuen, 1993), Chinua Achebe *Morning Yet on Creation Day* (London: Heinemann, 1975) and his *Hopes and Impediments: Selected Essays, 1965–1987* (London: Heinemann, 1988). For an excellent

17

discussion of the tensions between the national and the international, see James Mayall, *Nationalism and International Society* (Cambridge: CUP, 1993).

16. See Arjun Appadurai, 'Disjuncture and Difference in the Global Cultural Economy', *Colonial Discourse and Post-Colonial Theory: A Reader*, pp. 324–39.

17. For more on the relationship between the sub-national and the national in postcolonial cultures, see T.V. Sathyamurthy, *Nationalism in the Contemporary World* (London: Frances Pinter, 1983).

18. Gellner, p. 55.

19. Timothy Brennan, 'The National Longing for Form' in Homi K. Bhabha (ed) *Nation and Narration* (London: Routledge, 1990) p. 57.

20. In particular, see Homi K. Bhabha, 'DissemiNation: Time, Narrative and the Margins of the Modern Nation', *Nation and Narration*, pp. 291–322.

21. See Marjorie Ringrose and Adam J. Lerner (eds), *Re-Imagining the Nation* (Buckingham: Open University Press, 1993), and Andrew Parker *et al.* (eds) *Nationalisms & Sexualities* (New York & London: Routledge, 1992).

22. Wilson Harris, *The Palace of the Peacock* (London: Faber, 1960) and *The Guyana Quartet* (London: Faber, 1985).

Crippled by Geography?
New Zealand Nationalisms

Mark Williams

Writing on nationalism in 1983 Ernest Gellner used New Zealand as an example of a country in which national sovereignty was the outcome of geographical isolation rather than cultural distinctiveness:

> Most New Zealanders and most citizens of the United Kingdom are so continuous culturally that without a shadow of a doubt the two units would have never separated, had they been contiguous geographically. Distance made the effective sovereignty of New Zealand convenient and mandatory, and the separation does not provoke resentment in anyone's breast, notwithstanding the technical violation of the national principle.[1]

It is a familiar image of New Zealand, homogeneous and *British*, and goes with a picture of the country as harmonious, civil, pastoral and decent that has captivated New Zealanders themselves as much as foreign observers like Gellner. It's there in Katherine Mansfield's stories, albeit as a reproach as much as an affirmation. Gellner's representation of New Zealand is not wholly inaccurate; 'most' New Zealanders, even today, are British in origin and in 1983 many, perhaps 'most', remained British in sympathy.[2] It is, however, insufficient. Nationalism in New Zealand, even in 1983, possessed a considerable history, vigorous internal dissensions and various, often incompatible, motivations. It isn't my purpose here to berate Gellner for his Eurocentrism and thus rescue New Zealand from a persistent stereotype. I simply want to

19

demonstrate, chiefly by reference to the literary culture, that even in a society as seemingly simple, moderate and homogeneous as New Zealand, nationalism is a very complicated phenomenon indeed.

Until the early 1950s, Maori of the Ngati Whatua tribe inhabited a *pa* (village) on a rich estuary a mile or so from the city centre. The few acres at Orakei were all that remained to a tribe that had dominated the Auckland isthmus before the arrival of the Europeans. Much of the traditional food supply of the tribe was derived from the nearby beaches and at low tide the Maori would still gather shellfish from the mudflats. In 1950 the city fathers decided that the Maori at Orakei needed to be better housed and supplied with modern conveniences. Accordingly, the remaining Ngati Whatua land was compulsorily purchased and the people were resettled in State-built houses on the hills around the estuary where their village had been. Thus they were brought under the sphere of European advantage by a State which regarded itself as the 'friend' of the citizens.[3] W. H. Oliver advances another reason behind the clearance at Orakei of 1950–51. The Queen was to visit in 1953 and her route would pass by the *pa*-site; by that time the evictions had been effected and the houses of the *pa* had been burned.[4] Yet this was a period of the 'benevolent' extension of the State into the lives of disadvantaged or non-conforming citizens (the novelist Janet Frame had spent nearly a decade in psychiatric wards being 'cured' of her loneliness and alienation by the administration of multiple shock treatments). Pakeha (European settler) opinion at the time held that the Maori, unlike the native peoples in other settler societies, were fortunate to be the recipients of a policy of benign assimilation. They were to be 'raised' to the level of European civilization.

In 1976 the Government of the day determined that land at Orakei, formerly owned by the Ngati Whatua tribe, should be sold for a housing development. The Ngati Whatua people thereupon occupied part of the land in question. Many Pakeha joined the Maori protesters in an occupation at Bastion Point that lasted 506 days. These were the people who would later lead the more extensive and more violent protests against the 1981 tour of New Zealand by a South African rugby team. The conservative National Government of Prime Minister Robert Muldoon refused to compromise with the Maori land protesters and eventually sent in a heavy force of police to effect an eviction. The arrest of the 222 protesters by 600 police presented the country with a series of powerful images of massive State power directed at dignified protest.[5] In spite of a partial settlement of the Maori claim made by the Government in 1978, 'Bastion Point' remained a source of inspiration and resentment throughout the struggles of the 1980s.[6]

Three distinct nationalisms, not simply three phases of New Zealand nationalism, are involved in the events described above: post-settler Pakeha nationalism, Maori nationalism and bicultural nationalism. Each of these nationalisms in turn discloses its own separate phases of development, revisionary tendencies and internal differences sufficiently marked that we might perhaps speak of micro-nationalisms.

From a Maori point of view, the clearing of the Ngati Whatua people from their village restaged in miniature the whole process of colonization. The Pakeha understanding of that act, however, was not colonialist but nationalist. The early settlers were envious and afraid of the numerous, land-rich and sometimes mettlesome Maori.[7] They had to tread carefully in their efforts to enlist a reluctant colonial administration to help pry vast acres away from the tribes.[8] The wars fought against 'rebellious' Maori over land in the 1860s were long, bloody and inconclusive in outcome.[9] A century later the descendents of the settlers had established their rule and presence. They acted largely without reference to external authority (although the concern for the Queen's view indicated that the colonial cringe had not entirely disappeared). This confidence in themselves and their secure destiny as a people was indicated as much as anything by the will to bring a 'backward' people under the dispensation of modernity with which they invested this late dispossession.

The act of dispossession was a late expression of the Pakeha nationalism that appeared in the wake of the First World War and found its classic form in the 1930s and 1940s. This was not simply a matter of settling the country, clearing virgin land, and bringing it within the sphere of organized commerce, ownership and labour. All this had been accomplished under the imperial culture that continued largely unquestioned until the First World War. At issue was the long struggle of a displaced British people to feel 'at home' in New Zealand and this required the evolution (or construction) of a single coherent Pakeha culture. This in turn required of the Pakeha New Zealanders that they disentangle their identities from Britain, an act of separation the novelist and playwright Maurice Shadbolt locates in the Anzac soldiers' (the

21

Australian and New Zealand Army Corps) sense of betrayal by British officers in the trenches of Gallipoli.[10]

An effect of Pakeha nationalism was the elision of the differences that had marked the various immigrant cultures in the colonial period. In nineteenth-century New Zealand the various immigrant groups—Scots, Irish (Protestant and Catholic), English —maintained the distinctiveness that still marked those separate cultures in Britain.[11] The consolidation of the idea of Britain as a homogeneous unit among European New Zealanders (so that the word England came to designate a general origin) marked the consolidation of a specifically 'Pakeha' culture; that is, one which distinguished itself from the Maori rather than in terms of the imported internal differences within the British polity. By seeing themselves in relation to the Maori rather than in relation to Britain, the Pakeha were advancing their claims to authentic belonging in New Zealand. This process of indigenization of the settlers is marked by the evolution of the meaning of the term New Zealander which meant Maori in the early nineteenth century and white descendant of the settlers by the latter part of that century. (Conversely, the term 'Maorilander' meant white inhabitant of New Zealand in the colonial period, not Maori.)[12] The late-twentieth-century habit among the European New Zealanders of accepting the designation Pakeha carried yet further the task of self-naturalization.

What was also required was the construction (or invention) of a national consciousness and the means of representing that consciousness through literature, the arts and cultural production. The crucial expression of this effort to formulate such a consciousness was carried through in the 1930s and 1940s in the work of a group of writers and painters—Allen Curnow, Denis Glover, Charles Brasch, all associated with the Caxton Press established by Glover in Christchurch in 1936—who set about overcoming the colonial sense of distance, isolation and inferiority by establishing a distinctive local literary tradition, something which would be, in a phrase of Curnow's, 'different, something/Nobody counted on'.[13] This was the period of the establishment of a post-settler Pakeha nationalism, sometimes characterized as the post-provincial period.[14]

In order to achieve a specifically New Zealand tradition the Caxton poets felt that it was necessary to distinguish their *serious* efforts to fasten a poetic to New Zealand conditions from the ephemeral and colonial poetic outpourings of their female

22

predecessors. The characteristic styles of existing schools of New Zealand poetry were held to be marred by colonial deference, the decorative use of native flora, Georgian diction and outmoded verse forms. Nationalism in the lexicon of the Caxton poets, especially Curnow and Glover, was identified with realism, masculinity and scrupulous attention to the immediate world. The poet, according to Curnow, went on expeditions in search of a reality that was 'local and special'.[15]

Indeed, for Curnow, the artist could only interpret experience by way of the nation which formed not so much a determinant of consciousness as an extension of the body. The nation, for Curnow, constitutes a kind of second body in the sense that it grounds consciousness in the ineluctable real.[16] To come to the sense of one's condition as a New Zealander is analogous to coming to accept the world without faith. Curnow's nationalism is informed by his lapsarian temper.[17] His early verse is driven by the conflict over religious faith which led to his abandoning plans to become an Anglican minister. He considered loss of faith to be the precondition to a mature acceptance of the human lot, but it also involved a loss of the richness that had gone with belief. In a similar way he saw coming to terms with settler existence as a necessary acceptance of diminished possibility. The world encountered on arrival in the islands of New Zealand had its limitations and frustrations, but it was the realm of the real and he strongly favoured in his anthologies and criticism those poets whom he judged to have accepted that condition and reflected it accurately in their verse. He trenchantly condemned any sign of aversion towards what he called 'the New Zealand referent' in favour of an arid internationalism.[18]

There was a prose equivalent of the cultural putsch carried out in poetry by Curnow and the Caxton poets in the immensely influential short stories of Frank Sargeson. In the classic form of the Sargeson story of the 1930s and 1940s, which became the classic form of the *New Zealand* short story for at least three decades, masculine bias, a muscular style and sympathy for the 'ordinary bloke' are signs of an underlying faith that the un-educated, outback male whose speech and attitudes are furthest removed from English models came closest to establishing a specifically New Zealand voice. In a curious irony the intense fascination with maleness and mateship that Sargeson foisted on New Zealand fiction owed to his homosexual nature, which only recently has been openly discussed in New Zealand.[19] As with

23

W.H. Auden and some of his followers in England, sexuality and politics were closely allied in a literary preoccupation with the working man. In Sargeson's case, leftist politics and literary nationalism collide in the body of the strong, inarticulate male.

Curiously also, the discovery of an authentically New Zealand voice by the writer is associated with separation from the parental gods of the Mother country, in this case Methodist rather than Anglican. It is as though the act of separation from the parent culture required to assert a nationalist literature cannot be accomplished without a repudiation of inherited gods. For Sargeson, as for Curnow, the writing that is deemed to be most significant, that is, most likely to be both expressive and productive of that desired national consciousness, is one which reflects most accurately the referents of the place at hand, and those referents may be geographical, social or linguistic. The problem is that the national consciousness thus conjured into existence reflected uncannily the preoccupations of its discoverer: it is represented in Sargeson's stories by a New Zealander who is typically masculine, Pakeha, and hotly pursued by punitive Calvinist demons.

This masculinity of tone and attitude found expression in a series of confident dismissals of established women poets like Eileen Duggan (New Zealand's most internationally famous poet in the 1930s)[20] and novelist Robin Hyde, and of a notoriously 'Georgian' anthology of New Zealand poetry, Quentin Pope's *Kowhai Gold*. Yet it rested on profound anxieties and was, in fact, a measure of underlying doubt. In a famous poem, 'The Skeleton of the Great Moa in the Canterbury Museum, Christchurch', Curnow looked to a child 'born in a marvellous year,/[who will] learn the trick of standing upright here'.[21] In this poem about adaption and the failure to adapt, about the amount of time it takes for an organic national culture to take shape after the brutal wrench of transplantation, New Zealanders are seen as crippled by geography. Distance has rendered them ill-fitted for survival, like the extinct bird propped up with wires in the provincial museum. The 'trick' of self-sufficiency has yet to be fully mastered.

The New Zealand identity fashioned by the mid-century nationalists rested on the romantic view, influential in Britain between the wars, that national consciousness was a result of the organic response over time by a given people to a specific landscape. The modernism they used to attack their 'Georgian' precursors was always insecure.[22] Essentially, they inherited and adapted to local purposes the species of modernism informed by romantic organicism associated with D.H. Lawrence; onto that they grafted the leftist social conscience and the realism of the Auden Group.

Who were the people who would possess the organic consciousness they desired? Not the Maori, who already possessed it. What the European immigrants needed to do after a century in which the imagination had continued to 'recoil' from immediate realities, was to tap into and extend their consciousness of belonging in these islands.[23] The Pakeha, observes Curnow in the introduction to his enormously influential 1960 *Penguin Book of New Zealand Verse*, 'has generally felt his own New Zealand tradition to be enriched and dignified by association with those older Pacific navigators and colonists, his forerunners and fellow-citizens.'[24] The taint of colonization is here projected backwards onto the Maori so that the European New Zealanders are simply extending an ancient line of voyaging and settling rather than interrupting, as colonizers, an established world. Curnow begins his anthology with a selection of Maori *waiata* (songs) in translation. The point is to establish a ground for the ensuing European poetry which is still in the process of catching up with indigenous belonging.[25] The Maori poems, says Curnow, 'represent a significant part of our commonly diffused consciousness of ourselves as New Zealanders.'[26] Those to receive the desired consciousness of national identity to which the anthology acts as midwife, then, are the descendants of the white settlers, purged at last of their colonial longings, their sad sense of displacement. The anthology, by the very act of deferring to a Maori priority, extends the process by which the term New Zealander, which meant Maori in the nineteenth century, came to mean European in the twentieth century.

The nationalism in the arts in mid-century New Zealand was predicated on the need of local writers and artists to attend to the particularities of the place in which they found themselves and to find formal means of registering those particularities. In other words, lack of contiguity with Britain was producing fundamental changes in the descendants of the settlers half a century before Gellner found no substantial differences between New Zealanders and the British from whom they derived. The nationalism produced by this need was not of the radical kind that emerged in many of the former British colonies after the Second World War. It was a reluctant nationalism, given at times to mourning the

25

distance of New Zealanders from Europe, insistent on maintaining European 'standards', and wishing to preserve the heritage of European, particularly British, culture while seeking to add something new and distinctive to that heritage. It was, however, a movement sufficiently powerful to tap into the collective psyche of the Pakeha and establish itself in the culture generally. Certainly, by the 1960s this movement had become the literary establishment and would remain so until well into the 1970s.

During the 1970s the organizing energies and ideas, economic as well as cultural, which had directed the country towards a less colonial self-understanding and self-reliance in the immediate post-war period came to be identified with reaction and conservatism. The cultural nationalism of the 1930s poets which had resulted in a more assertive and distinctive literature, represented in the classic periods of the literary magazines *Landfall* and *Islands*, had become predictable. The emphasis on realism, geography, and tradition-building which had produced vital new work in the 1930s and 1940s had become entrenched prejudices, inhibiting the development of new ways of writing.[27] The very names of the established journals 'Landfall' and 'Islands' signalled the habit of looking inward, nurturing a tradition which was already stale and boring. The nationalism that grew out of the Depression and the Second World War and which had shaped New Zealand identity so utterly in the post-war period had exhausted itself and, in the economic sphere, very nearly bankrupted the country.

A measure of this conservatism is to be found in the curious unacknowledged congruences, noted by Roger Horrocks, between the prevailing thinking about literature and the conservative economic policies of the Prime Minister Robert Muldoon, who was hated by the majority of literary people.[28] In the literary scene nationalism, realism and pragmatism (the writer's craft was learned by observation, experience and practice rather than from abstract theory), the qualities which had given force and direction to the mid-century writers, had become shibboleths. These were precisely the values which governed the political and economic scene. Muldoon claimed an intimate and comprehensive knowledge of the local economy. His familiarity with its workings was detailed and precise, not abstract or theoretical. Hence, he alone was qualified to govern its operations, not the academics in Treasury who would apply foreign doctrines to local situations. Muldoon extended protectionist policies long after they became unsustainable, thus isolating and distorting the economy.[29] His popular support rested his preference for paternalistic protections coupled with right-wing foreign policy, including support for the South African rugy tour which divided the country in 1981. New Zealand by the early 1980s was confused, with no independent policies, and moribund, ideologically as well as fiscally.[30]

This is the context in which bicultural nationalism appeared in the late 1970s, in a mood of weariness with the existing formulations of national identity, especially that associated with the masculine realists of the 1930s and 1940s. The preconditions for the bicultural movement had been established across a number of fronts from the late 1960s. Women writers had often been treated dismissively by male editors of journals and anthologies in the masculine literary climate favoured by the mid-century nationalists.[31] Janet Frame was an exception, but her writing tended to be subsumed under the head of the ruling critical realist style; the feminist side of her work was generally ignored.[32] By the mid-1970s a number of women writers had won an eager and substantial reading public for writing by and about women. Similarly, Maori writing, which in the 1960s had meant only Hone Tuwhare's poetry, showed a prolific growth from the early 1970s. The novelist Witi Ihimaera has described the difficulties he encountered trying to convince Pakeha editors to publish his work: '"Who will read your book?",' he was asked. Ihimaera replied, '"Maori people would",' and was told in turn, '"Maoris don't read books"'.[33] By the mid-1970s Ihimaera, Patricia Grace and other prose writers had demonstrated that there was a significant audience for writing by Maori, reflecting a specifically Maori view of the world.

In the early 1980s New Zealand society underwent a dramatic political and cultural shift as the old nationalism born of settler discontent gave way to a more confidently bicultural kind of nationalism. The chief expression of this—admittedly contested[34] —new nationalism was a concerted effort to remake New Zealand by eradicating the settler heritage, renouncing the 'racist' policy of assimilation, and overcoming the legacy of colonial guilt by making New Zealand into Aotearoa (the Maori name for the islands), a truly bicultural country. Culturally, much of this effort was directed at the mid-century nationalists who were now seen to be tainted by paternalism, hierarchy and exclusiveness (more bluntly by racism and sexism). But the mood of revisionism existed in a larger context of a broad repositioning of New Zealand in cultural and economic terms as well as in terms of its relations to the rest of the world.

The new Labour Government elected in late 1983 promptly reversed all the policy directions pursued by Muldoon. Sporting contacts with South Africa were banned, radical anti-nuclear laws were passed, a woman was appointed Minister of Police. An undertaking was made to honour the Treaty of Waitangi, the 1840 contract between the British Crown and the Maori people and the founding document of modern New Zealand. A tribunal had been established in 1975 to investigate claims by Maori people going back to 1840 and to make recommendations to Government about settling those claims. In 1988 the Government declared the Treaty to be 'part of the basic law' of New Zealand, concluding a decade-long struggle to have its constitutional force and legal bearing acknowledged.[35] By banning nuclear-armed ships in its harbours New Zealand began at last to assert its independence in the world, precipitating the breakdown of ANZUS (the military alliance between Australia, New Zealand and the United States) in the process.

All this coincided with the publication of Keri Hulme's novel *the bone people* (1983), which attributed the violence in New Zealand life to the legacy of colonization, the erosion of cultural connections and meanings among Maori, and envisaged a redeemed New Zealand/Aotearoa refashioned around the indigenous presence, a spiritualized land possessed of a special destiny. Also indicative of this mood was a new edition of *The Penguin Book of New Zealand Verse*, edited by Harvey McQueen and Ian Wedde, which appeared in 1985. Wedde's introduction strategically revised Curnow's 1960 *Penguin Book of New Zealand Verse* in favour of biculturalism and a shift from the hieratic to the demotic as a means of realizing 'the growth of the language into its location'.[36] Instead of a selection of Maori traditional song attached to the front of the book, the 1985 *Penguin* included substantial selections of poetry in Maori alongside the English-language material. The book was a sign of the determination in much of the literary culture, in the educational establishment and in many areas of government and law to carry through a thoroughgoing programme of biculturalism. The period of Pakeha nationalism was at an end.

Or was it? The cultural redrawing and redirection undertaken in the mid- and late-1980s revisited existing kinds of nationalism. The idea of New Zealand as a specially blessed country, a model of harmony and social justice, after all, had a long history, going back to the nineteenth-century advertisements aimed at potential settlers and which presented the country as a new Eden. Moreover, as Jonathan Lamb observes, Wedde's method of including Maori poetry in the *Penguin Book* (and his rationale for doing so as outlined in the introduction) displays Pakeha envy of Maori originality and serves to make 'the authentic' [Maori poetry] connive in the 'authentication of the originally inauthentic' [Pakeha poetry].[37] The purpose of the copious selections of poetry in Maori is to make the *Pakeha* feel at home. After a century and a half the English language has been indigenized and Pakeha poets have at their disposal a language—New Zealand English—that is original, as Wedde puts it, 'where it is'.[38]

C.K. Stead has observed that this is a theme that looks back to *Kowhai Gold*, where native flora and fauna served as decorative signs of New Zealand identity.[39] Perhaps it is more accurately seen in an *evolutionary* context of making use of Maori myth, legend and romanticized approximations of oral traditions in Pakeha writing that goes back to the colonial period. Jessie MacKay's 'Rona', the fairy-filled landscapes of Trevor Lloyd, the stories of Roderick Finlayson—all these show how at each stage of settler history, from the colonial to the post-provincial, the Pakeha have reinvented the Maori in terms of the current paradigm.[40] In his 1985 anthology Wedde is not guilty of colonial romanticizing, but inevitably his efforts to represent Maori poetry without cultural arrogance participate in the ongoing exchange between two (partly phantasmal) cultural entities, Maori and Pakeha, each of which achieves homogeneity only in relation to the other.

As is usual in any ambitious attempt at cultural redefinition there were explicit and hidden agendas, conscious and unconscious ones. The result was less a single coherent programme of revision and redirection than a complicated and in some respects contradictory set of reassessments. The bicultural movement of the mid-1980s brought together several discrete, in some ways opposed, cultural attitudes. Most of these for a time found a place within the general programme of reform on which the Labour Government embarked. Zealous anti-racists and unreconstructed socialists jostled with free market reformers. The Government was able to appeal to the Greens with its anti-nuclear legislation, all the while preparing the ground for the selling off of forests to foreign interests. The most radically right-wing economic programme outside Chile was carried forward by a government which as late as 1985 resolved that it was 'socialist' in character.[41] Labour continually traded on consoling images of pristine landscape and invested a great deal rhetorically and constitutionally in addressing Maori grievances, all the while busily creating an economic climate that savagely disadvantaged Maori people. This was less the effect of deep cynicism than of profound confusion of purpose. The schizoid atmosphere of the period prepared the way for the full-blown mania that was to follow in the late 1980s when the share markets collapsed, the Labour Government disintegrated, and the various groups who had supported it discovered how antagonistic they had been all along.

All this needs to be seen in the context of the reshaping of the economy and of New Zealand's relations with the wider world forced on the country by its insolvency. When the Labour Government came to power in late 1983 the country's credit lines were exhausted and its reserves were depleted. Moreover, the outgoing Prime Minister, Robert Muldoon, precipitated a financial crisis by refusing to devalue the currency. The new Government was faced with a crisis report from Treasury insisting on radical measures—floating the dollar and rapid deregulation —aimed at rescuing a desperate situation. The real source of the problems was the byzantine structure of protections for the local economy erected by Muldoon. The Treasury recommendations were followed and the entire structure of supports, subsidies and controls was rapidly dismantled. The pastoral industries, the legacy of New Zealand's status as a supplier of cheap food to the British market, were suddenly stripped of the subsidies which had protected them against the loss of that market once Britain had joined the EEC. The financial markets were deregulated and the New Zealand dollar was floated. Government monopolies were broken up and progressively privatized. The consequences of these changes were felt particularly by Maori who made up much of the unskilled labour force. The reforms of late 1980s made more than 50 per cent of young Maori unemployed.

Biculturalism as it developed in the 1980s, at least among its Pakeha enthusiasts, displayed a desire not unlike that of the 1930s nationalists to shift the emotional ground of identity from British to local sources. In the 1980s, however, a resurgent Maori culture, not Sargeson's outback males, was seen as the guarantor of something truly distinctive and indigenous. Paradoxically, for all its championing of the victims of colonialism everywhere, biculturalism in New Zealand exhibited the same introversion that the mid-century nationalists had shown (more so perhaps in that Curnow, Brasch *et al.*, had insisted on the need to draw on the heritage of Europe while seeking to establish a distinctive local tradition as a kind of branch of the great trunk of existing tradition). Biculturalism, moreover, lacked a sophisticated theoretical framework with which to analyse and respond to the changes that were occurring in New Zealand culture, especially where the origins of those changes were global.

Postmodernism was ambiguously located in this respect. A long-standing local tradition of postmodernism had championed the margins against the literary authority of Curnow's poetics, of the realism that dominated the short story form, of the hieratic nationalism of *Landfall*. The internationalism of this group, however, tended to be concentrated on American poetry and its adherents were sometimes reverential rather than innovative in the importation of postmodern American poetics into New Zealand.[42] In the mid-1980s a more hip, theory-oriented postmodernism arrived, loudly advertising its debt to Roland Barthes and applying post-structuralist methods to local poets with sometimes excruciating consequences. These young postmodernists, centred around an Auckland broadsheet *AND*, were equally opposed to the ruling literary nationalist paradigm, but they were more closely attuned to the the relations between culture, in the broadest sense of the word, and the economy than any previous literary clique or movement.

The postmodernism of the mid-1980s, in spite of an element of leftist rhetoric in post-structuralist guise, was aligned with the generational push in business, politics and the bureaucracy which valued risk-taking and change and felt that the consensus established in the early post-war years about security and prosperity had outlived its use. As Colin James characterizes the latter, '[t]he unifying thread . . . was a shared temperament, an impatience with the status quo and with restraints, openness to new ideas, to change, to risk, to trying things out.'[43] Leigh Davis, a young poet and critic who took a post in Treasury on completing his MA, presented himself as a postmodernist of the markets. He delivered talks on the state of the literary magazines in the manner of a company director addressing the shareholders at an annual board meeting, noting market penetration of the various journals.

There was an element of dandyish parody in this, using the language of the financial markets in poetry and criticism and affecting three-piece pinstripe suits in contrast to the beards and sandals associated with local poets since James K. Baxter. But the connection between postmodern poetry and the new wave of economic policy of the mid-1980s was also serious and far-reaching. The little magazine which formed a vehicle for promoting the new postmodernism, *AND*, modelled itself on the Treasury report to the incoming Labour Government, *Economic Management*, which called for structural reforms in the economy. *AND* set about applying similar reforms to the literary market place, producing somewhat dandified versions of official economic diagnosis and prognosis: 'The job is to document the conditions of a peculiar kind of boredom and disenchantment with much present New Zealand writing'.[44]

Where the Treasury report asserted that 'the economy is beset with serious structural difficulties',[45] Davis in the first number of *AND* noted that 'the discourse of the literature is vulnerable to being replaced, and like dominoes a whole series of related changes are seen to occur as a consequence.'[46] Treasury complained that 'the attempt to cushion the economy from the effects of the deteriorating terms of trade did not prevent the community having to face a real relative income loss and a dramatic increase in the rate of unemployment.'[47] Davis protests against the effects of intellectual protectionism: '[a] change in the idea inputs of New Zealand literature, a growth in its consciousness of literary theory, would help curb the literature's tendency to recidivism.'[48]

Maori people by the late 1980s were preoccupied with much more prosaic effects of the Treasury-led efforts to restore economic health by a programme of radical reform. This programme impacted on a Maoridom inheriting more than a decade of vigorous challenge to the Pakeha status quo. The third strain of nationalism considered in this essay is the postcolonial position of the Maori, or at least of all those Maori who rejected the assimilationist policies of successive Pakeha governments since the mid-nineteenth century. Maori nationalism is a term identified with the Maori Renaissance of the 1970s and 1980s: a remarkable outpouring of expressive works by Maori people in all the arts. But it was also associated with the more overtly political term, Maori sovereignty, which signified the desire among Maori for a return not only of their alienated land but also of the cultural and political autonomy they had lost through 150 years of domination by the Pakeha.[49] In this sense the idea of a Maori 'nation' expressed the will among some Maori to govern their own affairs without having to defer to what they saw as an alien European colonial imposition. They were reacting against the assimilationist policies that had governed Pakeha thinking from the early colonial period to the late 1970s, according to which Maori values and practices here were considered suitable only for the *marae* (the meeting ground), for ceremonial purposes or tourism.[50] In 1976 the political party Mana Motuhake was launched to 'liberate the people from domination and manipulation so that Maori society is a being for itself and not a colony inhabited by another'.[51]

For some, this meant a resurgence of Maori culture and the return of land taken against the letter and spirit of the Treaty of Waitangi which Maori saw as establishing a partnership between two peoples. For a more radical group, the Treaty, far from vesting sovereignty in the British Crown, guaranteed Maori sovereignty permanently. The Maori as the *tangata whenua* ('people of the land') were the host nation and the Pakeha (all those who came as a consequence of colonization) were 'guests', with the obligation to behave with the proper respectfulness of guests towards their hosts. As the Pakeha had manifestly not behaved appropriately, but had seized control of the country from its rightful owners and alienated them from their land and treasures (Maori treasures, *taonga*, are specifically protected by the Treaty), the Pakeha should be given the option of accepting Maori sovereign authority in Aoteaora or leaving.[52]

The problem is (to adopt a rather simplistic dichotomy) that the two sides of the argument by the close of the 1980s had come to occupy different conceptual and linguistic universes. (Some would argue they always had.)[53] The Pakeha side sees the Treaty as having vested sovereignty in the British Crown and thereby established one law and one people. If, however, as Ernest Renan puts it, a nation 'is a soul, a spiritual principle', Pakeha are in a difficult position when they champion the one nation idea.[54] The past they share is not coterminous with that of the other they thereby seek to include. That which *is* shared is a cause of disputes. When Patcha say they want all New Zealanders to live together, laying the seemingly unappeasable ghosts of history, they mean that the difference of ethnicity is less significant than that of nation-making by way of colonization and settler presence. They can countenance reparation for past wrongs, but their tolerance is easily exhausted. Part of the reason behind Pakeha willingness to see the Government settle outstanding claims, albeit at considerable cost to the taxpayer, has been a fear that Maori demands might be perpetual. For their part, most Maori see the Treaty as obligating the Pakeha side to ongoing responsibilities: of dialogue, reparation, power of sharing, and of joint administration of Crown lands, national parks and so forth.

Yet to state the oppositions between the races in such terms is to grant a greater homogeneity of purpose and identity to both sides than has ever been the case. Pakeha, after all, is not strictly a racial description. Although the epithet has acquired positive connotations and has been adopted by many white New Zealanders, it has the limit that it signifies what a given person is *not* rather than what he or she is.[55] The idea of a Maori nation has always been problematic within Maoridom itself. At the time of the signing of the Treaty, as Michael King observes, 'Most of the Maori population saw itself not as Maori, but as members of *hapu* (sub-tribes) or tribes'.[56] Nineteenth-century Maori 'Kingite' (nationalist) movements tended to be conservative in character and localized in their appeal.[57] For Maori the term nation involves cultural experiences and understandings radically different from those of Western peoples, a point Powhiri Rika-Heke argues in her essay later in this collection. Nevertheless, Maori themselves have found precedent for their struggles against Pakeha in the experience of other oppressed peoples possessed of an acute consciousness of their special destiny. Nineteenth-century movements to establish Maori autonomy often looked to the example of the ancient Hebrews. In his 1985 novel *The Matriarch*, Witi Ihimaera updates this 'cross-cultural' tradition by associating the anti-British activist Te Kooti and his violent attempt to wrest independence from the European state with the Italian Risorgimento, as received through the colourful romantic nationalism of Verdi's operas.

Part of the problem today is that tribalized Maori, particularly those belonging to powerful or wealthy tribes, have a strong interest in maintaining that situation. The Treaty recognises tribes and chiefly authority (*rangitiratanga*) rather than the Maori people as a nation.[58] Hence the Ngai Tahu tribe which claims large parts of the South Island finds itself at odds with those who want a pan-Maori sharing of resources. Urban Maori with little or no connection to a tribe or *hapu* and no links to ancestral land, are more receptive to the radicals advocating Maori nationalism and contesting the conservative force of the traditional chiefs.

Nevertheless, in spite of the differences that have emerged among Maori people since the 1970s there have been sufficient

34

causes of general concern to provoke a concerted response. The chief unifying factors have been economic and political—land, unemployment, legal discrimination—but there has also been a powerful expression of commonality through literature and the arts. Maori nationalism has been allied with the bicultural nationalism of Pakeha liberals but less concerned with general issues of national identity. Maori have been concerned with the specific interests of Maori. Indigenous nationalism is an expression of the desire of Maori people to speak for themselves, to assert their rights to alienated land and to gain the power to determine their own lives. In this broad sense postcolonial Maori nationalism since the 1970s has expressed itself forcefully in both political and cultural terms, ranging from the Land March of 1975, through Ihimaera's novel *The Matriarch* to the occupation of disputed land in Wanganui in 1995.[59]

The situation in the 1990s is particularly fraught and complicated in spite of the achievement of some settlements with individual tribes.[60] Ironically, those very settlements have revealed the differences and antagonisms within Maoridom that were less apparent so long as Maori people as a whole were struggling against an overwhelming collective sense of wrong. Ironically also, while Maori nationalism in the mid-1990s still enjoys considerable prestige among Maori activists enthusiastically removing the heads of colonial administrators memorialized in public statuary, Donna Awatere, the figure most closely identified with the term in the 1980s, now acts as spokesperson for the political party of Roger Douglas who oversaw the right-wing economic restructuring in that decade. Maori sovereignty, according to Awatere, now means the right of Maori people to decide what they will do with their money without the intervention of State agencies, a view which neatly dovetails with Douglas' preference for unbridled individual responsibility.[61]

One manifestation of current tensions within Maoridom is to be found in the two versions, book and film, of Alan Duff's *Once Were Warriors*. The novel was widely resented among politically engaged Maori for its insistence that Maori cease blaming Pakeha for their problems and expecting government aid as salve. Traditional Maori culture is presented in the novel in decidely ambiguous terms: it is positive when coupled with a sense of self-reliance and discipline; it is corrupting so long as the obsession with the mana of warriors results in violence and family disintegration. The book also contains a stinging critique of traditional Maori life by way of central character Jake Heke's resentment of the enslavement of his tribal ancestors by Maori and their low status within Maoridom. The film rewrites the book to reinscribe mainstream Maori opinion. The slave theme is downplayed; the traditional associations of Maori culture are presented as a cure for the ills of the present. The scene of the *tangi* (funeral ceremony) on a *marae* in a tableau redolent of Maori warmth and sorrow, the heart feelings of an expressive and innately spiritual people, allows the consolations of authenticity partial triumph over the anxieties of modernity.

The cultural situation in the 1990s inherits these inevitable confusions and dissensions as the past is continually recast and reinterpreted in the light of contemporary anxieties and preoccupations. Nowhere is this unease more forcefully displayed than in contemporary New Zealand cinema. Here the troubled and divided psyche of the nation is represented in a series of images radically at odds with the tourist vision of New Zealand as an idyllic retreat from the anxieties of modern life. The film of *Once Were Warriors* opens with the pastoral convention reduced to a billboard above a naturalistic world of urban decay and violence. Jane Campion's *The Piano* invests the landscape with the gothicized contents of the settler psyche; the shapes of unconscious guilt, repression and anxiety are figured in the dense forestation as much as the violences of the plot. Curiously, these images return to a 1930s theme, strongly present in John Mulgan's novel *Man Alone* (1939), of New Zealand as a harsh inimical environment falsely represented as Edenic.

New Zealand's 'cinema of unease', far from signalling a sudden leap beyond provincial preoccupations, recasts in new images themes that have run through the literature from its beginnings.[62] At its heart lies the disenchantment that is part of every colonizing experience, when the hopes of a new and better world at the end of the voyage confront the inevitable disappointments of the actual. The disappointments that ensued, for those on the shore as well as for those who looked shoreward, have produced the various nationalisms of New Zealand's brief history. What connects them is the desire to compensate for what was lost the moment settler foot touched settled ground.

Nationalism, as Gellner observes, 'engenders nations, and not the other way round.'[63] New Zealand has produced not one but several nationalisms, each with different priorities and constituencies. The protracted and sometimes violent struggle among these nationalisms has produced competing and contradictory versions of the nation's meaning, destiny and identity.

Notes

1. Ernest Gellner, *Nations and Nationalism* (London: Basil Blackwell, 1983), pp. 134–5.
2. In 1951 92 per cent of the population were of British descent. In 1981 Europeans were 86 per cent, Maori up to 9 per cent and rising. Pacific Islanders were up to 3 per cent. Source: census figures quoted in Colin James, *The New Territory: The Transformation of New Zealand 1984–92* (Wellington: Bridget Williams Books, 1992), pp. 9, 37.
3. James uses the term 'the "friend" state', *The New Territory*, p. 18. Although a conservative National Government was elected in 1949, what James calls 'the prosperity consensus' prevailed until the 1970s. This consensus was extended to Maori. As James puts it, 'In the 1950s and 1960s the policy response to the Maori migration into mainstream New Zealand urban society was to put the state to work to level up Maori in land development, education, housing, health and general welfare, to make them equal with Europeans in terms of the consensus', p. 13.
4. W.H. Oliver, *Claims to the Waitangi Tribunal* (Wellington: Waitangi Tribunal Division, Department of Justice), p. 44.
5. The events at Bastion Point and their implications for the Waitangi Tribunal are discussed by Paul Temm, Q.C., in *The Waitangi Tribunal: The Conscience of the Nation* (Auckland: Random Century, 1990), pp. 61–7.
6. In fact, tensions still remain. Recently a long-simmering dispute between State-house tenants in the area and the Ministry of Housing flared up over the refusal by tenants to pay rent in protest against the application of market rates and in support of a land claim before the Treaty of Waitangi Tribunal. When the Government tried to sell the disputed grounds of a local school to an Asian Christian group, Ngati Whatua protesters blockaded the land, the Asian purchasers withdrew, and the Government was obliged to sell the land to the Maori protesters at a discounted price.
7. The pre-contact Maori were, of course, 'settlers' as much as the Pakeha. I have used the term in line with the convention that applies it to 'settler societies' such as Australia, Canada, South Africa and New Zealand and to the British colonists who migrated to those societies in the nineteenth century.
8. According to Keith Sinclair, the early settlers despised the Maori, 'but in many parts of the country they also feared and hated them', *A History of New Zealand* (Auckland: Penguin, 1988), p. 117.

9. James Belich argues that the Maori military effort was 'a unique feat of resistance to nineteenth-century European expansion', *The New Zealand Wars and the Victorian Interpretation of Racial Conflict* (Auckland: Auckland University Press, 1986), p. 291.

10. Maurice Shadbolt's play *On Chunuk Bair* dramatizes the view that the New Zealand soldiers at Gallipoli first formed a national consciousness by the discovery that their British officers did not have their interests at heart. In fact, New Zealand nationalism predates this. It goes back to the Liberals and the progressive nationalism of the 1890s. However, while the latter nationalism is rooted in the myth of New Zealand as the Eden that England might-have-been transposed to the antipodes, the former is rooted in resistance to England and the imperial connection. Hence it is more significant as a defining moment.

11. Donald Harman Akenson, *Half the World from Home: Perspectives on the Irish in New Zealand 1860–1950* (Wellington: Victoria University Press, 1990), pp. 6–7.

12. W.F. Alexander and A.E. Currie in their introduction to a 1906 anthology, *New Zealand Verse* (London: Walter Scott), use the word 'Maorilanders' to designate the European New Zealanders, not the Maori themselves. Modest about the quality of the work anthologized, the editors nevertheless see it as the halting beginnings of a national literature and see New Zealanders (i.e., the Pakeha) as distinct from England. Harry and Elizabeth Orsman in *The New Zealand Dictionary* (Auckland: New House, 1994) enter under Maorilander: 'obs., a New Zealand-born white'.

13. Allen Curnow, 'The Unhistoric Story', in *Collected Poems 1933–1973* (Wellington: A. H. & A. W. Reed, 1974), p. 79.

14. See, for example, Lawrence Jones' use of the latter term in his *Barbed Wire & Mirrors: Essays on New Zealand Prose*, Te Whenua Series No. 3 (Dunedin: University of Otago Press, 1990), especially pp. 140–203.

15. Allen Curnow, introduction to *The Penguin Book of New Zealand Verse*; repr., in Allen Curnow, *Look Back Harder: Critical Writings 1935–1984*, ed. Peter Simpson (Auckland: Auckland University Press, 1987), p. 133.

16. This idea, drawn from Santayana, finds fullest expression in Curnow's 1964 essay, 'New Zealand Literature: The Case for a Working Definition', in Wystan Curnow (ed) *Essays on New Zealand Literature* (Auckland: Heinemann Educational, 1973), p. 141.

17. On Curnow's lapsarian temper see K.O. Arvidson, 'Curnow, Stead and O'Sullivan: Major Sensibilities in New Zealand Poetry', *Journal of New Zealand Literature*, No. 1 (1983), pp. 31–51.

18. See Curnow's remarks on James K. Baxter in 'New Zealand Literature: the Case for a Working Definition', p. 146.

19. Kai Jensen discusses Sargeson's homosexuality in 'Frank at Last', in Mark Williams and Michele Leggott (eds) *Opening the Book: New Essays on New Zealand Writing*, (Auckland: Auckland University Press, 1995), pp. 68–82.

In the past it could be slyly referred to, as in R. A. Copland's *Frank Sargeson New Zealand Writers and their Work* (Wellington: Oxford University Press, 1976), p. 7.

20. See Peter Whiteford, *Eileen Duggan: Selected Poems* (Wellington: Victoria University Press, 1994), p. 13. On Curnow's treatment of Duggan see Michele Leggott's essay, 'Opening the Archive: Robin Hyde, Eileen Duggan and the Persistence of Record', in *Opening the Book*, pp. 279–90.

21. 'The Skeleton of the Great Moa', *Collected Poems*, p. 142.

22. Their own diction was not immune, as Iain Sharp points out in a review of Eileen Duggan's *Selected Poems in Landfall*, new ser., 3, 1 (Autumn 1995), pp. 130–33.

23. Curnow, *Penguin Book, Look Back Harder*, p. 135.

24. Curnow, *Penguin Book, Look Back Harder*, p. 135.

25. Jonathan Lamb makes this point in 'Problems of Originality: or, Beware of Pakeha baring Guilts', *Landfall* , 40, 3 (September 1986), p. 357.

26. Curnow, *Penguin Book, Look Back Harder*, p. 135.

27. Dennis List's parody of the Caxton poets' reverence for geography ('INEFFABLE YEARNING SEIZES ME/for the long-forsaken Canterbury Plains') reveals the impatience among the younger writers, quoted by Alan Brunton in 'Holding the Line: Contested Contexts in RecentVerse', *Opening the Book*, p. 254.

28. See Roger Horrocks, 'No Theory Permitted on these Premises', *AND/2* (February 1984), pp. 119–21.

29. Farmers were given subsidies to produce increasingly unmarketable commodities. Wages, prices, the exchange rate and imports were all directly regulated by the Government. At the same time Robert Muldoon extended the social welfare legacy of the first Labour Government (1935–49) by offering State-funded pensions to all New Zealanders over 60 years of age.

30. Foreign debt in 1974 was 6.7 per cent of GDP, by 1984 it was 47.6 per cent. Source James, *The New Territory*, p. 55.

31. There is some dispute about this. C. K. Stead asserts that 'during his lifetime [no] editor in New Zealand, either of a literary periodical or an anthology, has ever discriminated against a woman writer on the basis of sex', 'Wedde's Inclusions', rev. of, Harvey McQueen and Ian Wedde (eds), *The Penguin Book of New Zealand Verse, Landfall*, 39, 3, (September 1985), p. 291.

On the other hand, Anne Else, also in *Landfall*, 39, 4, (December 1985), p. 444, claims that the critical response in *Landfall* to the work of women writers in post-war New Zealand consisted 'at best of circumscribed, half-comprehending praise, and at worst of energetic misogynistic attack'. The truth is somewhat mixed. Some women fared well, Ruth Dallas in particular, and *Landfall* editor Charles Brasch's conservatism was probably just as important as gender. However, the explicitly masculinist tone of the literary culture meant that qualities deemed feminine were habitually posed as negatives to the desirable masculine ones of muscularity, realism, understatement and directness of treatment.

32. The references to her work as hysterical, tormented or strange (code-words for mad) that persisted after she achieved international recognition indicated lingering suspicion of female genius.

33. Witi Ihimaera interviewed by Mark Williams, in Mark Williams and Elizabeth Alley (eds) *In the Same Room: Conversations with New Zealand Writers* (Auckland: Auckland University Press, 1992), p. 220.

34. The most trenchant opposition to biculturalism in the literary scene in the 1980s came from C. K. Stead. For a discussion of this, see my 'C. K. Stead and the New Literary Order', *Meanjin*, 53, 4 (Summer 1994), pp. 695–703.

35. Quoted in *The New Territory*, p. 65.

36. Wedde, *Penguin Book*, p. 23.

37. Lamb, 'Problems of Originality', p. 357.

38. Ian Wedde, *Penguin Book*, p. 23. Elizabeth Gordon traces the emergence of a uniform national form of English in 'The Development of Spoken English in New Zealand', in Graham McGregor and Mark Williams (eds), *Dirty Silence: Language and Literature in New Zealand* (Auckland: Oxford University Press, 1991), pp. 19–28. Until the 1970s New Zealand English was considered as a continuum of registers from 'broad' through 'general' to 'cultivated'. The last was synonymous with the RP accent and had high prestige. Since the 1970s the cultivated and broad ends of the spectrum have been increasingly stigmatised with speech mainly falling in the 'general' range. Jeanette King suggests that in the late 1980s this model has been superseded by the emergence of two main varieties, 'Maori English' and 'Pakeha English', each of which occupies a continuum and is also related to the other, 'Maori English: A Phonological Study', *New Zealand English Newsletter*, no. 7 (1993), pp. 33–47.

39. C.K. Stead, 'Two Views of *The Penguin Book of New Zealand Verse*, I: Wedde's Inclusions', *Landfall*, 39, 3 (September 1985), p. 299.

40. McKay's Victorian romantic treatments of Maori myth are written in Tennysonian metres. 'Rona' is included in Alexander and Currie's *New Zealand Verse*. On Lloyd, see, for example, the painting 'The Death of a Moa' (1925), in *Two Centuries of New Zealand Landscape Art* (Auckland: Auckland City Art Gallery), p. 63. Lloyd's use of Maori fairy figures (*patupaiarehe*) links him with the *Kowhai Gold* school and recalls the Celtic Twilight poets. The representation of Maori in Roderick Finlayson's fiction is discussed by Bill Pearson 'The Maori in Literature, 1938–65', in *Essays on New Zealand Literature* 1973, pp. 99–100.

41. Quoted in James *The New Territory*, p. 141.

42. Alan Loney argues that the influence of American poets 'can be seen as a mature cultural process in which the participants are variously mature, responsible, intelligent, sensitive and skilled', 'The Influence of American

Poetry on Contemporary Poetic Practice in New Zealand', *Journal of New Zealand Literature*, 10 (1992), p. 94.
43. James *The New Territory*, p. 8.
44. Leigh Davis, 'Set Up', *AND/1* (August 1983), p. 3.
45. *Economic Management*, quoted in James, p. 150.
46. Davis, 'Set Up', p. 3.
47. *Economic Management*, quoted in James, *The New Territory*, p. 150.
48. Davis, 'Set Up', p. 3.
49. My use of the Maori plural for the word 'Maori' indicates at least some of the superficial success of this programme. Maori insisted that Maori words in English usage be pluralized according to Maori convention and this has been widely adopted.
50. James notes that a 1960 report on the future of the Maori showed an unconscious expectation that Maori people would become 'in effect brown Europeans' and it recommended greatly expanded spending on economic and social programmes to accelerate 'integration'; James, *The New Territory*, p. 13.
51. Mana Motuhake manifesto, quoted in James, *The New Territory*, p. 38.
52. Donna Awatere, *Maori Sovereignty* (Auckland: Broadsheet, 1984).
53. See D. F. McKenzie, *Oral Culture, Literacy & Print in Early New Zealand: The Treaty of Waitangi* (Wellington: Victoria University Press with the Alexander Turnbull Library Endowment Trust, 1985).
54. Ernest Renan, 'What Is a Nation?', in Homi K. Bhabha (ed), *Nation and Narration* (London: Routledge, 1990) p. 19.
55. This has been exacerbated by the current practice of using the terms 'non-Maori' or *tauiwi*, which more directly than Pakeha designate what one is not. The recently restructured Arts Council, now called Creative New Zealand, divides funding and administration under two main heads: Maori and non-Maori. The latter term attempts to include those immigrant groups other than European New Zealanders—Pacific Islanders, Chinese—who do not easily fit into the category of Pakeha without abandoning bicultural principle or practice. Senja Gunew has observed in Australia that the prestige of multi-culturalism prevents attention being paid to Aboriginal grievances over land ('Denaturalizing Cultural Nationalisms: Multi-cultural Readings of "Australia"', in *Nation and Narration*, p. 104). The obverse of this is true in New Zealand where the priority given to *tangata whenua* makes it difficult to represent the increasing complexity of the cultural picture as demographics change under the impact of immigration. Akenson comments on the long-standing difficulties of biculturalism in respect of the Irish in *Half the World from Home*, p. 6.
56. Michael King, 'Between Two Worlds', in W.H. Oliver (ed), *The Oxford History of New Zealand* (Oxford: Clarendon 1981), p. 272.
57. Sinclair, *A History of New Zealand*, p. 116.
58. Some Maori identify *rangitiratanga* with sovereignty, claiming therefore

it was never alienated. They argue that had their ancestors ceded the latter, the word *mana* rather than *kawanatanga*, a literal translation of governorship, would have been appropriate.

59. Motua Gardens, a block of land over which local Maori claimed ownership, was occupied by Maori for several months during 1995. The land was adjacent to the Wanganui City Council Chambers, part of a municipal park. Under threat of eviction the protestors eventually left peacefully.

60. The most notable settlement has been that reached with the Tainui people of the Waikato region who lost much of their land in the confiscations that followed the 1860s Land Wars. Tainui agreed to a settlement which included NZ$170 million, some Government-owned land and an apology from the Crown.

61. In another irony, Maori kiwifruit farmers are protesting at the Kiwifruit Marketing Board's monopoly which prevents them directly marketing their produce internationally on the grounds that the Treaty of Waitangi overrides the existing legislation. This puts the Maori involved in the camp of the Douglasite free-marketeers who also want to break up the producer boards.

62. The phrase appears as the title of a 1995 documentary on the history of New Zealand cinema, directed by Sam Neill and Judy Rymer.

63. Gellner, p. 55.

(Un)belonging Citizens, Unmapped Territory: Black Immigration and British Identity in the Post-1945 Period

Sarah Lawson Welsh

'A place on the map is also a place in history.'

Adrienne Rich

'Who belongs and what do we belong to [are] question[s] being asked with a new urgency in Europe where boundaries and state entities are shifting and where ethnic and national loyalties are changing the political structure of Europe with rapidity.'

Anne Curthoys

In Britain recently, the concept of national citizenship has come under particular scrutiny. There have been calls from the political right and from sectors of the black community for Government aid to black Britons considering voluntary repatriation to the West Indies. In December 1993 the unceremonious deportation of a number of Jamaicans from Britain received huge media coverage. In July 1995, a renewed controversy broke out over an article in *Wisden Cricket Monthly*, titled 'Is it in the Blood?'. The author, Robert Henderson, claimed that British sportsmen 'with black skin won't play for the country with the same fervour as those with white', as the desire of 'unequivocal Englishm[e]n' to play for England is 'instinctive, a matter of biology'. Henderson concluded: 'a multi-national nation . . . is a contradiction in terms.' More generally, there has been a reinvigorated and very visible

43

promotion of a resolutely monocultural 'Britishness' in the ideologies of the New Right. All of these, I would suggest, point to a crisis in citizenship, culturally and politically; in Stuart Hall's terms, 'a contestation over what it means to be British'.[1]

It is important to historicize the present crisis, if it can be so termed, for it is part of the backwash of a much larger historical phenomenon: the decline of Britain's formal Empire[2] in the nineteenth and early twentieth centuries, and more specifically, the new challenge to the former imperial centre's sense of itself which was presented by the 'children' of Empire 'coming home' —the emigration of colonial, dominion and former colonial subjects from the New Commonwealth and Pakistan to Britain in the post-1945 period.[3] With the loss of her formal Empire, Britain was forced to confront a radically redrawn world map which had significant ramifications for her own role and self-image, shifting her own sense of place on the map as well as challenging those versions of national identity around which the Empire had been built and sustained. However, it was the immigration into Britain of 'so many of its ex-subjects during and after the decolonization period'[4] which was to precipitate the most seismic shift in the former imperial centre's sense of itself. Ultimately, the presence of these 'new ethnicities'[5] would lead to a newly inflected sense of 'Britishness', one which was both more complex and more ambivalent.

There has been a black presence in Britain for centuries. Black soldiers, seamen, servants and students served or studied in Britain and some stayed on and settled. Cities such as Liverpool, London and Bristol which had particularly strong links with the trans-atlantic slave trade, have some of the oldest black communities in Britain and there is evidence to suggest that these populations were increasing significantly from the late nineteenth century onwards. For example in Liverpool, the census figures show a black population of 3,000 against a total population of 750,000 in 1911, 5,000 by 1918 and 8,000 by 1948.[6] However, the most significant immigration was to occur in the post-1945 period. Under the 1948 British Nationality Act, New Commonwealth and Pakistani citizens were free to enter and settle in Britain; however, the majority of the emigrants were propelled by more specific socio-economic factors. Some stayed on after serving in the Second World War. Many others were 'invited' to Britain, actively recruited through a series of overseas campaigns designed to supply labour to those (mainly service) industries in the British economy experiencing shortages in the post-war period. Later emigrant groups entered Britain in direct response to more precise and localized socio-political factors.[7] However, as Bernard Porter has pointed out, although 'a multi-racial Britain was one of the main results of empire, [it] was one for which the empire, despite all its high multi-racial pretensions, had very poorly prepared her people'.[8]

In this diasporic trajectory, former subjects of the British Empire moved from the 'margins' of Empire to a familiar centre—the Motherland—only to find that the version of Britain and British-ness mapped out for them under Empire bore little resemblance to the much harsher Britain they now encountered at first hand. This was a Britain of class difference and the colour bar, a society with racial prejudices of endemic proportions, riddled with social and economic inequalities. The new immigrants often found themselves at the bottom of the pile, subject to the worst working conditions, the most overcrowded and unsatisfactory housing, and denied full access to a range of rights many believed were theirs by right as British nationals. It was this version of Britain and of the British, as experienced and encountered by the immigrant, which was to confuse and unsettle the host society's own version of nation.

For example, in an early review of one of the novels of emigrant life by West Indian writers such as Samuel Selvon, George Lamming and Andrew Salkey, all of whom emigrated to Britain in the 1950s, the reviewer commented on the 'strangeness' of the London portrayed in these novels: 'Mr Salkey, concentrating on the impact of London on an educated Jamaican, succeeds in making parts of that city as foreign to the English as Babylon or Buenos Aires—but then today they are'.[9] The emigrants of the initial contact period, finding they were 'not (officially) on any map' were forced to create new temporal and spatial maps on which to record their presence in Britain and experiences of Britishness[10]. In so doing, they began to redraw the very map which had failed to include them, contesting, in powerful and subversive ways, the axes upon which British citizenship had formerly rested.

Almost forty years on, such novelists as Salkey, Lamming and Selvon are still relatively invisible, not widely known or read, although the work of succeeding generations of black writers and artists in Britain is at last receiving wider recognition. The larger issue at stake here is visibility on the map, whether the map of black representation in the media or in British politics, or the cultural map of Britain more generally. In many ways black people occupy an ambivalent space in British society: they are both on and not on the map. As the term 'fringe' used in a cultural context suggests, their temporal and spatial mappings of a very different Britain, British experience and Britishness are still often marginalized, delegated to the fringes. Yet it is precisely the presence of a British-born and/or self-defined black British population which is central to the current questions of citizenship: Who is British?, Who belongs and to what do we belong?

Black Britons then, both belong and radically 'unbelong' on the map; in Salman Rushdie's words 'they . . . are at one and the same time insiders and outsiders in this society'[11], manifesting a British form of what W.E.B. DuBois termed the 'double consciousness' of the black in a predominantly white society. Britain's black population, more than any other former immigrant group, continues to present discordant and 'discrepant attachments', incompatible and overlapping versions of nation which act to contest the former imperial centre's sense of itself and which radically disrupt the monocultural premises upon which these notions of Britishness are based. In short, the black British presence asserts a diasporic and local identity simultaneously; it invokes both difference from and economic and political integration into British life; it critiques notions of a monocultural or static 'Britishness', and because of its overlapping and intersecting constituencies, exposes the myth of discrete cultural 'essences' within multiculturalism. Most importantly, the black British presence radically destabilizes the demarcation (and thus policing) of state boundaries and skews the axes of citizen/alien, British immigrant, us/other on which notions of British citizenship currently rest. I propose then to look at the kinds of complex, contradictory 'British' cultural and national identities which have emerged over the last four or five decades in the former immigrant communities of Britain and to consider some of the ways in which these groups contest the former colonial centre's sense of itself. I will also look at how a number of black cultural practitioners are, in a post-colonial context, seeking not only to map their discordant and discrepant attachments to and experiences of Britain and its 'elsewheres', but are, in the process, radically redrawing that map.

One particular concern of this chapter will be to interrogate the term 'black British' and to consider the cultural production of identity in (and in relation to) black literary praxis in Britain.

Taking some recent black British poems as my textual locale, I will trace some of the tropes of 'belonging' and 'unbelonging' in this literature. Black British literature has long exploited its potential to deconstruct, destabilize and subvert old orthodoxies—not only in subject matter but also linguistically and formally[12]. However, my interest here is in the use of black British as a term of classification and the 'changing boundaries of this category'.[13] The use of black British involves more than political correctness or taxonomic niceties; indeed, I argue that how writers *place* themselves in relation to these fluctuating boundaries can be highly significant.

As literary discourse is one of the competing discourses which construct difference around the term 'black', the use of the frequently contentious term black British needs to be thoroughly deconstructed.

The term black is problematized because it intersects cultural, social class and political class identities; in various contexts it is appropriated as an ideological taxonomy. Equally, the term British needs to be interrogated, resonant as it is with the traces of a colonial and imperial past. At this locus some crucial questions need to be raised. How do the two components (i.e. black and British) connect? Is black British identity and culture more *black* than *British*? Or is the British hegemonic over black? In cultural terms, how important to the category black British is its grounding in a radical discourse and praxis? Is black British necessarily oppositionally positioned *vis-à-vis* the majority culture or is it also deeply implicated in the same? Is it possible for 'difference' to form the basis for asserting a collective identity in anything other than a negatively defined way? Has the use of the term black British opened up the creative perspectives and opportunities available to the black artist in Britain, or has it restricted them? Finally, in a postmodern context, what is the future for a black British identity? Is movement 'towards a world where identities are conceptualized as open, fluid and inclusive'[14] and away from a notion of ethnicity as a self-defined identity constituted by group construction around shared experience plus 'boundary maintenance', possible or desirable (and for whom?) in a black British context? Stuart Hall and David Held argue that:

> [I]n real politics, the main, if not the only arena in the West in which questions of citizenship have remained alive until recently, has been the discourse about race and immigration,

questions which challenge any notion of fixed boundaries of the 'community'.[15]

I would argue that these 'questions of citizenship' are also being raised in relation to literary praxis in Britain. Huge advances have been made in the wider publication and visibility of black British writing in the last twenty years. For example, in 1976 James Berry made this passionate declaration in his introduction to an anthology of black poets in Britain, *Bluefoot Traveller:*

> There is no nourishing atmosphere for the development of black distinctiveness [in Britain]. Neither does Britain show any desire for cultural fusion . . . Westindians here are . . . grossly underexplored, underexpressed, underproduced and undercontributing.[16]

This situation no longer pertains with such force, as Berry's later introduction to the 1981 edition of *Bluefoot Traveller* acknowledges. However, the term black British, although increasingly the focus of attention in the social sciences, urgently requires further interrogation in the literary and cultural arena.

Rather than privilege critical analyses of this subject, I will look instead at how the issues of culture, citizenship and nationality are interrogated in the work of two black poets 'resident in Britain'. I use this clumsy expression not as part of any exclusionary practice which denies that such writers can be both black and British, but in response to interesting differences in the categorization of these poets by their publishers, Bloodaxe and Virago. The cover of Fred d'Aguiar's recent collection *British Subjects* (1993) declares the poet's impeccable postcolonial credentials as the journeyer, the cultural traveller, the *unheimlich*:

> Born in Britain, brought up in Guyana, and now living in London and America . . . being and feeling British but not being made to feel at home.[17]

In contrast, Merle Collins' collection *Rotten Pomerack* (1992) states more starkly: 'Merle Collins is Grenadian . . . she lives in London.' It would be interesting to hear how the poets classify themselves, given the overlap of Caribbean and British identities in their work.[18] Certainly many of the poems themselves contest the kind of symbolic boundary control exerted by publishers' retention of uni-national classifications of writers, by figuring instead multiple, transcultural, transnational 'belongings'.

Whereas d'Aguiar's first two collections were largely concerned with re-imaging a Guyanese childhood, the punningly titled *British Subjects* focuses much more centrally on the ambivalences attendant on this traversing of continents and cultures and on the complexities of being black and a British citizen. In 'Home' the poetic voice reflects:

> These days whenever I stay away too long,
> anything I happen to clap eyes on,
> that red telephone box somehow makes me
> miss here more than anything I can name.
>
> my heart performs a jazzy drum solo
> when the crow's feet on the 747
> scrape down at Heathrow. H.M. Customs . . .
> I resign to the usual inquisition,
>
> telling me with surrey loam caked
> on the tongue, home is always elsewhere,
> I take it like an english middleweight
> with a questionable chin, knowing
>
> my passport photo's too open-faced
> haircut wrong (an afro) for the decade;
> the stamp, british citizen not bold enough
> for my liking and too much for theirs.[19]

The euphoria of 'belonging' in Britain in the opening stanza rapidly gives way to a literal and metaphorical grounding at Heathrow, where even the customs officers speak 'with surrey loam caked/on the tongue' as if to underline the notion of citizenship as literally earthed, rooted, grounded in the very soil which is Britain.

Here, the national collectivity (which is Britain) is metonymically rendered as 'soil' with all the resonances of a much-battled over and revered territory. There are distinct echoes here of Shakespeare's 'sceptred isle . . . other Eden, demi paradise . . . this blessed plot, this earth, this realm, this England'[20]; in 'Home', however, these allusions are ironized and gently undermined by the literalized images of clogging, caking and parochial 'surrey loam'. In a single stanza, d'Aguiar deftly invokes, only to deconstruct, one of the key narratives of nationhood; the mythologizing of territory, frequently metonymically rendered, usually idealistically but here, literally and somewhat bathetically, as 'soil'.

A further ironic resonance here, is that the *ius soli*, the ancient right of the soil entitling all those born on British soil to claim British citizenship, is no longer a reality. Since the 1981 Nationality Act, British citizenship has been instead, effectively a gift of Government and for many, an increasingly elusive one.

The recognition in 'Home' that 'home is always elsewhere', at once removed, displaced, deferred is a common enough trope in postcolonial literatures, especially in relation to those who continually cross boundaries, whether territorial boundaries or the 'dominantly construed'[21] and ever shifting boundaries of race, gender and class. In this way, d'Aguiar's poem can be seen as part of that 'growth [in] hybridity and "counter-narratives"' which Homi Bhabha notes as 'pertaining to those who cross boundaries continually'.[22]

However, d'Aguiar's poem deals in more deliberate ambivalences; in response to the categorization of the poem's persona as 'unbelonging', the poetic persona playfully notes: 'I take it like an english middleweight/with a questionable chin'. This image of 'an english middleweight', is cleverly constructed in terms of its hints of controlled aggression—more putative than actual, thus invoking another racial stereotype: young black equals 'has potential/for violence'.[23] The vague, generalized nature of the image 'english middleweight', (what does an englishman look like?) also begs the question: 'what does a British citizen look like? The customs officer's easy assumption that skin colour and ethnicity are key factors in determining who is British and who is not, uncovers the normative biases of this particular form of boundary control.[24]

As the persona of another poem, E.A. Markham's 'Racial prejudice day—a white poem' enunciates, with bitter sweet irony:

> Makes you proud, yes
> to be of this company . . .
>
> You see

we've got this great asset
(and it's truly national:

the polls agree) of recognizing
the foreigner. The skin,

you know, helps. We don't like
him: what to do, what to do?[25]

In principle, citizenship is colour-blind; it eludes such narrow construction on the basis of ethnicity and colour; in practice however, the conflation of these terms has had very real material consequences, impacting on the lives of many black people in Britain through a range of racist assumptions and exclusionary practices.[26] As Avtar Brah has pointed out, the reality in Europe is that 'Citizenship rights . . . are currently underpinned by . . . racial divisions'[27]

Returning to d'Aguiar's poem, another significant slippage is evident in the phrase 'questionable chin'. This invokes dual meanings: the chin may be questionable in boxing parlance, in the sense of not being able to withstand a good punch (with the possibility of verbal as well as physical abuse); however, traces of scientific racism, the colonially endorsed practice of measuring and recording so-called 'racial characteristics' as indices of inferiority are also registered. There is, as the following lines make clear, another sense of 'questionable'; both needing to be questioned and being suspect in some way, here not British enough for the customs officer with the possible adjunct of 'criminal tendency'.

The lines 'the stamp, british citizen not bold enough/for my liking and too much for theirs' speak the complexities and ambivalences of black British citizenship most powerfully. As d'Aguiar signals in his poem, the reality for many black British citizens is not one of sharply defined polarities but is instead one of discordant belongings and shifting boundary demarcations along a continuum between the polarities of black/colonial/other/alien (i.e. belongs elsewhere) and white/one of us/British/citizen.[28] The *placing* of the black British citizen is problematic precisely because black identity has traditionally been one of the oppositional identities defining what is Britishness by providing alterity: i.e. what it is not. As Perry Anderson has noted, a nation is ineluctably 'shaped by what it opposes . . . but the very fact that such identities depend constitutively on difference means that nations are forever haunted by their various definitional others'.[29]

It is possible to speak of a simultaneous presence and absence of former immigrant groups in Britain in the post-1945 period. I mean by this that black Britons have long suffered from invisibility on the map of Britishness despite their *presence* in Britain. The growing visibility of their own creative and experiential mappings of nation, of the complex state of (un)belonging in Britain, has been central to the problematizing and unsettling of received versions of Britishness as well as in undermining notions of a fixed, unchanging construction of nation. However, we are currently seeing a powerful counter-current to this process in the new racism, the resurgence of New Right ideologies and reinvigorated mobilization of 'powerfully homogenizing versions of the nation that act to constrain, oppress and eviscerate' Britishness.[30] Both Enoch Powell's 1968 'Rivers of blood' speech and Margaret Thatcher's equally infamous 'Fear of swamping the British character which has done so much to civilize the world' speech of 1978 were echoed during 1993 in MP Winston Churchill's renewed calls for the 'urgent halt[ing]' of (black) immigration 'if the British way of life is to be preserved'.[31] As Brah points out, the New Right's use of the metaphors of 'nation', 'family' and 'the British way of life', [all constructed as unequivocally white] 'invoke pathologized notions of Afro-Caribbean and Asian households, constructing these groups as "other" to the "British Character"'[32] and 'way of life' of which Thatcher and Churchill speak. What these powerfully homogenizing versions of nation fail to recognize or admit is that the nation as a collective is a shifting and changing entity, constantly defining and redefining itself. How to define the nation and where it is going, what it means to be British in the 1990s, are clearly important questions within a literary and cultural as well as a political arena.

Merle Collins' 'The sheep and the goats' and 'Schizophrenia' in her collection *Rotten Pomerack*[33] are useful points of comparison for d'Aguiar's 'Home'. The persona of 'The sheep and the goats' is not distinguished as immigrant or returning traveller on arrival at Heathrow. Perhaps this is deliberate in order to enforce the point that black individuals are often subject to a homogenizing racism at immigration control, based on the racist premises that 'all blacks look the same', are all 'other' (i.e. not British/British enough) and are potentially a 'problem'. In Collins' poem the arrival is couched in terms of animals waiting to be sorted and selected, an image precipitated by the persona's memory of her mother's proverbial saying 'this is where you separate the sheep from the goats' but also reflecting the process of immigration control itself:

> Standing in the queue
> at the airport terminal
> london heath-
> row
>
> i tried to decide
> which were the sheep
> and which the goats
>
> a sudden movement
> a twitch nervous toss of head
> to shoulder
> a forceful kicking
>
> twitching leg
> quick glance through the pages
> of a pass-
> port
> taut tug
> at the hands of a fearful child
>
> and on
> the
> other
> side
> the sheep
> serene

Collins' interrogation of the politics of immigration, just one of the many State-endorsed exclusionary practices in Britain today and a particularly powerful form of 'boundary control', continues with a similar recognition to d'Aguiar's 'Home' that citizenship, is in complex and contradictory ways, arbitrarily constructed in relation to ethnicity:

a few there
look like us
here
but this is clearly where
you separate
the sheep
from the goats

However, an ability to 'speak the language' is recognized by the poem's persona as one of the symbolic boundary guards of this collectivity, one of the ways in which its boundaries are policed:

at the desk
the officer's eyes
proclaim
a cold dislike of goats
so throats are cleared
for bleating
this is where one begins
to learn
new speaking

When he stamped my pass
i looked down expecting to see
SHEEP

Both poems testify, in different ways, to the ways in which ideologies of nationalism and racism, grounded in the discourses and practices of imperialism, have sought to reduce or conceal the multi-inflected senses of transnational, cross-cultural, historicized and gendered 'belongings', as well as the intersecting political and *class* identities, which constitute Britishness today. The legal category British citizen, metonymically represented by the British passport, fails to account for the complexity of these intersecting identities: rather it subsumes them.[34]

The full citizenship rights accorded to British subjects in 1948 have been 'persistently eroded through . . . increasingly restrictive immigration legislation'.[35] Moreover, the tiered system of unequal 'belongings' which has long been a feature of twentieth-century British immigration policy, has arguably never been more pronounced. As Collins reflects in her poem 'Schizophrenia', some are more British than others and the shared rights and equality of citizenship supposedly conferred by a British passport, can seem more illusory than actual:

> holding a passport that named him British
> he was an English man, he thought . . .
> until they moved to England . . .
> learning to search their mirrors
> for the faces the real English saw
> learning that Irish was a little less
> than English
> that black had
> no place at all in British.

At the heart of this issue of British citizenship is the overlapping of nation and State. Two recent studies[36] call for the urgent need to separate nation from State in any consideration of British citizenship. As Sheila Allen notes:

 The British *nation* is a myth, relying heavily on Anglo-Saxon origins and ignoring the different racial, linguistic, cultural and national composition of those living [here] over many centuries. The British *state* is a reality. In its imperial mode [it] defined all those living in the U.K. or . . . its colonies as British *subjects* with varying rights according to gender and race/ ethnicity. The post-imperial phase . . . through immigration control legislation and . . . legal categories of nationality, has produced a progressive reduction of rights for those not holding full British Citizenship, with gender and patriality playing crucial and continuous roles in the construction of Britishness by the British state. The de facto exclusion of the Black British from such constructions raises important political and sociological questions.[37]

This also raises important questions in the literary and cultural arena where a growing number of writers are also speaking of 'British Identities' with all the complexity, contradiction and difficulty this term implies.[38] For example, in his now famous, polemical essay, 'Commonwealth literature does not exist' (1983) Salman Rushdie writes:

55

I have constantly been asked whether I am British, or Indian. The formulation 'Indian-born British writer' has been invented to explain me. But my new book deals with Pakistan. So what now? 'British-resident Indo-Pakistani writer'? You see the folly of trying to contain writers inside passports.[39]

Turning to a specifically British context, Fred d'Aguiar develops this idea further in a passage which cleverly appropriates and reconfigures the language of international borders, travel and terrorism in his essay 'Against Black British Literature':

[T]he creative imagination knows no boundaries. Borders and passports do not confine it nor do attempts to hijack with neat terms said to be for the liberation of one section of it from the tyranny of another section . . . Creativity . . . cannot be contained for long in any fashion or vice-hold which the process of naming and compartmentalizing seeks to promote. Black writers are British not in terms of their imagination but because of naturalization or birth. [And] Britishness is altered in turn by this fact.[40]

D'Aguiar's argument for the creative imagination's transcendence of all boundaries is, however, weakened on two grounds. He refuses to interrogate in any sustained way what he calls the 'whole question of identity'; instead, rather simplistically, he terms it 'an evasion of the issue of imaginative license'.[41] More importantly, d'Aguiar also fails to take account of the material conditions of black cultural praxis in Britain: that is, the very real implications of the exclusionary politics of publishing and other areas of the arts, the designation of black cultural practices to 'ethnic' or 'fringe' categories and the racializing of cultural production. In all these and other ways, racist practices and inequities impact on black artists lives by constructing 'British' as resolutely white.

However, both Rushdie and d'Aguiar note the problematics of categorization and of the term black British as used to denote black cultural praxis in Britain and usefully discuss its implications. For example d'Aguiar argues that:

It is critical that black writers examine the labels ascribed to or embraced by them. Otherwise the labels stick. They become impossible to shake off and ultimately may police the imagination that gave rise to them . . . in its dual function as adjective and noun [the term, 'Black British'] serves to enclose and prejudice the real scope of th[e] creativity [to which it refers][42]

Rushdie's polemical dissection of the totalizing category 'Commonwealth literature' and his worries about the marginalizing implications of black nationalisms as expressed in what he calls 'self consciously black literature'[43], are equally instructive in considering the politics of the label black British:

> The dangers of unleashing such a phantom [as Commonwealth/Black British literature] are . . . manifold. There is the effect of creating a ghetto, and that, in turn does lead to a ghetto mentality amongst some of its inhabitants. Also, the creation of a false category can and does lead to excessively narrow, and sometimes misleading readings of actually worth looking at, what is going on . . . the term is not used simply to describe or even misdescribe, but also to divide.[44]

Both writers argue for a full recognition of the complexity of black cultural identities which are resistant to homogenizing categories and totalizing theoretical practices. Rushdie in particular, hints at the danger of the 'grand narratives' of a reified black presence and black cultural production in Britain, 'drowning' or 'flattening' out local, regional and temporal narratives which are also black and British.[45]

There is a recognition, especially in Rushdie's essay 'Minority literatures', that black problematizes the term black British considerably by intersecting cultural, social class and political class identities. If black British is more black than British, then what kind of black are we talking about here? Andree McLaughlin argues that:

> Prevalently Black people in Britain do not define themselves as 'Britons' despite the centuries-old Black presence on the island nation . . . Based on a history of antagonism whereby Blacks have not been recognized as legitimate and equal inhabitants . . . and are continuously fighting for [their] right to be [in British society], Black people reject British self-definition and correspondingly adopt Black identity.[46]

This is echoed by Mikey Massive of the *Caribbean Times:*

It's an insult to a black person to be referred to as English . . .
[A] lot of people feel . . . we're never going to achieve respect
in this country. Our numbers here are too small and insigni-
ficant. So they feel our primary loyalty should be to our original
countries. The kind of nationalism we're interested in is
achieving economic autonomy for Africa and the Caribbean.[47]

However:

[T]o novelist Mike Phillips, such talk . . . is a dangerous
distraction. 'You get people who know they're not going back
to the Caribbean, who know their fate is bound up with
this country—so why talk about "are we really Caribbean or
not?" This stuff about a Caribbean identity is really just an
attempt to claim some racial pride. The trouble is, in Britain,
such attempts have always been short-circuited by U.S. style
nationalism and the discussion of 'blackness' imported from
the U.S. Malcolm X has to be a revered figure for us because
he's a black hero. But in terms of our own history, his
arguments make no sense at all.'[48]

Paul Gilroy has been among those to question Afro-centrism and
the various forms of black nationalisms in Britain. He calls the
latter:

[S]trategies that do nothing but postpone the encounter with
white power . . . [when the real issue is] the relationship
between 'race', nation and class in the post-industrial world
. . . Besides, 'black nationalism' gets constructed, like other
nationalisms, as [unhelpfully] fixed, closed and exclusive[49].

Mike Massive's call for a return to the specificities of a black British
experience, or more accurately experiences, is, I think, a crucial
one. So is the recognition of such critics as Stuart Hall, that the
concept of 'blackness' as well as black British cultural identity,
continues evolving. Cultural identity, Hall reminds us:

is a matter of 'becoming' as well as 'being'. It belongs to the
future as much as to the past. It is not something which already
exists, transcending place, time, history and culture. Cultural
identities come from somewhere, have histories. But like
everything which is historical, they undergo constant

transformation. Far from being fixed in some essentialized past, they are subject to the continuous 'play' of history, culture and power.[50]

The gesturing towards a more open and multifaceted definition of black cultural production in Britain in Rushdie and d'Aguiar's essays and the clear articulation of a dynamic and transformative diasporic aesthetic in Hall's essay, correlates in many ways with Paul Gilroy's preferred 'Black Atlantic Identity'.[51] This is an identity comprised of a history of African origins, slavery, the Caribbean and the culture of Europe, an identity which is simultaneously black and European, cosmopolitan and local, diasporic and—albeit relatively recently—rooted. The result is a '"transnational", "translocal" open identity,'[52] which would seem to support Kum-Kum Bhavnani's point that in a postmodern context, all identities are undergoing movement 'towards a world where identities are conceptualized as open, fluid and inclusive'.[53]

Hall asks that we see diasporic cultural production as powerfully syncretic and transformative, rather than constituted purely of what he calls 'narratives of displacement'[54]. This framing of black cultural praxis is supremely postmodern as well as characteristically post-colonial. In response to those who might wish to contest this framing I would argue along with Hall that 'cultural identity belongs to the future as much as to the past' and that means taking account of current movements towards cultural syncretism and hybridization in British culture, the kind of 'cut and mix' aesthetic that Dick Hebdige[55] has formulated in relation to black musical forms in Britain and Gordon Rohlehr[56] has theorized as aesthetic code-switching along a continuum of styles, in relation to Caribbean literature. It is important to historicize the development of a recognizably black British culture, to trace the ways in which it has 'produce[d] and reproduced itself anew'[57], but it is also important to look at what is happening at present as this culture continues to evolve.

Until recently, a major part of black British cultural practice has been oppositionally grounded *vis-à-vis* the majority culture—and necessarily so, for a major imperative of this emergent culture has been to find a space from which to speak and to represent black experiences. However, while acknowledging the powerfully 'subversive force' of this praxis, its decentring, destabilizing, carnivalizing potential in relation to what Kobena Mercer calls the 'master codes of the dominant culture [including the] nation-language of [this] master discourse: Standard English',[58] I would also argue for a new sense of black British cultural practice as freed from this oppositional framework: one which admits 'interstitial' or 'intercultural' positionalities without marginalizing them as necessarily 'other' to 'Britishness', one which inhabits a more fluid realm of accommodations, and hybridizations, shifts and negotiations, where the fixed, the monocultural, the uni-vocal have no place.

It is perhaps brutally realistic to read the present 'contestation of what it means to be British' simply as crisis, given the attendant resurgence of New Right ideologies and ever rising numbers of racist attacks in Britain. However, perhaps this will also be a powerfully transformative stage in what Rushdie has called 'a critical phase in Britain's post-colonial period'.[59] The contested national space which is Britishness is often constructed as a battleground of clashing ideologies; however it might also be figured as an arena of ongoing negotiations, a situation analogous in some ways to the complex negotiations between black and white 'worlds' which forms the putative closure to many eighteenth- and nineteenth-century slave narratives.

Crucially, what is being contested here is not merely black British identities but the nature of *British* national identity itself and concomitantly the redefinition of the nature of British culture and literary praxis. Gilroy's notion of a 'politics of transfiguration' which 'emphasizes the emergence of new desires, social relations and modes of association within the racial community . . . and between that group and its erstwhile oppressors'[60], may seem unrealizable as yet; but in the cultural arena the nation is already being re-imagined, re-mapped, re-formed, rewritten; the very unfixed nature of postcolonial nationalisms means that such versions of nation, such cultural identities can be made and remade.

The ambivalences of being black in Britain and the complexities which can attend culturally locating oneself in relation to Europe, are currently being explored in a wide range of media by black artists in Britain. They include: the filmmaking of the Black Audio Collective and Gurinder Chader, director of *Bhaji on the Beach*; the dramatic pieces of Tara Arts, a theatre group which explores British Asian experience by borrowing from both cultures to create a kind of 'total theatre'; the novels and screenplays of Hanif Kureshi; the poetry of Moniza Alvi and David Dabydeen; the photography of David A. Bailey who sees his work as in critical dialogue with Western traditions of representation, setting up an art which is 'uncomfortably English . . . defined by that problem of belonging' and of Armet Francis, who produced 'Children of the Black Triangle'; the paintings of Tam Joseph and the installations of Keith Piper and Donald Rodney. Similarly, poet Maud Sulter recently held an exhibition of her paintings at the 1994 Edinburgh Festival, paintings which appropriate Western art objects and Germanic/Alpine locations and super-impose them with African artefacts in order to comment on the appropriation of peoples from one socio-political location to another in the transatlantic slave trade, the ways in which African cultures have been silently assimilated by European modernism, the resurgence of volatile nationalisms in Germany and elsewhere in Eastern Europe, and how these impact on her own life in Britain. Alongside these cultural productions should be placed the growing number of oral testimonies and histories of this particular diasporic experience.[61] In these diverse ways, black British artists are re-mapping Britain and re-inflecting Britishness; they are bringing new cultural valencies to the constitution of British identities, reinscribing and relocating the nation in terms of diverse and discordant new voices, bringing to bear new words and forms, opening up possibilities for a more complex sense of Britishness and a cultural praxis, enriched by that complexity.

Notes

1. For the *Wisden* controversy, see Mike Marquesee, 'Fear and Fervour', *The Guardian*, July 4, 1995, pp. 2–3. Stuart Hall's quote is from 'New Ethnicities' in J. Donald (ed), *'Race', Culture and Difference* (London: Sage Publications for the Open University, 1992) pp. 252–259

2. By 'formal Empire' I mean those territories formally annexed and ruled or governed by Britain, denoted, at the time, by the colour red on maps of the world. Formal Empire differs from informal Empire in involving direct rule of colonized territories as well as control of them in an economic sphere (e.g. of trade); informal Empire tends to include only the latter. Formal Empire may include territories with nominally self-governing status (e.g. in relation to domestic policy) but the imperial power still controls foreign policy. It should also be noted that 'im-perialism', 'colonialism' and 'postcolonialism' are all highly contested terms which may be defined and understood in very different ways (see note 3 for my preferred definition of 'postcolonialism' in this chapter). Because these are broad terms, denoting a multiplicity of ideologies,

practices, experiences and legacies over varying periods of time, it is possible, and perhaps most accurate, to see imperialism and colonial practices not just in a historical context but also as present-day phenomena. American economic and cultural imperialism in the twentieth century is a good example of informal Empire. The vestiges of colonial attitudes in Britain led E.P. Thompson to dub Britain 'the last colony', as does Salman Rushdie, examining the spectre of racism in what he calls the 'New Empire in Britain', an Empire (re-)constituted by its former colonial subjects, now re-colonized, re-subjugated at the former imperial centre.

3. It should be noted that the processes of decolonization, formally defined as movement toward political independence but usually also involving the assertion of psychological and cultural autonomies, took place—and are still taking place—at different times and at different rates in different colonies or former colonies. Ashcroft, Griffiths and Tiffin in *The Empire Writes Back* (London & New York: Routledge, 1989) use the term 'post-colonial' to signify 'all the culture affected by the imperial process from the moment of colonization to the present day' (p. 2), and this is my preferred usage; other commentators use the term more narrowly to signify post-independence status. It is important to realize that some of the New Commonwealth immigrants entering Britain in the post-1945 period, came from territories which were still British colonies (in the case of the British West Indies, many territories did not gain independence until the 1970s and 1980s); others came from British dominions which were semi-autonomous territories, defined earlier in the century by Lord Balfour as 'autonomous communities within the British Empire, equal in status, in no way subordinate one to another in any aspect of their domestic or external affairs, though united by a common allegiance to the crown'; the remainder (such as those from India which gained independence in 1947) came from former British colonies.

4. Bernard Porter, *The Lion's Share: A Short History of British Imperialism* (London: Longman, 1984 [second edition]) p. 351.

5. Donald, pp. 252–259.

6. Marij van Helmond and Donna Palmer, *Staying Power—Black Presence in Liverpool* (Liverpool: HMSO, 1991) p. 16.

7. Most of the East African citizens of Asian ethnicity, for example from Kenya and Uganda, who came to Britain in the 1960s emigrated as a direct result of persecutory 'Africanization' policies in those countries at that time.

8. Porter, p. 351.

9. Anon, review of Andrew Salkey's *Escape to an Autumn Pavement* (London: Hutchinson, 1960) in *Times Literary Supplement* (15 July, 1960) p. 445.

10. A striking example of this process of radical 'mapping' of black presence and black experience in Britain, can be found in Linton Kwesi Johnson's

poems, 'Di Great Insohreckshan' which charts the Brixton riots of 1981 and begins: 'it woz in april nineteen eighty-one/doun inna ghetto of Brixtan' and 'Mekkin' histri', *Tings and Times: Selected Poems* (Newcastle Upon Tyne: Bloodaxe, 1991) pp. 43–44.

11. Salman Rushdie, *Imaginary Homelands* (London: Granta, 1992) p. 19

12. As Elleke Boehmer has pointed out: 'Nationhood is so bound up in textuality, in "definitive" histories and official languages and mythologies, that to compose a substantially different kind of text, using vernacular forms that are part of a people's experience, is already to challenge the normative discourses of nationhood'. Susheila Nasta, *Motherlands* (London: The Women's Press,1991) p. 10.

13. See Floya Anthias and Nira Yuval-Davis, *Racialized Boundaries* (London and New York: Routledge, 1993) p. 9.

14. Kum-Kum Bhavani, 'Towards a Multicultural Europe? "Race", Nation and Identity in 1992 and Beyond', *Feminist Review* 45 (1993) pp. 30–45.

15. Anthias and Yuval-Davis, pp. 30–31.

16. James Berry (ed), *Bluefoot Traveller: An Anthology of Westindian Poets in Britain* (London, Limestone, 1976) p. 9.

17. The cover does this rather than stressing the peculiarly 'privileged' insight potentially deriving from what Paul Gilroy has termed 'this intercultural positionality'. Gilroy, *The Black Atlantic* (London: Verso, 1993); originally published as 'It Ain't Where You're Coming From, It's Where You're At . . . The Dialectics of Diasporic Identification', *Third Text* 13, (1991).

18. This is an issue d'Aguiar acknowledges in his polemical essay 'Against Black British Literature', in Maggie Butcher (ed), *Tibisiri* (Sydney: Dangeroo Press, 1989), pp. 106–114.

19. Fred d'Aguiar, *British Subjects* (Newcastle-upon-Tyne: Bloodaxe, 1993).

20. William Shakespeare, Richard II, ed. Peter Ure (London: Arden 1976) pp. 50–53.

21. Sheila Allen 'Race, Ethnicity and Gender' in Haleh Afshar and Mary Maynard (eds), *The Dynamics of 'Race' and Gender* (London and Bristol, PA: Taylor and Francis, 1994) p. 100.

22. Anthias and Yuval-Davis, p. 6.

23. As E.A. Markham has the white persona of 'A mugger's game–a black poem' say in James Berry [ed], *News For Babylon* (London: Chatto and Windus, 1984) p. 37.

24. Incidentally, another normative bias is also exposed here; the privilege of the dominant national collective within 'British' to use 'English' as a synonym for 'British', a usage which would be contested by many Scots and Welsh.

25. Berry, p. 36.

26. Salman Rushdie and many others have noted the racialization of the term 'immigrant' to signify 'black immigrant'. Also the use of 'Muslim' to signify Asian Muslim, as Anthias and Yuval-Davis and Avtar Brah have pointed out recently: 'Re-Framing Europe: Engendered Racisms,

Ethnicities and Nationalism in Contemporary Western Europe', *Feminist Review* 45 (1993) pp. 9–29.

27. Even in Britain, the criterion of patriality for citizenship (parent or grandparent born in Britain), has created a two-tier system where to be non-patrial means being 'subject to immigration control, deportation and restriction to taking up employment' (Brah, p. 23); it is possible to be British-born, but because non-patrial, still not enjoy full rights of citizenship for the first ten years of one's life.

28. James Clifford's concept of 'discrepant cosmopolitanisms' captures some of this sense of 'discordant belonging'. He summarizes: 'unresolved historical dialogues between continuity and disruption, essence and positionality, homogeneity and differences (cross-cutting 'us' and 'them') characterize diasporic articulations. Such cultures of displacement and transplantation are inseparable from specific, often violent, histories of economic, political and cultural interaction, histories that generate what might be called discrepant cosmopolitanisms': 'Travelling Cultures' in Lawrence Grossberg, Cary Nelson and Paula A. Treichler (eds), *Cultural Studies* (London and New York: Routledge, 1992) p. 99.

29. Perry Anderson in A. Parker, M. Russo, D. Sommer and P. Yaeger (eds), *Nationalisms and Sexualities* (London and New York: Routledge, 1992) p. 5.

30. Parker *et al.*, p. 3.

31. Winston Churchill, 'Give Us Winning Policies, Churchill Tells PM'; Press Release, 28 May 1993.

32. Brah, p. 18.

33. Merle Collins, *Rotten Pomerack* (London: Virago, 1992).

34. Even though as James Clifford has rightly pointed out, it is a fallacy to believe 'culture (singular) equals language (singular). This equation implicit in nationalist culture ideas has been thoroughly unravelled by Mikhail Bakhtin for whom language is a diverging, contesting, dialoguing set of discourses that no "native"—let alone visitor—can ever learn'. (Grossberg *et al.*, p. 99).

35. Brah, p. 23.

36. Anthias and Yuval-Davis *Racialized Boundaries*, Afshar and Maynard, *The Dynamics of 'Race'and Gender*.

37. Afshar and Maynard, p. 99.

38. Brah, p. 26.

39. Reprinted in *Imaginary Homelands* (London: Granta, 1992). In this seminal essay Rushdie discusses on the one hand, the critical bias towards readings of postcolonial writings as expressions of nationality and the concomitant restrictive pressure on the writer to attend to what he calls the 'bogey of authenticity', and on the other, warns of the dangers of literary ghettoization attendant on the totalizing category 'Commonwealth literature'.

40. Butcher, p.109.

41. Butcher, p. 107.
42. Butcher, pp. 6, 12.
43. Salman Rushdie, 'Minority Literatures in a Multi-Cultural Society' in Kirsten Holst Peterson and Anna Rutherford (eds), *Displaced Persons* (Sydney: Dangeroo, 1988) pp.9–16.
44. Rushdie, *Imaginary Homelands*, pp. 63–66.
45. As Merle Collins writes in 'Visiting Yorkshire—Again': 'an art called Black/exists/for england/in some region called the fringe' (*Rotten Pomerack* p. 18).
46. Andree Nicola McLaughlin, 'The Quest for Humanhood and Wholeness: Wild Woman in the Whirlwind' in Joanne Brixton and Andree Nicola McLaughlin (eds), *Wild Women in the Whirlwind —Afra-Caribbean Culture and the Contemporary Literary Renaissance* (London: Serpent's Tail, 1990) pp. 147–180.
47. Massive, quoted by Mike Bygrave, 'Movement of the People', *The Guardian*, 20 August 1994, pp.28–33.
48. Bygrave, p. 33.
49. Gilroy, quoted by Bygrave, p. 33.
50. Stuart Hall, 'Cultural Identity and Diaspora' in Patrick Williams and Laura Chrisman (eds), *Colonial Discourse and Postcolonial Theory: A Reader* (Hemel Hempstead: Harvester, 1993) pp. 392–403.
51. Gilroy's concept is usefully theorized by Barnor Hesse in 'Black to Front and Black Again', in Michael Keith and Steve Pile (eds), *Place and the Politics of Identity* (London and New York: Routledge, 1993) pp. 162–182.
52. Bygrave, p. 33.
53. Bhavnani, p. 39.
54. Williams and Chrisman, p. 392.
55. Dick Hebdige, *Cut and Mix: Culture, Identity and Caribbean Music* (London and New York: Routledge, 1987).
56. Gordon Rohlehr, 'The Problem of the Problem of Form: The Idea of an Aesthetic Continuum and Aesthetic Code-Switching in West Indian Literature' in *Anales del Caribe* 6 (1986) pp. 218–277.
57. Hall, in Williams and Chrisman, p. 402.
58. Hall, in Williams and Chrisman, p. 402.
59. Rushdie, *Imaginary Homelands*, p. 129.
60. Gilroy, 'It Ain't Where You're Coming From', p. 11. In *The Black Atlantic*, within the context of his analysis of the particular nexus of economic, cultural, political and human 'exchanges' historically initiated by the Atlantic slave trade, the 'rhizomorphic, fractal structure of the transcultural, international formation I call the Black Atlantic', Gilroy reiterates Hall's point about the constant re-transformation of cultural identities: 'The history of the Black Atlantic yields a course of lessons as to the instability and mutability of identities which are always unfinished, always being remade' (xi).

61. See Zhana, *Sojourn* (London: Methuen, 1989); Elyse Dodgson, *Motherland: West Indian Women and Britain* (London: Heinemann, 1984); Chapeltown Women Writers Group, *When Our Ship Comes In: Black Women Talk* (Castleford: Yorkshire Arts Circus, 1992).

Anglo-India after the Mutiny: The Formation and Breakdown of National Identity

Máire ní Fhlathúin

> Infuriated beyond measure by the death of their officer, the Sikhs (assisted, I regret to say, by some Englishmen) proceeded to take their revenge on this one wretched man . . . [W]hile still alive, though faint and feeble from his many wounds, he was deliberately placed upon a small fire of dry sticks, which had been improvised for the purpose, and there held down . . .
> Vivian Majendie, *Up Among the Pandies*[1]

> [We] . . . had disgraced ourselves as Englishmen forever . . .
> Rudyard Kipling, 'The Mark of the Beast'[2]

The question of national identity is more difficult and ambiguous on the periphery of the British Empire than at its English centre. In the latter half of the nineteenth century, the Anglo-Indian community in India was compelled to inhabit the uneasy outer limit of Englishness, the space where it became associated with the opposing quality of Indianness.[3] The idea of the Englishman in India was based on the two forces of distance and control, and his successful construction of Anglo-Indian identity depended on his ability to hold these in balance. But part of the legacy of the Indian Mutiny was the Anglo-Indians' realization that their actions in controlling Indian insurrection were sometimes such that the critical distance between native barbarity and colonizing civilization became unmaintainable. The values upheld by the community involved them in actions which overstepped the limits

67

of their shared identity, an identity which was thereby shown to be inherently unstable. This essay examines some theoretical formulations of the relations between colonizer and colonized, and attempts to use these in a reading of Anglo-Indian identity.

In discussing Anglo-Indian Orientalism as a distinct form of Western Orientalism, B.J. Moore-Gilbert argues that the Anglo-Indian society defined itself in opposition to the home country as well as in opposition to India: 'the discourse of the exiles in India characteristically tended to consider itself as different to that emanating from Britain.'[4] From the time the term 'Anglo-Indian' came into general use, in the early nineteenth century, the community became a unit, increasingly separate from the mother country. This separation was the cause of deep anxiety surrounding the question of identity. To maintain the self-image which justified their possession of colonized lands, the Anglo-Indians needed to uphold the values of reason and civilization, those values associated with British rule which differentiated them from their subjects. But to control their Indian dominions, to suppress insurrection and sustain the colonial order, they engaged in actions which would clearly be regarded by the home country as less than civilized. The identity they claimed was therefore inherently unstable, liable to fracture along the fault-line of violence and superstition. Anglo-Indian reactions to the Indian Mutiny, both in the common memory and in Rudyard Kipling's fiction, display a continuing obsession with these qualities; and the prevalent motif is that of an 'Englishman' driven to un-English madness, compelled to abandon his identity by his very efforts to maintain it.

Edward Said's critical study *Orientalism* provided the framework for subsequent analyses of the colonial encounter, a structure in which European classification of the Oriental reflexively justifies the European's image of himself. In this process, the European is invariably in a position of power; he is the reader, the scientist, while the Oriental is the subject of study: 'Every statement made by Orientalists or White Men (who were usually interchangeable) conveyed a sense of the irreducible distance separating white from colored, or Occidental from Oriental; moreover, behind each statement there resonated the tradition of experience, learning, and education that kept the Oriental-colored to his position of *object studied by the Occidental-white*, instead of vice versa.'[5] Said's second use of the word Orientalism, to describe the West's unconscious knowledge of the Orient which perpetuates such ideas as 'the separateness of the Orient, its eccentricity, its backwardness, its silent indifference, its feminine penetrability, its supine malleability . . .' also maintains the balance of power.[6] There is no room in his analysis for the idea that Western knowledge or control might prove inadequate, or that the self-serving representation of the Orient should fail, and recoil on its perpetrator.

Homi Bhabha's work recognizes some of these limits of Orientalism; he sees in Said 'the suggestion that colonial power and discourse is possessed entirely by the colonizer', and describes this suggestion as 'a historical and theoretical simplification'.[7] His essay 'Signs Taken For Wonders' describes one instance where the Word of British power, in the form of the Bible, is studied by a group of Indians.[8] In the course of their adoption of what they call the 'book of God', they change its message to suit their own ideas, explaining that they will 'conform' to all the 'customs' of Christianity, except that they will not take the Sacrament, 'because the Europeans eat cows' flesh, and this will never do for us'.[9] Bhabha explains the effect of this questioning of the colonizer's power by referring to the 'uncertainty' which is produced by the juxtaposition of the European text and the Indian version of it which reflects Indian concerns. In fact, there is no longer, in his reading, a single clear voice of authority; it is replaced by a 'hybrid' discourse which is not 'a third term that resolves the tension between two cultures' but a force which 'afflicts the discourse of power; an uncertainty that estranges the familiar symbol of English "national" authority and emerges from its colonial appropriation as the sign of its difference'.[10] The creation of this hybrid discourse is offered by Bhabha as a strategy of colonial insurrection: 'By taking their stand on the grounds of dietary law the natives resist the miraculous equivalence of God and the English . . . When the natives demand an Indianized gospel they are using the powers of hybridity to resist baptism . . .'[11] Bhabha's development of this theory, and the critical discussion it has engendered, have concentrated on one aspect of its use—to the neglect of another, perhaps equally interesting. Bhabha sees it as a weapon in the colonial struggle: 'Then the words of the master become the site of hybridity—the warlike, subaltern sign of the native—then we may not only read between the lines, but even seek to change the often coercive reality that they so lucidly contain'.[12] But the focus of his work is on the colonized subject, the native, the oppressed —and in critical discussion of his theories, their limitations are decried because the 'theoretical bias' in his study is 'obviously detrimental to research on the culture of the colonized'.[13]

Such discussion overlooks, as Bhabha has to a great extent overlooked, the question of the colonizer. In the course of his evaluation of Said's work, he writes that 'it is difficult to conceive of the process of subjectification as a placing within Orientalist or colonial discourse for the dominated subject without the dominant being strategically placed within it too'.[14] But, while Bhabha gives instances of native questioning of authority, he fails to give an instance of the English reaction to that questioning. Both colonizer and colonized are constrained by the limitations of the colonial discourse, and any uncertainty in that discourse must threaten the colonizer as much as it liberates the colonized. So, when Bhabha claims that 'colonial specularity, doubly inscribed, does not produce a mirror where the self apprehends itself; it is always the split screen of the self and its doubling, the hybrid . . .'[15], the question remains: how does the colonizer react to this? What kind of portrait does the colonizer see in the combination of the ideal self and the hybrid produced in the colonial encounter?

Within this theoretical framework, it is possible to explain the formation and breakdown of Anglo-Indian identity as a process involving just such a corruption of the self-image. Indian insurrection threatened the Anglo-Indians' control of India, but did not alter their status; their response to that insurrection, however, was such that the undesirable elements of irrationality and uncontrolled violence, long associated with the Indians, had to be recognized as part of their own image. In Kipling's fiction, such incidents of insurrection and response become central experiences for his characters, moments when they abandon the idea of Englishness and replace it with an unidentifiable hysteria.

While the Mutiny was in itself a traumatic event in the history of British India, it was doubly so by virtue of the fact that it was generally attributed to the mistakes of the Anglo-Indian administration, civil and military. Moreland and Chatterjee's *Short History of India* attributes final responsibility to the army officers, who 'trusted their men blindly, and were resolutely opposed to any interference from outside; even Dalhousie [Governor-General, 1848–1856], who described the discipline of the army, officers and men alike, as scandalous from top to bottom, had felt unable to effect a reform; and it was this want of discipline that made the Mutiny possible.'[16] The histories also note that the Anglo-Indian establishment showed a criminal lack of understanding of Indian traditions, in such areas as caste and religion[17] and were reckless in imposing such decrees as the requirement that sepoys previously invalided as 'unfit for foreign service' should be 'utilized for the performance of cantonment duties'.[18] The most obvious, if contested, example of this was the affair of the greased cartridges, where soldiers were ordered to use animal fat, from cows (sacred to Hindus), or pigs (considered unclean by Muslims), to grease their rifles, orders which needlessly offended many. Contemporary accounts follow the same pattern, but reveal even more of the emotional confusion and shock caused by the Mutiny:

> The Officers are not to blame. The whole Mutiny from beginning to end is almost unaccountable, but if any one is to blame, it is the Indian Government, made up of men who have never been out of Calcutta in all their lives and who know positively nothing of Native soldiers. Our Officers have had only too much faith and confidence in their men, and many a gallant fellow has gone to his last home from this feeling, almost amounting to infatuation.[19]

This type of explanation reduced the Mutiny and its aftermath to a problem of management and understanding of the Indians. It ignored other, perhaps equally important, factors such as those pointed out at the time by Karl Marx, who 'stressed British incomes in India, rapacious land tenure policies, and evidence that tax collectors resorted to torture'. The response thus focused on the idea of the Indians as a potentially murderous rabble which needed more careful watching, and disregarded any question of 'economic exploitation'.[20] The Anglo-Indians became wary, determined that the lack of knowledge and control of India which gave rise, in their view, to the Mutiny, should be made good.

On the surface, the Mutiny seemed only to intensify the Anglo-Indians' view of themselves as distinct from the Indians. In the words of Lewis Wurgaft, 'The Mutiny, in the works of British and Anglo-Indian historians, became a psychological drama in which the native propensity for sudden and violent expression was opposed by the iron will of their rulers. The frenzy of the mutineers was conventionally contrasted to the restraint and persistence of the masters they betrayed.'[21] Equally haunting, however, was the memory of how the uprising had been suppressed. Accounts of the reprisals carried out by British forces are

common, both as documented incidents and as hearsay—
Brigadier-General James Neill's infamous directive on the use of
prisoners at Cawnpore, to lick the blood of British women from
the rooms where they had died, is merely the best known. Julia
Inglis describes the fate of more than a thousand rebels who were
'cut to pieces, no quarter being asked or granted. Their bodies
had just been covered over with earth, and it sickened me to feel
they were so near us.'[22] Many years after the event, soldiers told
stories of how the 'rebel Pandies' who had no fear of hanging
'squealed like rats when they were tied to the cannon's mouth'.[23]
But along with the straightforward records of official retaliation,
there exists a more interesting set of atrocity stories dealing
with unlicensed revenge. These often stress the presence and
responsibility of Sikh soldiers, who had not joined in the uprising.
W.H. Russell describes his encounter with a man who claims to
have accepted the surrender of fifty-seven sepoys, disarmed them,
and 'told some Sikhs, who were handy, to polish them off'.[24]
Vivian Majendie gives the eyewitness account which opens this
essay, of a captured sepoy being burned alive by Sikhs, with the
active assistance of Englishmen. Majendie clearly holds all the
perpetrators in equal contempt, and contrast their actions with the
nineteenth century ideal of 'civilization and humanity'.[25] By the
time this story is re-told, however, in Russell's diary intended for
the home market, the participation of English soldiers is no longer
mentioned in it. 'There were Englishmen looking on, more than
one officer saw it', Russell says—but their responsibility, in his
version, is limited to their failure to interfere. By concentrating
on the Sikh presence, he can express horror at the soldiers' actions
while still maintaining the vital distinction between native cruelty
and Anglo-Indian restraint.[26]

This memory of British revenge, as well as the insecurity
engendered by the Mutiny, may be read in Kipling's work. When
he returned to India at the age of seventeen, twenty-five years
after the Mutiny, he found a community still haunted by its
images. Later still, in 1895, he wrote, ' '57 is the year we don't
talk about and I know I can't.'[27] It had a perceptible effect on his
fiction, from such particular details as Kim's referring to 1857 as
'the Black Year' to a more general colouring of his work.[28] Mark
Paffard argues that his work 'echoes the Mutiny . . . chiefly by
sustaining the possibility of unpredictable violence'.[29] But the
violence is not associated only with Indian rebellion, it is also
found in the ranks of the Anglo-Indians.

In his depiction of Anglo-Indian rule, Kipling was drawing on the popular mythology of the 'Punjab Style' of government. The term refers to the theories and practices of Henry and John Lawrence, who held various administrative posts, mainly in north-western India, from 1836 to 1869, when John Lawrence ended his term as Viceroy. Kipling's child-like natives, stern, paternal rulers and emphasis on action over bureaucracy are the product of a shift in the British perception of India which was in part a reaction to the Mutiny. After this, there occurred 'a major reorientation in imperial policy', i.e., the change of focus from the cities and central India to the recently-annexed north-western province of the Punjab.[30] This was accompanied by a growing preference for the stereotypical native of the Punjab, an un-civilized, warlike peasant, over the educated city-dwellers who were increasingly resentful of British rule. 'To the government the essential point was that these martial races of the interior belonged to pre-industrial societies of feudal landlord and peasant, blissfully untouched by the political ideas that the big cities were breeding.'[31] This particular view is reflected in that strand of Kipling's work which presents the Indians as essentially dependent: primitive, superstitious and, in the end, amenable to the wiser rule of the European.[32]

This view of the Indians naturally influenced the Anglo-Indian perception of the type of government needed to control them. The events of the Mutiny had intensified the strong impulse towards authoritarian rule which had always been present in the Anglo-Indian treatment of India. But the figure of the authoritarian, paternal administrator entered into Anglo-Indian legend with the romanticizing of the Punjab Style, which had its greatest success during and immediately after the Mutiny. Kipling himself lived and worked in the Punjab for his time as a journalist in India, and would have observed the 'frustration' of the Anglo-Indian administration with the bureaucracy which was by that time replacing the methods of the Lawrence brothers.[33] His fiction celebrated their achievements, indirectly, by replicating in his self-sacrificing heroes the qualities of these men. The essence of the Punjab Style was in local rule, giving responsibility to the junior officers of the administration rather than having them continually working in the shadow of their superiors. It was, in theory at least, opposed to all forms of bureaucracy. The 'responsibility system' gave these men enormous power, which was used to subdue hostile regions by the display of superior force and the pitiless suppression of any sign of unrest.[34] The emphasis is always on personality, and personal authority; the might of the British Empire concentrated in the person of the administrator. John Lawrence considered that 'the great object of the Government should be to secure the services of able, zealous, and high-principled officials'.[35] Again, this finds its echo in Kipling's fiction, as just such an official instructs his people from his deathbed:

> Such of you as live in our borders must pay your taxes quietly as before. I have spoken of the villages to be gently treated this year. Such of you as live in the hills must refrain from cattle-lifting, and burn no more thatch, and turn a deaf ear to the voice of the priests . . . And you must not sack any caravans, and must leave your arms at the police-post when you come in; as has been your custom, and my order . . . I speak now true talk, for I am as it were already dead, my children—for though ye be strong men, ye are children.[36]

The personal control of the Punjab Style was soon to be superseded, as the legislative programme of the 1860s and 1870s imposed bureaucracy and ensured the separation of judicial and executive power.[37] The influence of the system, however, endured, in the personality cult which grew around such figures of the Punjab as the Lawrence brothers and John Nicholson. When the rest of India was staggered by the outbreak of the Mutiny, John Lawrence and his assistants kept control of the Punjab, as well as sending the army that won back Delhi from the mutineers. His success ensured that he and his lieutenants were remembered, imitated and idealized. These elements of the personality cult—the ability to control with force, the capacity to inspire fear, the knowledge of Indian ways and the assumption of moral right (which played a large part in the legends of the Punjab)[38]—are those attributed by Kipling to the character who was the embodiment of his creator's ideal of the Englishman, Strickland the policeman.

Kipling describes the exploits of this character with an enthusiasm which makes it clear that Strickland is his model of what a governing Englishman should be. The narrator of the various stories where he appears (internal links make it clear that there is one common narrator) regards him with awe, and explains the basis for his success: 'He held the extraordinary theory that a Policeman in India should try to know as much about the natives as the natives themselves.'[39] He, unlike the other Europeans, would disguise himself as an Indian, a sweeper or a groom, and go among them, spying and listening to their talk. In so describing his character, Kipling was drawing on stories of the heroes of the Punjab—compare Martin Gubbins' praise of Henry Lawrence, 'from his habit of freely mixing with [the natives], few succeeded better than himself in arriving at just conclusions, and in eliciting the truth.'[40] Kipling's contempt for bureaucracy is equally clear: the narrator recounts how Strickland disguised himself as a *fakir* to solve the 'great Nasiban Murder Case', only to incur the resentment of the bureaucrats, who asked, 'Why on earth can't Strickland sit in his office and write up his diary, and recruit, and keep quiet, instead of showing up the incapacity of his seniors?' Kipling and his narrator are clearly in complete agreement with Strickland's methods. But it is not enough that he should *know* the habits of the natives. At least as important is the mental attitude he brings to his quest for learning. In order to keep himself safe, he must prevent himself being absorbed into the lives of those he should be observing. He keeps the Indians away from him by the force of their respect: 'not a native in the Province would wittingly have touched "Estreekin Sahib's" gear for the world'.[41] The maintenance of authority is dependent on the Anglo-Indian's moral superiority, and his ability to distance himself from those he would control. The stories show him as Kipling's voice of justice and of reason, the man who restores order to the chaotic world of India. But as he was Kipling's pattern of what an Englishman should be, it is through his figure also that the subconscious disquiet and insecurity felt by Kipling, and by the Anglo-Indian community, are displayed. In the very stories which seem to show Strickland the Englishman at his most unshakeable, we see his strategies of control being undermined.

'The Mark of the Beast' describes an instance of this, when their uncontrolled private violence leads two white men to realize that they have placed themselves outside the boundaries of their communal identity. Their force consumes them as well as the Indians towards whom it is directed, and they succumb to irrationality and emotional hysteria. The story exemplifies the three stages in the formation and breakdown of identity: the Anglo-Indian community is defined as distinct from the surrounding country; this distance is threatened by native violence; lastly, the insurrection is defeated, at the cost to the protagonists of their own sense of themselves as civilized Englishmen.

The plot is straightforward: Fleete, a newcomer to India, insults a temple god, and is bitten in retaliation by a leper—a 'Silver Man'. During the following day, he loses most of his human characteristics, finally becoming a wolf-like creature who is referred to as a beast. In order to restore his humanity, Strickland and the narrator capture the Silver Man, and torture him with 'heated gun-barrels' (p. 204) to make him release Fleete from the evil spirit in him. They eventually succeed in this; the leper is sent away, and Fleete awakens in his true self, having no memory of the incident. The categories of man and beast are used to establish an opposition between the civilized society of Anglo-India and the primitive land outside it. The first paragraphs describe the Anglo-Indian community as it goes about its ordinary life. The New Year's Eve celebration is an occasion for solidarity, emphasized in the coming together of men 'from the uttermost ends of the Empire' (p. 195). The narrator's description of the event displays a strong sense of the community's strength, and of its imperial mission to civilize and colonize savage lands:

> Everybody was there, and there was a general closing up of ranks and taking stock of our losses in dead or disabled that had fallen during the past year. It was a very wet night, and I remember that we sang 'Auld Lang Syne' with our feet in the Polo Championship Cup, and our heads among the stars, and swore that we were all dear friends. Then some of us went away and annexed Burma, and some tried to open up the Soudan and were opened up by Fuzzies in that cruel scrub outside Suakim . . . [p. 196].

Indian society, on the other hand, is continually referred to in terms of the bestial and the sub-human. The Indians worship Hanuman the Monkey-god; and the leper is almost animal in his appearance: 'He was perfectly naked in that bitter, bitter cold, and his body shone like frosted silver, for he was what the Bible calls "a leper as white as snow". Also he had no face, because he was a leper of some years' standing, and his disease was heavy upon him. He does not speak, but makes "a noise exactly like the mewing of an otter"' (p. 197). When the narrator says the affair was 'beyond any human and rational experience' (p. 202), he is equating humanity and reason with his own world, the world of Anglo-India. The rest of the country, he implies, does not live by the same laws.

The opposition thus created is put at risk by Anglo-Indian ignorance—Fleete's inability to appreciate the importance of Hanuman—and by the Indian leper's retaliation. The account of Fleete's degeneration shows him gradually losing these rational qualities associated with Anglo-India. His drunkenness is the first cause of his misfortune; it make him lose control of himself and leads to the offence of insulting the god. With the leper's bite, he leaves the civilized plane altogether, sinking to the level of a beast, finally conscious of nothing but the need for raw meat and blood. It is as though his initial loss of that control—and self-control —which is almost the defining attribute of the imperial English-man has allowed India to seize him and drag him down to its own animal level. The intervention of Strickland would, on this reading, be an act of reclamation. By making the leper lift the curse, he releases Fleete from the beast-world of India. Thus he displays the power necessary to maintain order and civilization. The leper, also, is in some way redeemed: when he leaves the house in the morning, he is no longer mewing, and is wearing a sheet 'to cover his nakedness' (p. 206). It appears that the united community of the story's opening has been re-established, and that the civilizing function of the Empire has been affirmed in its victory over Indian evil.[42]

However, the return to normality has been achieved at the cost of Strickland and the narrator's membership of their community. They have a choice between acting within the law, maintaining the standards of civilization; or abandoning the stance of racial superiority they occupied at the start, and operating on the level of simple physical force. When they have brought Fleete away from the temple, the narrator says that 'the Managing Committee of the temple would in all probability bring a criminal action against us for insulting their religion. There was a section of the Indian Penal Code which exactly met Fleete's offence.' (p. 198) But even the mention of 'criminal action' and the 'Penal Code' looks absurd in such a context, and so it proves indeed. Instead of proceeding as the narrator suggests, within the bounds of civilized society, Strickland is forced to abandon the code which he, as a policeman, is supposed to uphold. 'I shall take the law into my own hands,' he says, and from this point on the cruelty of his actions mirrors that of the Silver Man: 'I understood then how men and women and little children can endure to see a witch burnt alive; for the beast was moaning on the floor, and though the Silver Man had no face, you could see horrible feelings passing through the slab that took its place, exactly as waves of heat play across red-hot iron—gun-barrels for instance.' (pp. 204–205) The pattern of atrocity and revenge displayed in the Mutiny stories has been recreated, but this time without the presence of the Sikhs to allow Anglo-Indian responsibility to be obscured.

In that situation, the story shows the impossible nature of the Anglo-Indian dilemma: to re-establish the necessary distance between themselves and the Indians; to maintain imperial control, they are compelled to use the tactics of illegal torture and brutality which the story has already figured as Indian. In the colonial encounter, the colonizers see a hybrid image of themselves, containing the undesirable elements assigned to the colonized. Reason, control and civilization are contaminated by superstition and hysteria, as the Anglo-Indians realize that their identity as Englishmen is no longer sustainable:

> Strickland . . . caught hold of the back of a chair, and, without warning, went into an amazing fit of hysterics. It is a terrible thing to see a strong man overtaken with hysteria. Then it struck me that we had fought for Fleete's soul with the Silver Man in that room, and had disgraced ourselves as Englishmen for ever, and I laughed and gasped and gurgled just as shamefully . . . [p. 207]

Kipling's characters, like the shadowy English soldiers who accompany the tales of Sikh retaliation, take the law into their own hands and, in so doing, place themselves outside of that civilization by which they define themselves.

Notes

1. Vivian Majendie, *Up Among the Pandies; or, A Year's Service in India* (London, 1859), quoted in Wayne G. Broehl, *Crisis of the Raj: The Revolt of 1857 through British Lieutenants' Eyes* (London: University Press of New England, 1986) p. 213.
2. Rudyard Kipling, 'The Mark of the Beast', in *Life's Handicap* (1891), ed. P.N. Furbank (Harmondsworth: Penguin, 1987) pp. 195–207 (p. 207). Further references to this story are given after quotations in the text.
3. Because my analysis deals with the British experience of India during the nineteenth century, I have retained the terms and names in general use at that time. Thus, I refer to the events of 1857–8 as the Indian Mutiny, 'Cawnpore' is used in preference to 'Kanpur', and the British

community in India are referred to as 'Anglo-Indians' (as they called themselves). The views and roles examined are exclusively those of Anglo-Indian men; the roles of women, and their self-images, are more complex in nature and cannot be considered here.

4. B.J. Moore-Gilbert, *Kipling and 'Orientalism'* (London: Croom Helm, 1986) pp. 5–9.

5. Edward Said, *Orientalism* (London: Routledge, 1978; repr. Harmondsworth: Penguin, 1991) p. 228.

6. Said, p. 206.

7. Homi K. Bhabha, 'Difference, Discrimination and the Discourse of Colonialism', in Francis Barker (ed) *The Politics of Theory,* (Colchester: University of Essex, 1983) pp. 1940–211 (p. 200). This essay has been reprinted, in a slightly revised version, in Bhabha's later collection *The Location of Culture* (London and New York: Routledge, 1994) pp. 66–84; further references to his work will be cited from this volume.

8. Bhabha, pp. 102–22.

9. *The Missionary Register* (London: Church Missionary Society, January 1818) p. 19, quoted in Bhabha, p. 104.

10. Bhabha, p. 113.

11. Bhabha, pp. 117–18.

12. Bhabha, p. 121.

13. Ania Loomba, 'Overworlding the "Third World"', *Oxford Literary Review* 13 (1991), 164–91 (p. 180). See also pp. 174–75; and Benita Parry, 'Problems in Current Theories of Colonial Discourse', *Oxford Literary Review* 9 (1987), pp. 27–58 (pp. 42–43).

14. Bhabha, p. 72.

15. Bhabha, p. 114.

16. W.H. Moreland and Atul Chandra Chatterjee, *A Short History of India,* 4th edition (London: Longman, 1957) p. 367.

17. See T.R.E. Holmes, *A History of the Indian Mutiny* (London, 1883) pp. 79–80.

18. Holmes, p. 79.

19. F. Roberts, *Letters Written during the Indian Mutiny* (London: Macmillan, 1924) pp. 51–52 (28 August 1857).

20. Patrick Brantlinger, *Rule of Darkness: British Literature and Imperialism, 1830–1914* (Ithaca: Cornell University Press, 1988) p. 202.

21. Lewis D. Wurgaft, *The Imperial Imagination: Magic and Myth in Kipling's India* (Middletown, Connecticut: Wesleyan University Press, 1983) p. 68.

22. Julia Inglis, *The Siege of Lucknow* (London, 1892) pp. 199–200.

23. Frank Richards, *Old-Soldier Sahib* (London: Faber, 1936) pp. 84–85.

24. William Howard Russell, *My Indian Mutiny Diary,* ed. by Michael Edwardes (London: Cassell, 1957) p. 215. This is an abridged version of *My Diary in India,* 2 vols (London, 1860).

25. Majendie (see note 1), pp. 213–14.

26. Russell, p. 87. Majendie is not named in his account, being identified only as 'my friend', but the story is unmistakably the same; the sentence, 'They had lost Anderson, our own men encouraged them, and I could do nothing', appears word for word in both versions.

27. Thomas Pinney (ed.) *The Letters of Rudyard Kipling*, 2 vols (London: Macmillan, 1990) II, 219.

28. Moore-Gilbert, p. 87. He cites this as an instance of the 'persistent emotional impact of the Mutiny' on Kipling's work.

29. Mark Paffard, *Kipling's Indian Fiction* (London: Macmillan, 1989) p. 9.

30. Wurgaft, p. 11.

31. V.G. Kiernan, *The Lords of Human Kind: European Attitudes Towards the Outside World in the Imperial Age* (London: Weidenfeld and Nicholson, 1969) p. 54.

32. See, for instance, 'The Tomb of his Ancestors', *The Day's Work* (1898), ed. Constantine Phipps, (Harmondsworth: Penguin, 1990) pp. 102–33.

33. Wurgaft, p. 26.

34. This remained the case for long after the Mutiny had been suppressed; forty-nine men were executed by the method of blowing away from guns after the Kuka rising of 1872—a decision of the Deputy Commissioner present, who was later subject to official censure. See Henry Cotton, *Indian and Home Memories* (London: Fisher Unwin, 1911) pp. 111–13.

35. Quoted in Kathryn Tidrick, *Empire and the English Character* (London: Tauris, 1990) p. 30.

36. 'The Head of the District', in *Life's Handicap*, pp. 111–32 (p. 114).

37. Eric Stokes, *The English Utilitarians in India* (Delhi: Oxford University Press, 1959; repr. 1989) pp. 268–71. Even then, membership of the Civil Service carried enormous powers, 'beyond comparison greater than those possessed by young men of the same age under any civilized Government'. Cotton, p. 78.

38. Tidrick, p. 11.

39. 'Miss Youghal's *Sais*', in *Plain Tales from the Hills* (1890), ed. H.R. Woudhuysen (Harmondsworth: Penguin, 1987) pp. 51–56 (p. 51).

40. Martin Gubbins, *An Account of the Mutinies in Oudh* (London, 1858), p. 199.

41. 'Miss Youghal's *Sais*', p. 53.

42. Further discussion of this reading may be found in Moore-Gilbert, p. 196.

Modern Ireland:
Postcolonial or European?

Declan Kiberd

The Irish were the first English-speaking people in this century to attempt a programme of decolonization; the first to walk in darkness down what is by now a well-lit road. The movement to restore the Irish language had begun as far back as 1893 with the foundation of the Gaelic League: in that year there were only six books in print in Irish and the language was spoken by a small sub-section of the population confined to remote and poor regions of the western seaboards.[1] Yet within a generation the cultural revival had created a new self-confidence among Irish people: many who took part in the Easter Rebellion against British rule in 1916 had been 'to school', so to speak, in the auditorium of the Abbey Theatre and in the classes of the Gaelic League. For them the Irish language and its literature were not simply luxuries to be repossessed in an independent Ireland, rather they were weapons in the revolutionary struggle. The mistake of nineteenth-century agitators had been to elevate the fight for Ireland into a self-sustaining tradition, while abandoning all those cultural elements—native language, dance, music and sport—which made the land worth fighting for.[2] But a new generation at the outset of the twentieth century believed passionately that self-government could only be restored after a sustained attempt had been made to decolonize the Irish mind and body.

That movement achieved a partial victory in the Anglo-Irish Treaty of 1921, which returned twenty-six of the thirty-two counties on the island to Irish hands. The victory was only partial, however, not just because six northern counties remained under British rule but also because the vast effort discharged in dislodging the British from the rest of the island seemed to have left the people with little energy to renovate their consciousness. Although programmes for teaching the Irish language in all schools were rapidly set in place, what was taught was all too often a standardized Civil Service Irish rather than the living dialects of the west, and much of the old imperial administrative and educational apparatus was maintained. Ireland became one of those postcolonial states which was, in the words of Benedict Anderson, 'insufficiently imagined'.[3] Part of the problem, of course, lay in the fact that what was being attempted was without many clear precedents and so there were few maps to guide the decolonizers along the unfamiliar road. Revivalist doctrine had, perhaps predictably, trumpeted the Irish as God's chosen people, 'like no other people on earth', and thus destined to be saviours of spiritual values for the modern world; but the disinclination to make comparisons with the experience of other peoples in the decades that followed, especially those people emerging from a briefer phase of colonial occupation, would enact a palpable price.[4]

Patrick Pearse, an executed leader of the 1916 Rebellion and founder of the first boy's school run on Gaelic League principles, had always feared that the shapers of an independent Irish state might consolidate the order which they had set out to overthrow. He had after all opened 'The Murder Machine', his essay on educational reform, with a warning that freedom was so little experienced or understood that 'the very organisations which exist in Ireland to champion freedom show no disposition themselves to accord freedom; they challenge a great tyranny but they erect their own little tyrannies.'[5] The danger was that people would mistake a repressive colonial machine for nature itself and proceed unbidden to employ many of the old categories of thought upon themselves. When Michael Collins, the guerrilla leader who signed the 1921 Treaty which copper-fastened partition, sent for British guns to help the Free State army to defeat the republican insurgents in Dublin's Four Courts, he did at the level of action what generations of Irish intellectuals would do at the level of ideas. Years later, after similar experiences in Africa, the revolutionary psychiatrist Frantz Fanon wrote:

> In its wilful narcissism, the national middle class is easily convinced that it can advantageously replace the middle class of the mother country. But that same independence which literally draws it into a corner will give rise within its ranks to

catastrophic reactions, and will oblige it to send out frenzied appeals for help to the former mother country.[6]

The nascent middle class in Ireland had, quite simply, emerged too late, missing out on the heroic period of the bourgeoisie in the nineteenth century, that phase when its members learned how to found heavy industries and factories. They arrived only *after* independence in the twentieth century and the vast majority of them never learned how to produce, only how to consume. They failed to transform the semi-developed economy inherited from the British regime.

The history of independent Ireland bears a remarkable similarity, therefore, to the phases charted by Fanon in *The Wretched of the Earth*.[7] In the early decades, nationalist leaders seemed to have soothed a frustrated people with endless recollections of the sacred struggle for independence. Commemorations abounded, the Irish version of this disease being the repeated political taunt, 'Where were you in 1916?' Poor leadership and scant resources condemned the nation for years to the status of an artisan economy, featuring local products and not fully or freely trading with Britain or the world beyond. Shoddy native manufacturers were protected by tariff barriers, just as writers who played up 'local colour' were elevated over talented modernists who refused to follow the approved line. When this way of living was revealed as untenable, the native leadership identified its historic role as intermediary for multinational companies; and thereafter it modelled its lifestyles on that of an international élite, whose members it invited to visit the countries as tourists in search of the exotic. At this point the literary exponents of local colour found themselves ratified by a new, even more influential, even more ecstatic, audience.

Certain counties such as Kildare and Meath were, for instance, described by the visiting Australian-Irish poet Vincent Buckley as 'playgrounds for the wealthy which the mere Irish strive to keep up to scratch'.[8] One result of all this was that the cultural life of the nation seemed less often geared to meet the people's own needs and more often addressed to the whims of foreigners. Eventually, many Irish people learned how to act like foreign tourists in their own country, while advertisements ('Discover Ireland: it's a part of what you are') which might once have been beamed at transplanted exiles in North America or Britain were directed at a native audience. This happened partly because more and more of the population had moved into cities and larger towns, but also because of the idea of Ireland seemed to appear increasingly in the guise of an 'other' to be penetrated from without. Those who took these signs at their word were sometimes dismayed to discover that much of the tourist industry was nothing more than an uneasy attempt to demonstrate to outsiders that there still was indeed a native Irish culture: yet the Gaeltacht (Irish-speaking area), like the 'native quarter' of a colonial city, appeared more as an effect of colonialism than a real answer to it.[9]

That disappointment had been anticipated by James Joyce in the closing sections of *A Portrait of the Artist as a Young Man*, which raise sharp, difficult questions about the meaning of a Gaelic culture which has been 'lost', a loss which can be established by the revivalists only in terms of a valued English scheme of things. What the revivalists sought to rediscover was merely a projection of imperial fantasy, eventually embodied in the person of the literary tourist Haines, a visiting Oxford student, in the pages of *Ulysses*. The mistake of the revivalists would be repeated in Africa and India in later decades: too often an 'African' or 'Indian' culture would simply be one which could be easily translated into forms comprehensible to European imperial minds. The revivalists failed to recognize that tradition in that sense is always syncretic; only a 'tradition' which was the invention of the colonizers could so facilely disintegrate to be supplanted by a ready-made modern equivalent.[10] The question put in the nineteenth century to the Irish—what distinctive civilization justifies your separatist claim?—would be raised again and again.

In Joyce's *Portrait* a Gaelic Leaguer named Mulrennan has an unsatisfactory encounter with a western peasant: both speak Irish at the outset but revert rapidly to English, though whether this is because the countryman's Irish-speaking is a mere act for tourists or because Mulrennan's Gaelic League phrase-book is easily exhausted, Joyce does not choose to clarify. At all events, he remains sceptical about the proposed return to a Gaelic past which entranced the more conservative members of the Gaelic League. In his modernist texts there is a double exposure: he indicts colonialism as do the revivalists themselves, but then he proceeds to indict the native culture for not living up to revivalist expectations of it, for not being an authentic *elsewhere*. The revivalists feel this lack too, but they respond by making the peasant the embodiment of sacred values which he himself would never claim to uphold, converting him into a fetish of unsatisfiable

[handwritten margin note: rediscovery a myth created by colonial powers]

desire. The revivalist thus comes close to the 'melancholy of the collector', the tantalizing hope that the next salvaged lyric, the next native speaker, will perhaps reveal the holy grail that he seeks. Yet these cultural trophies can offer no more than a fleeting charm, for to linger over any for too long would be to confront in them the selfsame emptiness which led the revivalist in desperation to invoke them. The tragic knowledge which awaits the revivalist is that which also attends the imperialist, who comes to the native quarter in hope of an epiphany. Desiring a pristine experience, Mulrennan is thwarted: hoping to recover the scope of an ancient culture from which he was cruelly separated, he finds instead a peasant whose inheritance is as broken as his own. There is no absolute *elsewhere* to be found, not even a final frontier where the theory of Irish innocence and the discontents of English civilization could come to a competitive point.

This was Joyce's perception: that Ireland is just another of those modern places where there is no *there* any more—and the visitor to the Gaeltacht who notices the *bialaan á la carte* in restaurants where Yorkshire Pudding tops the bill of fare can only agree. The nationalists who denounced England were more often than not denouncing an England inside each one of themselves. Their search for a pristine Ireland was a quintessential English search, because it involved them in the search for a corresponding England as well, if only so that they might repudiate it. Since 'Ireland' in such a construction was largely an English invention, those who took upon themselves the burden of having an idea of Ireland were often the most Anglicized of the natives.

This was the postcolonial elite which would in time create not industries so much as industrial authorities, not factories so much as fixers. Their schools remained obsessed with a hyperacademic form of learning, derived from the colonial period, which seemed to exist mainly to test new recruits for the swelling civil service. The curriculum emphasized languages, not only English and Irish but also Latin and Greek, 'resembling that of the English public schools of the mid-Victorian period'.[11] Science and technology tended to be secondary, and their study was often devalued. This ruling group mimicked the surface effects of Western consumerism, while its politicians bought votes at election time with borrowed cash: but it built no infrastructure with which to service the debt. Its educators scarcely concealed their snobbish contempt for those who actually made things with their hands.

This *trahison des clercs* might have been attributed to the failure to overhaul the 'murder machine' so that education could instead have served the community's needs. Hence, Nigerian children found themselves sweating through Corneille's *Le Cid* at much the same time that V. S. Naipaul in Trinidad was straining over Dickens, and Irish students were picking their way through the essays of Sir Arthur Quiller-Couch.[12] Ngugi wa Thiong'o reported from 1970s Kenya that the nation's children, after independence in 1963, were still taught to know themselves only through London and New York, and he recalled the complaint of a syllabus committee that 'students were still being subjected to alien cultural values which are meaningless to our present needs'.[13] Chinua Achebe noted that the post-Independence élite of readers, 'where they exist at all, are only interested in reading textbooks', and he recalled a pathetic letter from a Ghanaian reader of his novel *Things Fall Apart*, which took the form of a complaint that he had not included sample questions and answers at its end, 'to ensure his success at next year's school examination'.[14]

Such a system produced, with dire predictability, a people lacking in self-confidence and easily bullied by outsiders. Doctors, dentists, lawyers, engineers and architects were produced in over-abundance, to meet the career aspirations of the new élite, but most were then exported as free, instant experts to the former colonizers: and so it is with most Irish critics. The more gifted among them were often simply internalizers of the imperial mode. 'No Irishman', wrote Denis Donoghue, 'can ever assume that he is at the centre of anything.'[15]

In the post-colony, school students engaged in rote learning of old, familiar texts, on courses often taught by mediocre lecturers from the former colonial power rather than by persons of talent from the independent State. In Nigeria, Achebe noticed a similar tendency in college administrators: 'Given a chance, they will appoint a European over a Nigerian to teach at their university.'[16] Ngugi's account also rejected the widespread notion that Africa was a mere extension of the West. He recollected a question put by young lecturers in 1968: 'If there is need for the "study of historic continuity of a single culture", why can't this be African? Why can't African literature be at the centre so that we can view other cultures in relation to it?'[17] Eventually, of course, these reforms would be achieved, but one side effect of the intervening crisis was the extraordinary tardiness in the developing of a probing native criticism. The few native-born critics who emerged in the years immediately following independence often specialized in overseas literatures, while the leading native writers were most fully explicated by foreigners; and many lower-level postings in universities were occupied by foreign academics hoping desperately for a summons back to a more 'prestigious' assignment in the old country. Today, all that has changed, but in the intervening period much psychological damage was done.

'When exams matter so terribly', writes Paul Harrison in *Inside the Third World*, 'rote learning is encouraged and creative, adaptable thinking is surpressed. Anyone who has taught in a developing country cannot help noticing the problems of bringing out students' self-confidence and ability to make independent judgements.'[18] The student was often taught a covert self-hatred, seeing advancement as the poised imitation of English masters. V. S. Naipaul put it very well in his novel *The Mimic-Men*:

> We pretended to be real, to be learning, to be preparing ourselves, we mimic men of the New World, one unknown corner of it, with all its reminders of the corruption that came so quickly to the new.[19]

And the Barbadian novelist George Lamming was even more blunt:

> Supervising this complexity of learning to be a new man, in a new place, was an authority whose home was elsewhere.[20]

The Irish, being the first English-speakers to decolonize this century, were inevitably the first to make the expected wrong-turning, before, in Achebe's words, 'the great collusive swindle that was independence showed its true face to us'.[21] Achebe adds that at least Empire had its glorious heyday, its years of honour, but 'its successor, independence, did not even wait to grow old before turning betrayer'.

It seemed, at the outset, as if the Irish might genuinely renovate their student's consciousness. Eoin Mac Néill, a brilliant Gaelic scholar and co-founder of the Gaelic League, became the native Minister for Education of whom Pearse had long dreamed, a man who abolished payment of teachers according to examination results and who introduced open courses in literature, without the dead weight of prescribed and approved texts. But he did *not* abolish the hated examination system, and so schools faced the ultimate nightmare, an open course followed by a set test. The bleakness of such a freedom could not long be tolerated and, by June 1940, a new Minister, Éamon de Valera, reintroduced prescribed books. The anthologies of English literature thereafter studied, for the next three decades in Ireland, were described by one teacher as 'a monument to an essentially Victorian sensibility'.[22] While England in the 1940s and 1950s transformed itself into a welfare state and returned its syllabi to the modern world, the Irish continued for another decade to model their literary studies on the methods of Quiller-Couch.

The fact that religion, rather than English literature, was held to be the central subject of study in schools helped to prevent the emergence of a movement of literary critic such as followed F.R. Leavis in England. Even more regrettable was the fact that the courses studied paid scant heed to the considerable achievement of modern Irish writers in the English language. It may even have suited certain dogmatists in the Department of Education to misrepresent English culture by antique imperial curiosities, since that helped to feed a pet theory that Irishness was only to be found within the Gaelic tradition. If religion was the central subject in the humanities, then the Irish language and its literature were not far behind. English literature was nothing more than a pretext for the study of historical sensibilities. It was, therefore, hardly surprising that Ireland should have continued to produce some of the foremost exponents of *belles-lettres* still working in the English language.

The problem, as Daniel Corkery saw it at the end of the first decade of independence, was that such a system led to a cultural confusion of a kind that would be found later in Ghana when nationalists sang the Victorian Englishman J.H. Newman's hymn *Lead, Kindly Light* to welcome their leader Nkrumah back from jail. Corkery in his own career was a living symbol of such tensions, for he earned his daily bread as Professor of English at University College Cork, while in his leisure hours he wrote masterful essays on the poets of Gaelic tradition. Small wonder that he detected in many Irish schoolchildren a dispute between intellect and emotion. In the Ireland of his time Corkery detected not just a lack of native forms, but the want of any foundation on which to shape them: 'Our national consciousness may be described in a native phrase as a quaking sod . . .'[23]

Corkery attributed such self-doubt to the continuing prestige of English culture in Irish scholastic traditions. An English child, reading his or her own literature, found in it the focus of the minds and instincts of the English people; whereas an' Irish child, caught between a reality for which there were no obvious forms and a set of proffered forms which did not cohere with that reality, had to try to convert English locations and characters into Irish versions already known and loved. The outcome in Ireland was often a student blinded equally to the richness of both inheritances, constantly forgetting what little had been learned.[24] Ngugi's report from Kenya, of his childhood attempt to visualize Wordsworth's daffodils in the image of fish crowded in a lake, reads in places like a paraphrase of Corkery, a man whose work he did not in all likelihood know.

The apologists for English literature as traditionally understood might argue that such self-estrangement—the production of a divided consciousness—has been the object of all sophisticated literary study since the eighteenth century. As Gauri Viswanathan has written:

> It entails the suppression of the individualistic self, through self-examination and self-evaluation, to make way for the idealized self of culture. Division is the key to canonical power, inducing the reader to absorb another identity and respond in another voice. The tyranny of canons can be overcome only by deliberate estrangement from the texts that constitute them. But if education remains committed to our getting into texts rather than viewing them from the outside as strangers, the process of division will continue.[26]

This, however, seems only half the story. The British élite of the nineteenth century was inspired to self-improvement: they *began* as estranged, but soon separated themselves from the philistine middle class, and thus achieved their ideal selves. The Bombay élite, in contrast, were selected out of their society, and by the study of English literature set into such tensions with it that all their efforts at self-elevation were redirected to the reform of that society. Matthew Arnold never dreamed of estrangement *from a national culture,* merely from a philistine middle class, the better to pursue the ideal. Two generations after him, his American disciple Lionel Trilling did indeed ask his students to read the texts of modernism so that they took a step 'beyond culture', in ways which allowed them to view man as if he were an anthropological witness of himself. Trilling was, however, shrewd and sardonic enough to note the scandalous ease with which his students stepped back inside their charmed circle.[27] Had they stayed outside just a little longer, their understanding of other cultures, for instance, that of Islam, might have been enriched. The readers of English in colonies were asked a rather different question—to step outside their native cultures on the strict understanding that they would never thereafter step back in. *All* became victims of this process, but the spiritual disorientation reported by Ngugi, Achebe and Corkery was far more painful than the kind envisaged by Arnold for English schoolchildren.

It is, none the less, one of the recurring paradoxes of a decolonizing culture that Corkery's subtle account of a dispute between a child's intellectual schooling and emotional nature is a reworked version of T.S. Eliot's notion of the dissociation of sensibility. It lends a pervasive gloom to Corkery's entire opening chapter in *Synge and Anglo-Irish Literature*, a gloom not to be found in West Indian commentaries on the same crisis. (Perhaps the lack of a native language left the West Indians less prone to depression than their Irish, African or Indian counterparts, who felt that something good had been taken away.) Whereas Corkery can complain bluntly that 'Ireland has not learned how to express its own life through the medium of the English language'[28] (and this after the decade of *Ulysses, The Tower* and *The Silver Tassie*!), Lamming can welcome the novel form as 'a way of investigating and projecting the inner experience of the West Indian community'.[29] Lamming, indeed, sees this as the positive result of being caught between two cultures, a turning inward to examine the ground of one's perceptions, to find out how one knows what one knows. To him this is an event as important as the very discovery of the Caribbean islands.

Corkery is equally negative concerning the sheer number of expatriate Irish writers who function as prisoners of overseas markets. Yet Lamming can find exile a 'pleasure' rather than a dreary financial necessity: it affords him a welcome relief from a philistine class at home which reads solely for examinations, and an opportunity to discover overseas, perhaps for the first time, what it means to be West Indian. To write an investigation of the sources of West Indian consciousness virtually demands a strategic withdrawal from the place: to write at all is, in effect, to go into exile. This might have been the answer given by Corkery to Irish writers.

Corkery's piercing insights into aspects of Irish reality are of the kind possible only to one who has blinded himself to nine-tenths of that reality. His commentary on Synge ends on a note of near-farce, virtually denying the existence of Anglo-Irish literature, except perhaps as an exotic offshoot of the English parent plant.[30] He deserves praise though, for until the advent of Conor Cruise O'Brien in the late 1950s, he was the nearest thing Ireland produced to a postcolonial critic.

The years of the 'open syllabus' proved happy ones for the more imaginative teachers and students in Ireland who could afford to think little of examinations; and it may be no accident that they also coincided with that period when Ireland came to be regarded with affection and respect by peoples of the developing world. In such places, tens of thousands of Irish missionaries were made welcome in the 1920s and 1930s, since they came with no hidden political agenda. When Ireland entered the United Nations after World War Two, its position of non-alignment between the superpowers became a model for other emerging states; and when the foremost architect of that policy, Conor Cruise O'Brien, displeased the European imperial establishment by his handling of affairs in Katanga (formerly part of the Belgian Congo) in 1961, that phase in Irish history reached something of a climax. Editors in London were sharpening fangs well-bloodied from recent clashes with the Egyptian leader Gamal Abdul Nasser. 'And who,' sniffed Prime Minister Macmillan in London, 'is Conor Cruise O'Brien?' At Dublin Airport, a suddenly jobless O'Brien gave his answer: an unimportant, expendable civil servant. But then, eyebrows arched, he declared that he had just received the backing of a less expendable man, Prime Minister Nehru of India, leader of a sub-continent.[31] That moment in Irish history was soon lost. For his part, O'Brien soon afterward embarked on a revision of the anti-colonialism of his younger years, although it was some time before he went public with it. As late as 1969, in his masterly study of the French–Algerian writer Albert Camus, he came out in support of Jean-Paul Sartre's attack on French colonialism in Algeria and was suitably caustic about Camus' acquiescence. Camus had said that, if forced to choose between revolutionary justice and his mother, he would in the end opt to save his mother. 'Not every intellectual has to make the same choice,' commented O'Brien, 'but each must realize how he is a product of the culture of the advanced world, and how much there is that will pull him, among the "Algerias" of the future, towards Camus' fall.'[32]

By 1969, however, Western intellectuals were repenting of their support for national liberation movements, as the new states of

Africa and Asia sank into chaos, censorship and even dictatorship. Those who saw such problems as the predictable legacy of colonialism were drowned out by a new kind of commentator, often from a former colony, who gravely assured his old masters that these troubles were largely due to the inherent incapacity of such people to govern their own affairs. Chinua Achebe was scathing about this 'bunch of bright ones' who came along in this way to say, 'We are through with intoning the colonial litany . . . We are tough-minded. We absolve Europe of all guilt. Don't you worry, Europe, we were bound to violence long before you came to our shores'. Many liberal Europeans were greatly relieved by this exculpation. Achebe called it 'this perverse charitableness, which asks a man to cut his own throat for the comfort and good opinion of another', but he did not fail to note how many European thinkers praised the 'sophistication' and 'objectivity' of these new analysts.[33] Their thesis of the self-inflicted wound proved immensely consoling to readers of the 'liberal' Western press, especially when penned in the elegant essays of a V.S. Naipaul. 'No Indian can take himself to the stage,' wrote the Indian–Trinidadian Naipaul, 'where he might perceive that the faults lie within the civilization itself, that the failures and cruelties of India might implicate all Indians.'[34] An Indian economist might point to the many effects of colonial underdevelopment which this thesis excluded, and might seek to occupy a space somewhere between the secular Naipaul and the militant holy men. But it was the secular, anti-nationalist revisionists who held the high ground. Naipaul was feted in Western journals, having told their readers that after their rulers withdrew from their holdings, things only went from bad to worse.

In Ireland, Conor Cruise O'Brien began to sing the same song, but in the future tense, by way of justifying a continuing British presence in the six counties of the north. He repented publicly of his anti-partitionist past, becoming a favoured columnist in the London and New York press, 'a voice of sanity in the Irish mess'. He translated the mess of Ireland into a rational, enlightenment discourse which made good sense to his international readers. Witty, urbane, amusing, he shared with Naipaul a coolly analytical brain and a mind formed by close study of the European classics. After the outbreak of renewed violence in Northern Ireland, he revised his view of the Camus-Sartre debate and concluded that Camus had been right. The man who had once echoed Lenin's disappointment that the 1916 rebels had risen too soon to launch an international revolution now made it very clear that he no longer considered the Easter Rising to have been a positive thing. Yet his career, for all its twists, has an inner logic, that same logic which he had detected in the work of Albert Camus. Both men had found themselves caught on the cusp between Europe and the developing world. Both responded deeply to these twin tugs, because they could feel the pulls so deeply within themselves. What O'Brien said of Camus was, perhaps, even more applicable to himself: 'he belonged to the frontier of Europe, and was aware of a threat. The threat also beckoned to him. He refused, but not without a struggle.'[35]

The leaders of modern Ireland also 'refused', but only after a period of uncertainty and doubt. The roots of this change may be found in the career of O'Brien's own youthful model, the writer and pundit Seán O' Faoláin. He was a brilliant young protégé of Corkery, but one who eventually transcended and repudiated his former teacher in a much-publicized critique. That critique, however, remained unsatisfactory, because it invoked only the values of European individualism, values which, however admirable in themselves, had often been invoked in order to justify the colonial enterprise from which the country was but slowly emerging.[36] O'Faoláin and O'Brien represented the ideal of a liberal European Ireland, but free of its problematic past, whose only tense was the present and its needs. However, the persistent injustices in Northern Ireland, and the economic under-development of the south, meant that the conditions for such transcendence were never propitious.

It may be doubted, anyway, whether such transcendence, even if achievable would have been desirable: a postcolonial Ireland had many important differences from a mainly post-imperial Europe. Its people could hardly 'play at being Europeans', not because of invincible provincialism but because their traditions linked them to a much wider global network. The years of evolution from the nineteenth to the twentieth century had not been some kind of apprenticeship for an understanding of Europe: rather, the culture of Europe might offer an apprenticeship for a fuller understanding of the writings of Yeats, Joyce and Beckett. All three handled many classic themes of European art, but they did not feel tied to that tradition by any special devotion, and so their handling was irreverent, even insolent. Of nothing was this more true than of their treatment of English literary culture.

Living at such an angle to official English canons, Irish artists 'read England' as a prelude to 'writing Ireland'. They incorporated many of their re-readings of English authors into their creative texts, and revealed to a new generation of English readers a Shakespeare, Milton, Blake and Shelley richer and more various than the versions of these authors which had been promoted by previous critics. The English, to their lasting credit, took the lesson to heart. It was Irish *academics* who continued to ask their students to read Shakespeare and the others as they would have been interpreted by educated English persons in the year 1922. There was no attempt to imagine how the study of republican poets like Blake or Shelley in a university of Dublin or Cork might constitute a challenge to the Eliotic notion of a royalist, Anglo-Catholic canon. In 1922 the images of national possibility froze, with the country's teachers cast as the curator of a post-imperial museum, whose English departments were patrolled by zealous custodians anxious to ensure that nothing changed very much. Down the corridor, many of the curators of the postcolonial Gaelic museum, known as the Irish department, made equally certain that no radical revisions occurred, no compromising contacts with other cultures.

All of this required a vast degree of self-repression. If nineteenth-century critics in England had a full-time job stripping Shakespeare and other writers of their radical potentials, the academics of twentieth-century Ireland devoted themselves with equal solicitude to the deradicalization of native writing in both languages. Long before Irish nationalist politicians had erased subversive voices from Irish debate, the critics in the academies had performed parallel feats on the great national writers.

These critics were working hand-in-glove with the new administrative élite, which pursued a programme of insistent 'Europeanization' from the late 1950s onwards, after Ireland emerged slowly from a period of introversion characteristic of a neutral country in World War Two and its aftermath. If the major critical studies of Yeats, Wilde, Joyce and Beckett all tended to assume that each man became European (and therefore 'modern') to the extent that he played down his Irishness, then the political and economic commentators urged Irish people to measure their own performances and laws by an increasingly European criteria. To the sponsors of such an analysis, postcolonial theory proved anything but welcome, especially when its emergence seemed to coincide with the latest rebellion in Northern Ireland. In fact the two developments were scarcely linked, and many IRA apologists, confronted with the brute reality of a British military presence, angrily demanded the deletion 'post' from 'postcolonial'. But, in wider public debates, the difficulties and resistances facing those who advanced a postcolonial critique were compounded by predictable taunts of being 'fellow-travellers of terrorism.' These taunts went as far back as the 1972 referendum on entry to the European Economic Community. In the course of that campaign, the 'no' lobby—a compound of Labourite leftists, radical socialists, old-fashioned nationalists and Sinn Féiners—was accused of being infiltrated with subversives.[38] By 1987 when a constitutional challenge to the Single European Act was led by Raymond Crotty, a university based economist who pioneered the application of postcolonial theory to agronomy, the opponents of the Act were characterized by Joe McCartin, a member of the European Parliament, as 'knockers, Marxists, little ayatollahs, ex-clerics from England, and a Danish radical'.[39] Although the Act was carried by a majority of more than two-to-one, this was significantly lower than the five-to-one majority for EEC entry in 1972; and the actual campaign was strange indeed, as the 'pro-Europeans' indulged in xenophobic remarks against British, Danish and German radicals and environmentalists, while the 'anti-Europeans' continued to invite in speakers from most of the neighbouring nations.

One of the reasons for the increasing scepticism about European integration in the 1980s among the workforce could be found in the fact that EEC membership had coincided with the collapse of many traditional Irish industries from car assembly to textiles, from shoe-making to flour-milling: it did not go unnoticed that these had been the perennial centres of left-wing trade unionism in the past. Moreover, the chronic indebtedness of the State—by 1987 Ireland owed more per capita than either the Mexicans or the Brazilians, and all personal tax went on servicing the interest component of the national debt—led many commentators to ask whether Ireland might not be a Third World country.[40] A columnist writing in *The Irish Times* in that year listed those features which made the question at least possible to ask,[41] and a pundit in the British *Daily Telegraph* joked that the only thing keeping Ireland out of the Third World was the weather. There was, of course, a great deal more to distinguish Ireland from, say, Argentina or India: not only was per capita income far higher, but the country had undergone a thorough revolution in land-holding, the military was a subordinate arm of the government, and the multi-party elections held peacefully and at regular intervals saw orderly changes of power. Most of all, the country was listed as one of the top twenty-five economic democracies in the world.

Nevertheless, the strains between the various competing images of Ireland began to show in all kinds of tell-tale ways. For instance, through the mid-1980s two very different posters at Heathrow Airport in London spoke of two contrasting Irelands: one, sponsored by the Irish Industrial Development Authority, welcomed the Dublin-bound traveller to the home of 'The Young Europeans' and the best-educated workforce on the continent, while nearby a Bord Fáilte (the Irish Tourist Board) advertisement featured the massive frame of Bill Beaumont, former captain of the English rugby team, standing in a lush green landscape and urging his compatriots to 'Come on over and meet the little people'. Official Ireland's attempts to square this particular circle could lead to some discordant effects: once again the meaning of Irish history was recast and revised, this time in the guise of a dress rehearsal for EEC membership, when *The Irish Times*' star columnist Fintan O'Toole, who had heaped scorn on the postcolonialists for many years, led off the newspaper uneasily marking the seventy-fifth anniversary of the Easter Rebellion with the revelation that 'They Died for a Seat at the European Table'. Popular sentiment was not so easily fooled and, although the population remained broadly supportive of the EEC and its successor the European Union, people found their own ways to come to terms, however metaphorical, with the Irish past. According to singer Bob Geldof, who spearheaded the Live-Aid concerts, the immense generosity of even the poorest parishes in sending funds and aid to famine-stricken Africa was rooted, at least to some extent, in folk memories of the Great Hunger of the nineteenth century. These were ways of facing, without fully facing, the implications of Irish history.

Throughout recent decades, then, two major strains can be identified in Irish intellectual life: the European movement, rooted in government and the serious broadcast press, which sees itself as modernizing, secular, pragmatic and blessedly free of old-fashioned national pieties; and the postcolonial analysts, to be found on the left wings of both the Labour and Fianna Fáil parties and in somewhat higher profile among the artistic and intellectual circles. Various contests between both groups have added colour to public life over the period. For instance, Raymond Crotty's challenge to the Single European Act or the ongoing debate as to whether an

Irish neutralist policy which dates back to 1918 can be surrendered in a European superstate.[42] Recent creative texts reflect those tensions. Brian Friel's *Dancing at Lughnasa*, a hugely successful play at home and among the diaspora overseas, depicts a priest who, on returning from a life spent as a missionary on the equator, finds that Africans and Irish harvest rituals become hopelessly confused in his mind, even as the younger members of his family in 1930s Donegal prepare for emigration to modern Britain. On the other hand, it is only right to add that such plays as *In High Germany* by Dermot Bolger or the novels of Hugo Hamilton explore in a positive spirit that undeniable European element in the making of young Ireland today.

In many respects the debate, like many Manichean confrontations, has been melodramatized, for only a rudimentary thinker would deny that the Irish experience is at once post-colonial and post-imperial.[43] If many Irish suffered the economic and cultural woes of life under the imperial yoke, quite a few others happily took on the white man's burden in Africa and India. (Though some, like the Connaught Rangers who mutinied in India in 1920, while their brothers and sisters back home fought a war of independence, came to experience that ambivalence in a painfully personal fashion.) The real challenge today is to find a truly contrapuntal narrative which projects both aspects of the national experience and captures the complexity of being at once postcolonial and European, an experience which is not in fact unique now that the European Union has received applications for membership from the recently-liberated nations of Eastern Europe.[44] If the decisive relationship of the next century, as the Brandt Commission has stated, will be that between North and South, there is a sense in which that relationship is enacted every day on the streets and in the valleys of Ireland. In the 1990s, Ireland is proving to be a force field of continuing modernity as surely as it was a crucible for change in the 1890s.

Notes

1. On the general cultural situation see the excellent essays in Seán O Tuama (ed), *The Gaelic League Idea* (Cork: Mercier, 1972).
2. For a full version of this thesis read Douglas Hyde, 'The Necessity for De- Anglicizing Ireland', *The Renewal of Irish Literature*, ed. Charles Gavan Duffy (London: 1894). On state formation see Terence Ranger and Eric

Hobsbawn, (eds) *The Invention of Tradition* (Cambridge: CUP, 1983) and Declan Kiberd, *Inventing Ireland: The Literature of the Modern Nation* (London: Jonathan Cape, 1995).

3. Benedict Anderson, *Imagined Communities: Reflections on the Origin and Spread of Nationalism* (London: Verso, 1983).

4. Some tentative comparisons were made by Conor Cruise O'Brien, *The Shaping of Modern Ireland* (London: 1960) p. 10. In recent years there has been fuller documentation e.g. Peadar Kirby, *Ireland and Latin America: Links and Lessons* (Dublin: Gill and Macmillan,1992) and Brian Girvin, *Between Two Worlds: Politics and Economy in Independent Ireland* (Dublin: Gill and Macmillan, 1989).

5. Séamus O Buachalla (ed) *A Significant Irish Educationalist: Educational Writings of Patrick Pearse* (Cork: Mercier, 1980) p. 352.

6. Frantz Fanon, *The Wretched of the Earth*, trans. Constance Farrington, (Harmondsworth: Penguin, 1967) p. 120.

7. Fanon. See especially the chapters on national consciousness and national culture, pp. 119–200.

8. Vincent Buckley, *Memory Ireland* (Victoria, Australia: Penguin, 1985) p. 175.

9. Declan Kiberd, 'Absolute Tourism Corrupts Absolutely', *The Irish Times*, 1 September 1987, p. 8.

10. Vincent Tucker, 'The Myth of Development', unpublished paper, Department of Sociology, University College Cork, 1993.

11. Donald Harman Akenson, *A Mirror to Kathleen's Face* (Montreal: McGill–Queen's University Press, 1975) p. 76.

12. Paul Harrison, *Inside the Third World* (Harmondsworth: Penguin, 1981)

13. Ngugi wa Thiong'o, *Decolonising the Mind: The Politics of Language in African Literature* (London: Currey, 1986) pp. 97 & 100.

14. Chinua Achebe, *Hopes and Impediments: Selected Essays, 1965–1987* (London: Heinemann, 1988) pp. 27–28.

15. Buckley, p. 175.

16. Achebe, p. 64.

17. Ngugi, p. 89.

18. Harrison, p. 317.

19. V. S. Naipaul, *The Mimic-Men* (Harmondsworth: Penguin, 1969) p. 146.

20. George Lamming, in Andrew Salkay (ed) *Caribbean Essays*, (London: Evans Bros., 1973) p. 11.

21. Achebe, p. 58. The following quote is from p. 54.

22. John Devitt, 'English for the Irish', *The Crane Bag*, Vol. 6. No. 1, (1982) p. 106.

23. Daniel Corkery, *Synge and Anglo-Irish Literature*, (Cork: Mercier, 1966) p. 14.

24. Corkery, p. 15.

25. Ngugi, p. 10.

26. Gauri Viswanathan, 'The Empire Within', *Voice Literary Supplement*, New York (Jan–Feb 1989) p. 22.
27. Lionel Trilling, 'On the Teaching of Modern Literature', *Beyond Culture: Essays on Literature and Learning* (Oxford: OUP, 1980) pp. 3–27.
28. Corkery, p. 12.
29. Quoted by Gareth Griffiths, *A Double Exile: African and West Indian Writing Between Two Countries* (London: Boyars, 1978) p. 91.
30. Corkery, p. 11.
31. On this see Conor Cruise O'Brien, *To Katanga and Back: A UN Case History* (London: Hutchinson, 1962).
32. Conor Cruise O'Brien, *Camus* (London: 1970) p. 85.
33. Achebe, p. 64.
34. V. S. Naipaul, *India: A Wounded Civilisation* (Harmondsworth: Penguin, 1979) p. 148.
35. O'Brien, *Camus*, p. 84.
36. Within these general constraints, O'Brien was capable of adopting a somewhat oedipal attitude to O Faoláin: see Donald Harman Akenson, *Conor: A Biography* (Montreal: McGill–Queen's University Press, 1994) pp. 120–23.
37. Jorge Luis Borges, *Labyrinths* (Harmondsworth: Penguin, 1970) p. 216.
38. The phrase was used by Taoiseach Jack Lynch and other Fianna Fail ministers on many occasions in that year: see *The Irish Times*, passim.
39. *The Irish Times*, 26 May 1987, p. 10. Raymond Crotty's book on the Irish economy is *Ireland in Crisis: A Study in Capitalist Colonial Under-development* (Dingle: Brandon, 1986).
40. Thérèse Caherty, Andy Storey *et al.* (eds) *Is Ireland a Third World Country?*, Committee for Research and Documentation, Belfast, 1992
41. Declan Kiberd, 'The Hallmarks of the Third World?', *The Irish Times*, 18 August 1987. Among the items which I listed were: a history of economic plunder by the colonial power; a failure of the post-independence leadership to create heavy industry and a propensity on its part to ape the surface glamour of 'advanced' industrial societies, without generating the wealth necessary to underwrite such opulence; a consequent chronic indebtedness to foreign bankers; a tendency to imitate the cultural values of the former occupier; a code in which prestige derives more from land-ownership than land-use; an ever-swelling capital and resulting evacuation of the regions; limited social services and an over-production of doctors, dentists, lawyers, engineers and other professionals, destined mostly for export but produced to meet the career aspirations of the local élite; a politics in which the two largely conservative parties vie for office; external and internal instability as an outcome of the arbitrary redrawing of boundaries by the departing colonial regime. The *Daily Telegraph* article was written earlier in 1987 by Bruce Anderson in response to the columns generated by the general

election in February in Ireland: see Declan Kiberd, 'Fasten your Seat-Belts for the Third World', *The Irish Times*, 10 February 1987, p. 10.

42. On these campaigns see Crotty's partisan but vivid account, *A Radical's Response* (Dublin: Poolbeg, 1988).

43. For a full exploration of this bifurcated cultural inheritance, see Declan Kiberd, *Inventing Ireland: The Literature of the Modern Nation* (London: Jonathan Cape, 1995). See also David Lloyd, *Anomalous States: Irish Writing and the Postcolonial Moment* (Dublin: Lilliput, 1993).

44. Some interesting connections between Ireland and Eastern Europe have been explored by Seamus Heaney, *The Government of the Tongue* (London: Faber, 1988).

Portugal, So Great So Small. Colonial Obesity and Post-Revolutionary Anorexia

Paul Hyland

Frontiers are like knicker elastic, they expand or contract to fit whatever they contain or restrain. Once it seemed simpler, for the school atlas is an anthology of coloured patches each bounded by a firmly-drawn line whose end always meets its beginning however jagged its course; you can measure it on the map precisely, just as you can walk into Marks & Spencer and ask for waist 34 inch or Eurosize 16. But peoples, like people, have wildly neurotic notions of how they look, of how gross or slender they are. One Englishman's England is likely to be greater then another English person's Britain. Portugal's reflection should fit tidily enough between the bevelled edges of a long mirror, a cheval glass. Most Portuguese I meet smile resignedly and say of themselves, in a sort of chant, 'Once we were so great, but now we are so small.'

Children live in a confusing, arbitrarily shifting world, but gazing at fixed lines and contrasting colours on a globe—when it stopped spinning—would give them a god-like and profoundly false idea of what frontiers are, if they didn't know any better. As a child my most persistent nightmare was of Earth, a great globe which swirled with clouds and oceans, rolling unstoppably towards me out of incorrigible darkness long after my mother had switched on the light and made me sip water. 'The world's coming,' I'd scream, 'the world's coming.' I wasn't wrong. I saw it coolly, years later, exactly reproduced in NASA's photos from space.

Our image of Earth had not fully developed when Joseph

101

Conrad was young. His first bit of map drawing, described in his essay 'Geography and Some Explorers', 'consisted in entering laboriously in pencil the outline of Tanganyika on my beloved old atlas, which, having been published in 1852, knew nothing, of course, of the Great Lakes. The heart of its Africa was white and big.'[1] (There is, by the way, a Freudian misprint to delight postcolonial critics such as Chinua Achebe in the first edition of *Last Essays* by the author of *Heart of Darkness*: there it reads, 'The heart of its *African* was white and big'[my italics].) Some years earlier Conrad had written:

> It was in 1868, when nine years old or thereabouts, that while looking at a map of the time and putting my finger on a blank space then representing the unsolved mystery of that continent, I said to myself with absolute assurance and an amazing audacity which are no longer in my character now: 'When I grow up I shall go *there*.'[2]

Assurance and amazing audacity—a presumption that we can now see as culpable innocence—characterized the explorers and colonizers of the world. Not least the Portuguese who outfaced terrors we can't imagine when edging down Africa in the fifteenth century. At 26° north they met Cape Bojador on the Saharan coast. *Bojador* means 'bulging' or 'jutting', but the promontory was nicknamed the Cape of Fear for, south of that latitude, Arabs and Christians alike believed that you fell into the devil's power, your body blackened and the waters churned with anarchic currents and the whirlpools of chaos. In 1434 Gil Eanes, courtier and navigator, sailed on into the mind's darkness:

> Was it worth while? All is worth while
> If the soul is not small.

So Fernando Pessoa, the great modernist poet (1888–1935), wrote in 'Portuguese Sea', and continued:

> *Quem quer passar além do Bojador*
> *Tem que passar além da dor.*
> Whoever would go beyond Bojador
> Must go beyond pain.[3]

The mental pain stemmed from the loss, south of that cape, of the Pole Star. Beyond that point navigators simply lost sight of sky marks they knew, that fixed star that kept them sane, and risked sailing out of the known through a door into hell. But Gil Eanes dared to do it, astrolabe in hand, and returned home with tamer tales than expected and an intact white skin.

Whimsical meditations on the loss of the lodestar, on the mind and the world, on inner and outer journeys, on the entanglement of hearts within and without, lead us back to knicker elastic and how we stretch and shrink boundaries to most comfortably accommodate the known world, and the unknown, in our heads. I came across a farm worker who lived at the heart of the Isle of Wight, which measures just thirteen miles by twenty-three and gets smaller by erosion faster than it grows by accretion. He had driven from the farm to Newport market almost every week of his life with a cartload of corn or roots or livestock. In his 70s he was admitted to hospital in the coastal resort of Ryde following a heart attack. On recovery he was taken up to the flat roof for exercise. He took one look at the view and fixed the nurse with his glare: 'So tha's what they call the sea. My duck pond at hwome's better'n thaat'.

The farm had tied him all his life through war and peace. Before that moment on the hospital roof, and his little joke about the pond, what map of the Island, and of the Island in the world, did he carry in his head? And did it change, or was the information the waves carried irrelevant to his life? Before the globe was a village, each village was a world and every head was its own globe.

Portugal's parochialism works in just the same way, despite the fact that its destiny was to refashion our notion of the world. The north's view of the south is typical: it looks across the river Tagus and gives the south a name, Alentejo, from *além do Tejo*, 'beyond the Tagus'. The caricature of a pale-skinned Christian northerner looks down to (or on) the caricature of a dark-skinned Moorish southerner with enough conviction to enable me to argue that the Tagus divides Europe from Africa.

So what do these two small continents, north and south, have in common, apart from a long seaboard and an equally long border with, or against, Spain? They combine to shape a country whose frontiers have remained almost as they are, angry squabbles and pained intermissions excepted, since 1249, ratified by a treaty in 1297. These two Portugals have been one, and the same, for seven centuries. Only island nations can compete with that in the identity stakes. Portugal has a population one-tenth that of the United Kingdom in a territory little more than a third of the United Kingdom's size, or, to really put it in perspective, a little less than one-hundredth of the area of the United States. But the sum of Portugal's parts is greater then its boundaries can possibly embrace. And much greater than the flimsy idea—the port and golf, beach and sardines, poor-man-of-Europe caricature—that is carried in most non-Portuguese heads. In my head it adds up to at least two continents severed by a river.

Portugal's frontiers were Spain and the shore for some time. Then they became Spain and the horizon. The poet António Sardinha expresses the difference:

> Here is the end of all the ancient earth,
> Here begins the temptation of the sea.

So, at Sagres near Cape St Vincent (the *fim do mundo* or 'end of the world') tradition and many scholars hold that the Infante Dom Henrique (Prince Henry the navigator) established a school of navigation, his launchpad for exploration, discovery and later colonialism. That arc at the end of sight, the horizon, was both imaginary frontier and frontier of the imagination, beyond which 'the sea ends and the earth begins.' Always *além*, 'over there'. The new beginning (poignant tautology) and the new earth. I could argue, and my slender subtext does, that 'discovery' was predicated on the power of the imagination, and colonialism on the failure of it, the same touching but dangerous failure that allows us to think 'new beginning' and 'new world'.

Meanwhile, here is a handful of Portuguese landfalls: 1434, beyond Bojador; 1452, Açores; 1457, Cape Verde Islands; 1471, Guiné; 1482, beyond the Equator; 1487, Cape of Good Hope; (1492, Columbus voyaged to America); 1499, India; 1500, Brazil; 1513, China; 1520, Fernao de Magalhães circumnavigated the globe; 1522, Australia; 1543, Japan . . . Imagine a century's voyages stretching imagination's frontiers across a 'world' whose very meaning grew and grew, each caravel's wake like weak elastic, overstretched by the enormity of the world and the appetite for it.

At principal landfalls the navigators, starting with Diogo Cão who first crossed the Equator, took to planting stone pillars or crosses (*padrões*) like visiting cards. Each *padrão* bore the shield of Portugal.

The endeavour is large and man is small
I, Diogo Cão, navigator, left behind
This standard at the edge of the dusky beach
And sailed onward.[4]

From a small dinghy, I once gazed across the glittering skin of the
Congo's mouth, with its subtle and powerful machinery of
currents and counter-currents, towards Shark Point and Ponta do
Padrão where Diogo Cão had left his mark in 1482. It stood there
until it was used for target practice by a British man-of-war.
Fragments of it were prized as fetishes or *nkisi* by Angolans whose
folk memory held a strong image:

> Suddenly they saw a big ship on the sea. It had white sails
> which shone like knives. White men came out of the water,
> talking in a manner which nobody understood. Our ancestors
> were afraid, they said they were Vumbi; spirits come back to
> earth. They pushed them back to the sea with showers of
> arrows. But the Vumbi spit fire with a noise of thunder. Very
> many men were killed. Our ancestors fled away. The chiefs
> and seers said that formerly these Vumbi were the possessors
> of the land . . . The big ship came back and white men
> reappeared. They asked for fowls and eggs; they gave cloth and
> pearls. The Whites came back again. They brought maize and
> manioc, knives and hoes, ground nuts and tobacco. From that
> time until now, the Whites have brought us nothing but war
> and misery.[5]

I thought of that as I floated in the jaws of the river called
Nzadi, which the Portuguese corrupted to *Zaire*, and again as I
examined rusting half-sunk hulks at Banana Point's naval base,
relics of the Zairian President Mobutu's ill-fated intervention in
the Angolan civil war. I thought of it later, when I touched two
large fragments of Diogo Cão's *padrão de São Jorge* from the
Zaire's mouth, now back home among half-forgotten riches of
Empire in the deserted museum of the Lisbon Geographical
Society. I thought of it upriver from the port of Matadi, beyond
the whirlpool called Hell's Cauldron, beside the rapids that
finally blocked Diogo Cão's ascent of the Zaire; close to a dwarf
baobab tree growing in the steep rocky bank I ran my finger in
the crisp inscription he had carved there in 1487: '*Aqy chegaram
os navios*' . . . 'Here arrived the ships of the illustrious King Dom

João the Second of Portugal. Diogo Cão. Pêro Anes. Pêro da Costa.'[6]

Just as Columbus would later stumble on bits of America while out west chasing rumours of China, so Diogo Cão went up the Congo cul-de-sac hoping to find both the source of the Nile and the kingdom of Prester John, that fabulous medieval Christian priest-king of Asia, Marco Polo's Lord of the Tartars, who decamped (in the imagination) to Abyssinia in the fourteenth century and was still (mythically) ruling Ethiopia when Vasco de Gama left Africa behind and bumped into India.

Though they were looking for influence and trade rather than colonies, the Portuguese saw the Congo foothold, and others on the coast of as yet undiscovered continents, as an expansion of territory. This has been described as 'an enlarged version of their own kingdom, a kind of negative to be subjected to that developing agent which was Christian and Lusitanian civilization'.[7] I think of the fate of Mvemba Nzinga who, like his father the late king, had swallowed Portuguese bait. He fought his brother and the 'witchdoctors' for the Kongo throne, but his long reign, 1506–?1543, afforded him progressively painful lessons in the meaning of the *padrão*, and of patronage. He continued to welcome craftsmen and scholars, technicians and priests from Europe, but he wrote in eventual disillusion, 'Today Christ is crucified in the Kongo against his will'. Promise had long since turned to threat. He survived a Portuguese assassination attempt on Easter Day 1540. He protested at the import of alcohol, and at the export of slaves, even though they might be branded with *IHS*, Christ's monogram. He systematically questioned laws that trammelled his subject to suit Lisbon. 'In Portugal,' he asked with despairing irony, 'what punishment is given to the man who puts his foot on the ground?'[8]

In Portugal élite black scholars studied to become *mindele miandombe*, 'black whites'. Mvemba Nzinga's son studied theology and was consecrated bishop in 1521; one of his nephews became a professor and the director, as he says in a letter of 1526, of a 'public school for the humanities in Lisbon'. Not long before, dead black slaves were thrown to Lisbon's dogs until the Portuguese king, Manuel 'the fortunate' (1495–1521), ordered a grave pit to be dug. These extremes say at least as much about the polarity of Portuguese and Kongolese society as they do about imperialism.

Mvemba Nzinga's successors both rebelled and collaborated

more crudely. A powerful Kongo prophet—Francisco Bulla-matare, *bula matadi*, 'breaker of rocks', was the name also given to the Congo explorer H.M. Stanley four centuries later—aimed to expunge the Church. The old Kongo kingdom is now part of that Angola disputed, over the last thirty-odd years, by Portuguese, MPLA, Cuban, FNLA, Zairian and UNITA forces. During the second half of the sixteenth century, it grew to be so beleaguered by the Bateke people, the Bayaka and the Portuguese, that in the end its leaders repented and turned to Lisbon for help. In 1571 the young King Sebastião of Portugal responded to Kongo's penance; he sent a force to sustain survivors who had found refuge, and desperate degradation, on the Isle of Horses in the Zaire river. He sent smelters too to follow up tales of silver and gold.

The following year, 1572, Portugal's great poet Luis Vaz de Camões published his epic poem dedicated to King Sebastião: *Os Lusiadas*, 'the sons of Lusus' meaning 'the Portuguese'. Previously the nation had defined itself in contradistinction to 'barbarian' invaders, to Moors who had finally been expelled in 1249, and to Spanish, or Castilian aggressors, conclusively defeated at Aljubarrota in 1385. It defined itself as what was on this side, *aquém*, 'on the threshold of the beyond', as against what was beyond, *além*. With the discoveries, Portugal began to define itself in terms of both *aquém* and *além*. The cheval glass could no longer contain its thin Lusitanian reflection; it needed a hall of mirrors. Camões gave the Portuguese just such an exotic, and distorted, hall.

The randy, rugged, one-eyed poet had been banished to North Africa and then to India, given a hard time in Macau, wrecked on the Mekong river, and stranded in Goa and Moçambique before returning to Lisbon in 1570. He found the city emerging from the shadows of the plague, Portugal altered for the worst, the discoverers and empire-builders already undervalued, virtue wilted beneath the weight of unspeakable wealth, the heroic temper ebbing and irresponsibility reigning in the person of the sixteen-year-old King Dom Sebastião whom Camões believed badly advised.

Sebastião was *o desejado*, 'the desired one', even before his birth. His young father, who was the last survivor of ten royal princes, died a few days before his son was born. Inbred and asymmetrical, and named for his birth-day saint who survived martyrdom by arrows, Sebastião was nevertheless his grandfather's precious heir and hope incarnate. I've crept into the claustrophobic cork-lined granite cells of the Capuchin monastery, set among boulders near Sintra, where the adolescent king fuelled his sense of spiritual mission at the feet of his confessor. I've sat on the tiled throne, on a patio of Sintra's grand Paço Real, where Sebastião sat to listen to Camões recite *The Lusiads*.

Camões aimed to emulate and outdo the *Aeneid*, to put history into Vasco da Gama's mouth and to recount the real achievements of the Christian Portuguese, but to re-enact them on a world stage beneath Olympus, the gallery of the classical gods, thus making a new and better myth than Virgil's, a national epic and *mythos* that defined his people, both *aquém* and *além*, and celebrated their destiny. In *The Lusiads* Camões offered the king both advice and reproof, but in the first canto addressed him as a marvel of the age decreed by destiny and sent by God to strike new terror into Muslim hearts, and in the last canto pictured him levelling Morocco's fortifications; that is, reverting to Henry the Navigator's North African ambitions of 150 years before.

Dom Sebastião's very mind-set was anachronistic and, to cut a very short story short indeed, it was a medieval crusade which, despite all the advice, the wild but virginal king launched against the Moors in 1578. He went to aid the claimant to the Moroccan throne who had promised freedom of religion there in exchange for an army. Sebastião's mission was to expand the spiritual empire that Portugal was destined to rule. He would not allow for the possibility of defeat and therefore conceived no strategy for retreat. His army and the cream of the nobility perished in the sands between Tangier and Rabat at the battle of Ksar el Kebir, 'the great fortress'. But what of Sebastião who incarnated the longings of the people, did he die? Some said, and still say, not. Certainly the bones in the sarcophagus in Jeróminos monastery, in whose church the supposed remains of Vasco da Gama and Camões also lie, are not his. Philip, the Hapsburg King of Spain, bought them from the Moors to persuade the Portuguese that Sebastião was dead. It was an expensive funeral.

Sebastião's defeat was followed in 1580 by Camões' death. He is supposed to have said, 'Everyone will see that my country was so dear to me that I was content to die not only in it but with it'. Spain took Portugal for over sixty years (1580–1640). It was the ultimate tragedy and humiliation. The country's real size was reduced to that of an African sand dune. Camões' hall of mirrors was a grave-pit. Ironically, Dom Sebastião was still, and ever more strongly, equated with the identity and survival of Portugal. He continued, and continues, to be *o desejado*, 'the one-so-longed-for'. Fernando Pessoa spoke for him in the poem, 'D. Sebastian, King of Portugal':

> Mad, yes, mad for I wanted majesty
> such as fate never allows.
> My conviction did not fit within me;
> that's why where the desert lies
> my has-been self remained, not he who is.
>
> My madness, let others take it from me
> and all that went with it.
> Without madness what can man be
> other than a healthy brute,
> a postponed corpse that procreates?[9]

Sebastião perversely embodied national hope. Portugal, that had been *aquém* and *além*, was now only *além*: beyond the horizon and, most potently, beyond the grave: *o além*, the hereafter. With my English head I think of King Alfred, in a Wessex that by 878 had shrunk to a tiny island called Athelney in the Somerset marshes, before his successful assault on the Danish invaders; when he appeared to rally his people they 'received him after so great tribulation as one risen from the dead'[10]; but more, I think of Arthur asleep beneath the hill like many another once-and-future king.

When I first spoke to Portuguese about this it was too soon after the so-called revolution, or officer's coup, of 25 April 1974 to speak unashamedly about reactionary hopes; a woman told me, 'I suppose now nobody thinks he is going to come, but we are waiting for something, I don't know what, a kind of miracle perhaps. More or less as the Jews wait for the Messiah we are waiting for I don't know whom, but something or someone who gives us once more a very good life and all good things.'[11]

Prior to 1974, during the repressive New State presided over by the dictator Salazar for almost forty years (1932–1970), Camões' *mythos* had been appropriated by the propaganda ministry. Everyone knew what their posters told them, that Portugal's real size was that of its provinces (not called colonies), from Macau to Moçambique, the Açores to Angola. And Salazar did not disown Sebastianic inferences about his person: he too seemed austere, Franciscan, his vision was of sublime national destiny, his name began with 'S'. Now, once again, as in all periods of change, Sebastião looms. The novelist Almeida Faria, whose satirical *O Conquistador* brings a highly-sexed parody of the King back to life in today's Portugal, told me recently that 'in the last twenty years the myth of King Sebastião is getting bigger and bigger every day.'

In 1994 I discussed these things with Dom Duarte, Duke of Bragança and pretender to the Portuguese throne. Though the monarchy ended in 1910, he is often referred to as *Sua Alteza Real*, 'His Royal Highness'. He deplored the passivity engendered by Sebastianism, as usually misunderstood, but hoped for the return of Sebastião, for only then would Portugal understand its spiritual duty and take on its real size.

He talked seriously and passionately in terms we can trace back through the *History of the Future* by Padre António Vieira (1608-1697), to the sixteenth-century cobbler-prophet Bandarra who anticipated the coming of the redeemer king; to the vision of the epoch of the Holy Spirit in the writings of Joachim of Fiore (1145–1202); to the sign of Christ given to Afonso Henriques before his battle with the Moors at Ourique (1139), promising that his victory would guarantee Portuguese rule over the universal Fifth Empire. These prophecies are rooted in the book of Daniel which has fuelled similar ideas about other 'sleeping lords', about Charlemagne of France, Frederick II of Germany, and the spiritual kingdom anticipated by the Fifth-Monarchy men in Cromwellian England. Unusually, Sebastianism still goes deep. In the seventeenth century the figure of a resurrected king merged with the dream of a restored nation and reinforced Portugal's destiny as the ruler of the world for God.

I asked Dom Duarte whether, if by remote chance he ever gained the crown, he would assume the mantle of Sebastião. 'The fight is our duty,' he said, 'the victory is the business of God. In this sense, yes.' He talked about his advocacy for the Timorese, 'who are more Portuguese than we are,' under Indonesian oppression. He feels that he is Sebastião's heir, though he knows he must avoid mistakes like the battle of Ksar el Kebir. But still he told me, 'I would have done the same thing at the time, if the Moroccans had asked my help.'

The Portuguese who *are* in power seem to have given up notions of a destiny that encircles the earth with an empire, material or spiritual. After the revolution of 1974, hatched by officers who served in Guiné Bissau, Moçambique and Angola, and consequent decolonization, it was as if the nation turned its back on the horizon and the world. Starved by guilt, but swollen alarmingly by *retornados*, returned colonials, the Portuguese wished to forget, by wilful amnesia, all that was *além* and concentrate on all that is *aquém*.

Novelist and playwright Luisa Cosat Gomes talked to me about Portuguese identity as 'this big myth'. She said she had been joking about this myth, of which people are so fond, since she could remember. 'We've been identical for 800 years, but only after 1974 are we so worried about this identity. What is it that we seemed to have and don't have any more? I think what we have is ignorance.' People talk of the shame of leaving Africa but, she said, 'we never cared about Africa in 500 years, this can be proven.' The recurrent myth is that Portugal's destiny is to be universal. 'Now Portugal has closed its borders to Africa. We are not a soup of cultures. Portugal, the gate of heaven, and it's closed!'

António Lobo Antunes is one artist who looked hard at the protracted and painful colonial wars in Portugal's African colonies (1961–74) in his ground-breaking novel *South of Nowhere*; set in Angola, it enacts the trauma of his narrator who writes, 'I am caught between two continents that repel me'. The Portuguese made their choice: in 1986 the Treaty of Rome was signed within the cloisters of the very Lisbon monastery—Jerónimos—that had been built at the beginning of the seventeenth century in thanksgiving for Vasco da Gama's safe return from India. Portugal became part of the European Union. Its reflection fits within the cheval glass.

But that same year one of its greatest writers, José Saramago, published a novel of epic dimensions that rebels against Europe, not because its leftist author wants to re-establish an empire, far from it, but because he hates the imaginative poverty of the Community's pragmatic reductivism. In his book, *The Stone Raft*[12], the premise and supervening metaphor is that the Pyrenees split geologically/magically down the middle, the Iberian peninsula floats away into the Atlantic, almost collides with the Açores, spins disorientatingly and slides south between two continents, and between, of course, Angola and Brazil. It's Saramago's impassioned effort to redraw Portugal's psychic map, to align himself with the tradition of Iberian republicanism, to respond to the 'call of the south' and to distance his country from France, Germany and from Britain, its oldest ally—its oldest, ambiguous, exploitative ally.

In the scramble for Africa, Britain, with Cecil Rhodes on board and Cape-to-Cairo ambitions, colluded with Germany and Belgium to sabotage the *Mapa Cor-de-Rosa* ('the Pink-coloured Map') which drew a Portuguese belt across Africa from Angola to Moçambique. In 1890 a British ultimatum forced an outraged, betrayed Portugal to withdraw from all the territory in between. It so happened that my great uncle Dan Crawford (author of *Thinking Black*) was walking into Africa at that time of terrifying flux, on the way to becoming a white slave of the great emperor-chief M'siri, in present-day Shaba, Zaire, and the adopted uncle of one of M'siri's favourite wives, the half-Portuguese Maria Fonseca. *En route* he passed through Bié and met the explorer and slave-trader Silva Porto, not long before the famous old man, disillusioned and unable to broker peace, retreated to his private chapel and lay down on a bed of gunpowder barrels spread with the Portuguese flag. He lit a match.

Thus Portugal, that created the first modern Empire, and the one that lasted longer than most, lost the extra inches it might have gained around the middle of Africa. In India, pork sausages helped to save it from obesity. Nehru followed his demand for democracy in Portuguese Goa by invasion and annexation. The Portuguese authorities affected injured innocence. More significantly Salazar, who ordered his forces to resist to the death, discovered how remote he was from a military which quickly surrendered to the Indian army. When asked to send sausages to Goa, the general staff despatched pork ones quite overlooking the fact that 'sausages' was their own code word for cannon shells.

Now, I want to prod the map nearer home: note the Spanish town of Olivenza near Badajoz. It was Portuguese Olivença until 1801. Saramago's stone Iberian raft presupposes an accommodation with Spain that doesn't allow for it. The people there speak a language closer to Portuguese than Spanish. Elsewhere, apart from Tras-os-Montes where the dialect is a kind of Galician Portuguese, the linguistic boundary is dramatically distinct. The Olivença district is a hernia in the ancient frontier, a vestigial pocket of Alentejo that stirs many hearts more than any number of lost colonies. There General Delgado was buried, who had been an aide and then an opponent of Salazar, author of flamboyant attempted coups. In 1965, he had emerged from exile in Brazil, crossed from Morocco into Spain and made for a conspirators' conference, or a trap, at Badajoz. He hoped to be a Sebastião. Salazar's secret police, the PIDE, killed him with his secretary and hid him in a shallow grave in what had once been Portugal.

Nine years later, in the carnival atmosphere of an almost bloodless revolution, the monocled, kid-gloved General Spínola was cast as Sebastião. His book, *Portugal and the Future*, published in February 1974, was one of the sparks that set off the 25 April coup. He knew that the colonial wars could not be won and set out his ideas for federation in his book. As President of the Junta of National Salvation he announced the first of its aims: 'To guarantee the survival of the sovereign nation in its pluri-continental entirety . . .' The pluri-continental entirety that survives today is linguistic. Fernando Pessoa's modernist Sebastianic vision was of a universalism, cultural and spiritual; in the voice of one of his heteronyms, Bernardo Soares, he says, 'My country is the Portuguese language'.[13] It is a country of 150 million inhabitants. As Isabel Allegro de Magalhães writes, 'It is in the very fabric of our own language that we look for what is (or was, or was supposed to be) beyond [*além*]. That *beyond* has become, in a certain mode, literary texture. It reveals itself in the very stuff of our language, and in our ability to make something new with that same old stuff. A new poetic, perhaps, rather than a new patriotism.'[14]

The precipitate decolonization that followed the 1974 revolution was the latest in a series of events that slimmed Portugal to its 'real' size. Back in 1822, Dom Duarte's ancestor Pedro IV (whose royal family fled into exile from the Peninsula War) declared himself first emperor of an independent Brazil which dispensed with emperors altogether and became a republic in 1889. Today Brazilian television soap operas are a Portuguese addiction. Brazilian Portuguese is alive and evolving in a way that Portuguese writers envy. Where it once supplied gold Brazil now supplies style. The gold comes from nearer home. It is often said that Portugal was once the richest and most powerful nation on earth. Still they sigh, 'Ah, what nostalgia [*saudade*] we have for a future in which Sebastião may come. Once we were so great, but now we are so small.'

The novelist Lídia Jorge remarked to me, with biting lyricism, 'The will to be far and far and far, it is very Portuguese, a taste for the very far, without a name, not an Empire, a metaphysical dream, without ground, outside our time always.' But when Portugal cuts all that cackle and looks in the cheval glass today, what does it see and what must its artists paint? A wasted figure perched at Europe's edge, wistfully looking over its shoulder? A slender Brazilian colony gazing greedily at Brussels?

Notes

1. Joseph Conrad, *Last Essays* (London: Dent, 1926).
2. Joseph Conrad, *A Personal Record* (London: Dent, 1912).
3. Fernando Pessoa, 'Mar Português', *Mensagem* (Lisbon: Edição Ática 1934).
4. Fernando Pessoa, 'Padrão', *Mensagem* (Lisbon: Edição Ática, 1934).
5. Quoted in G.K. Haveaux, *La Tradition Historique des Bapendes Orientaux* (Brussels: I.R.C.B., 1954).
6. Paul Hyland, *The Black Heart: A Voyage into Central Africa* (London: Gollancz, 1988).
7. Georges Balandier, *Daily Life in the Kingdom of the Kongo*, trans. Helen Weaver (New York: Allen and Unwin, 1968).
8. Quoted in Sigbert Axelson, *Culture Confrontation in the Lower Congo* (Falkoping, Sweden: Gummesons, 1970).
9. Fernando Pessoa, 'D. Sebastião, Rei de Portugal', *Mensagem* (Lisbon: Edição Ática, 1934).
10. From the Latin of Asser's *Life of King Alfred*, written in 893.
11. Maria Salomé Ferro in Paul Hyland, *Tremor in the Raven's Throat* BBC Radio 4, 1988.
12. José Saramago, *A Jangada de Pedra* (Lisbon: Editorial Caminho, 1986), *The Stone Raft*, trans. Giovanni Pontiero (London: Harvill, 1994).
13. Fernando Pessoa (Bernardo Soares) *Livro do Desassossego1* (Lisbon: Edição Ática 1982), *The Book of Disquiet*, trans. Margaret Jull Costa (London: Serpent's Tail, 1991).
14. Isabel Allegro de Magalhães 'Here and Beyond: Structuring Spaces of Portuguese Contemporary Fiction,' paper delivered at the Institute of Romance Studies, University of London, 5 May 1994.

Constructing National and Cultural Identities in Sub-Saharan Francophone Africa

Dominic Thomas

To tell the truth, I must say the country concerned is *not on any map*. If you want to find it, it's in time that you must go searching.

Henri Lopes, *The Laughing-Cry*[1]

As the twentieth century comes to an end, we have become increasingly accustomed to images of world leaders gathering for economic summits. Little more than one hundred years ago, in 1884, the members of some fourteen international delegations representing the superpowers of the age assembled in Berlin to divide the African continent among themselves. We know today that this meeting triggered the 'scramble for Africa', and that it was nothing but a pretext for economic exploitation, veiled in arguments for Christianity and civilization. However, when the participants at the Berlin Conference divided Africa, they failed to consider the cultural, linguistic and ethnic boundaries which distinguished African peoples. The African leaders of postcolonial nation states have had to confront these complex realities in their attempt to construct national identity within the boundaries established by Western powers. As the various superpowers gather today, one cannot help but wonder why they have not been joined at the conference table by the leaders of politically independent African nations.

Defining African Nationalisms

The problems associated with the concept of 'nationalism' in the African context are inextricably linked to, and complicated by, the historical determination of the territorial borders following the Berlin Conference and its neglect for heterogeneous realities. In the African context, nationalism has come to signify the attempt to bring together peoples who were not linguistically, ethnically or culturally homogeneous within given territorial boundaries and to build the nation state. As James Coleman has argued, 'a colonial nationalist movement directs its efforts toward the attainment of two main objectives: (1) the achievement of self-government and (2) the creation of a cultural or political sense of nationality and unity within the boundaries of the area of the nation to be.'[2] It is the relationship between the cultural and the political that are of particular interest to me here, and I propose to explore it within the context of francophone sub-Saharan Africa. Many of the issues and arguments I raise will of course be pertinent to other areas of Africa.

The concept of nationhood describes various stages of communality and collectivity. Coleman's comprehensive description of the various manifestations of these 'nationalisms' is most useful:

Pan-Africanism: race, continent, or subcontinent.
Nationalism: colonial territory to a new state or nation.
Ethnic nationalisms/ethnicity: *historic*-ethnolinguistic collectivities with previous political unity; *situational*- large-scale collectivities acquiring identity and self-consciousness through supertribalization.
Tribalism/micronationalism: small-scale ethnolinguistic, kinship-defined collectivities.
Regionalism or localism: any collectivity which asserted itself against alien rule prior to the emergence of an organized territorial nationalist movement as the presumptive successor regime.[3]

While these various collectivities represent attempts to forge community, I would argue that it is essentially with the struggle for independence that the nation becomes an object of public consciousness, since it is at this historical juncture that nation-building becomes the responsibility of the State. Somewhat paradoxically, an important moment in the process of national consciousness in francophone postcolonial cultures came from the exposure of African soldiers, (collectively designated as the '*tirailleurs sénégalais*') fighting for France in Europe during the Second World War, to French denunciations of the invading German forces; the French invocation of nationalism as a response to this territorial invasion led many Africans to reflect on the analogies with the colonial situation in Africa.

Acquiring Power

As V.Y. Mudimbe has argued, 'Up to the 1920s, the entire framework of African social studies was consistent with the rationale of an epistemological field in its sociopolitical expressions of conquest . . . Socially, they were tools strengthening a new organization of power and its political methods of reduction, namely assimilation or indirect rule.'[4] Assimilation describes the French colonial policy which sought to impose French language and culture on its colonial subjects, while indirect rule refers to the British model which was fundamentally concerned with economic and political exploitation. These colonial models of dominance and authority (of power that is), were challenged by the *négritude* movement and the discourse it generated, and announced, as Mudimbe has argued, the first 'signs of an African will for power'[5]. The essential tenets of the *négritude* movement were to rehabilitate the idea of Blackness through the glorification of the African past, to dignify tradition and culture, and in the process to dispel the Western reductionist vision Africans had been subjected to for generations. This would also transform the superior–inferior relationship that had come to characterize Western and African relations, and simultaneously empower Africans. The *négritude* movement was soon politicized and came to play a significant role in the politics of nationalism both in the movement towards independence but also in the post-independence structuring of newly-independen*t countries.*

Maintaining Power

In order to avoid potential conflict, the Organization for African Unity (OAU) encouraged African leaders at independence to accept the existing colonial territorial borders, and to undertake the task of promoting national unity. Newly-independent governments identified the importance of recognition in the international community, and the juridical legitimacy it conferred upon the State. United Nations documents during the early 1960s are particularly revealing, in their concern with portraying their leaders fully engaged in government.

African governments simultaneously attempted to promote a national culture, common heritage, and collective memory in order to justify the construction of the nation state. As Coleman has explained, 'it is a posttribal, postfeudal terminal community which has emerged from the shattering forces of disintegration that characterize modernity . . . there must be a much greater awareness of a closeness of contact with "national" compatriots as well as with the "national" government.'[6] The task of constructing identities required a renunciation and denunciation of the French assimilationalist paradigm, and this dimension was implicit to much *négritude*. This was also one of the reasons why Marxism-Leninism proved attractive to a number of African countries (for example Mali and Congo), since the rejection of colonialism and imperialism that was so central to the writings of Lenin and Stalin, coincided with the opposition shared by Africans to the colonizing powers. Since independence, African countries have experimented with political systems as diverse as multiparty democracies, monarchies, single-party structures, military dictatorships and Marxist-Leninist parties. However, the frequency of *coups d'état* and the ease with which governments have been overthrown, underlines the fact that these structures were unstable and characterized by fragile alignments. Furthermore, the military in Africa soon relinquished its initial apolitical status, and entered the realm of politics.

One of the most influential and interesting leaders in postcolonial Africa was the *négritude* poet Léopold Sédar Senghor. Senghor served as President of Senegal for some twenty years (1960–1980). The Senghorian-négritude view of Africa played a determining role in the postcolonial nation-building process and division of power, to the extent that it offered a model of African unity and co-existence. Irving Markovitz has described Senghor's influence in the following terms: 'observers have called Senghor one of Africa's architects of a revigorated, dynamic socialism; they have held him responsible for a dramatic cultural and moral break with the values of Western civilization and the creation of a new, uniquely African civilization and systems of values.'[7] As Ali Mazrui

118

has shown, Zaire's President Mobutu Sese Seko transformed this 'paradigm of authenticity' and has 'argued eloquently that, while *négritude* as a literary movement was a rebellion against the contempt which others (e.g., Europeans) felt towards Africa, *authenticity* as a political stance was a rebellion against the contempt many Africans felt towards *themselves*'.[8] Allegiance to an African past and unity have provided key tenets to the policies of African leaders, as they implemented them with their own variations. Senghor's writings during that period reflect the transformations in his thinking as it evolved, as Mudimbe has described it, from *négritude* to Marxism and finally to universal civilization.[9]

As I have argued, national consciousness emerged during the colonial era as a unified attempt to rid the African continent of colonial oppressors. Africans from all over the continent joined forces in the colonized territories and formed a united front against the common oppressor. However, these alignments were not conceived as permanent associations and unity soon came to signify sameness, that is to say assimilation to the views and philosophies of the new postcolonial élites who controlled and manipulated power.

Manipulating Power

It is essential for us to explore the emergence of various power mechanisms in the African context, since, as Achille Mbembe has argued, 'to account for postcolonial relations is thus to pay attention to the workings of power in its minute details, and to the principles of assemblage which give rise to its efficacy'.[10] The term 'power' signifies a number of phenomena, but it is used here, as Henry Bretton defined it in his book *Power and Politics in Africa*, 'to connote any extension of will or physical ability beyond an individual or group to effect certain goals in relation to other individuals or groups'.[11] The manner in which power has been acquired, maintained and manipulated by the various agents is essential to our understanding of nationalism in the African context.

Patrick Chabal has addressed the question of power and violence in postcolonial Africa, and distinguished between two types of violence, namely 'active violence' and 'passive violence'. Whereas the former includes torture, execution, detention, et cetera, the latter designates incompetence, economic considerations, hunger, famine, embezzlement, and so forth. Indeed, as Max Weber has demonstrated, 'the use of force is regarded as legitimate only in so far as it is either permitted by the State or prescribed by it . . . the claim of the modern state to monopolize the use of force is as essential to it as its character of compulsory jurisdiction and of continuous operation.'[12] These types of violence feature prominently in a number of literary works, in their portrayal of what Chabal has described as:

> A political order that is exclusively governed by a moral economy founded on violence . . . This regression of the political toward raw violence in turn lowers human psychology to its most basic expression: it is a return to the survival of the fittest and to a political economy made up of rape, theft, barter and robbery.[13]

The suitability, or at least the effectiveness of the models I have discussed to the African context, can in part be gauged by considering the predicament of the postcolonies. Africans were only allowed limited participation in the leadership hierarchy under French direct rule, and therefore gained only little experience with power. This factor does not in itself explain the situation in the postcolony today, since the problems faced by countries that were subjected to British indirect rule, which did allow greater participation, are analogous.[14] However, if one examines these colonial mechanisms of rule, one can see how, after independence, they came to be duplicated in spaces that were not ethnically homogeneous, and thus generated the situation which characterizes postcolonial Africa. As Kwame Anthony Appiah has argued in his book, *In My Father's House*:

> In most places, however, the new states brought together peoples who spoke different languages, had different religious traditions and notions of property, and were politically (and in particular, hierarchically) integrated to different—often radically different—degrees . . . even the states with the smallest populations were by and large not ethnically homogeneous.[15]

The structures and alignments that were in place on the pre-contact African continent were all dismantled by the colonial powers. This process of erasure and domination ensured that any subsequent autonomous rule would have to be undertaken according to colonial alignments. The colonial authorities employed such terms as 'tribalism' and 'ethnicity' to further their *divide ut imperes* policy. However, it was not just the colonial measures undertaken to restrict nomadic existence and the process of 'fluid' exchanges which Jean-Loup Amselle has described in *Au coeur de l'ethnie* (*The Heart of the Ethnic Group*) but rather the colonial practices themselves (economic, regional, social) which generated a 'tribalist ideology' (encompassing factionalism, tribalism and micro-nationalism).[16]

The 'tribalist ideology' described by Amselle has come to represent the principal obstacle to the nation-building process to the extent that it has been politicized and employed by postcolonial rulers, in the same way that the colonial powers did, to fuel ethnic animosity and generate instability. As Crawford Young has argued, ' "Nation" as an imagined community of anti-colonial combat . . . was relatively unproblematic . . . But "nation", once independence was won, required the postcolonial state as vehicle: thus its imperative of "national integration".'[17] The initial model for nation-building consisted in bringing together heterogeneous peoples, and foregrounded the willingness to incorporate and validate this sociological plurality. However, in the name of 'national integration' and unity, governments have failed to recognize this diversity and accordingly to authenticate individual aspirations; the instability of postcolonial environments can thus be seen as an affirmation of peoples' refusal to assimilate their respective identities to a monolithic national paradigm.

In his book, *Technology, Tradition and the State in Africa*, Jack Goody attested to the conflict characteristic of pre-colonial Africa. While it is vital to recognize the often violent character of pre-colonial relations, it is the alienation, assimilation and violence associated with colonial rule which comes closest to the sophisticated and technologically advanced mechanisms of repression and exploitation (such as torture, propaganda, communication technology et cetera) that are at work in the postcolony today. Assimilationist policy was the order of the day under French rule, but similar philosophies have prevailed in the postcolony at the service of nationalistic, unifying policies, that are just as oppressive and exclusive. The territorial borders may have been artificial and arbitrary in their original conception, but they nevertheless became political, legal and administrative realities at independence. Indeed, as Denis Austin has stated, 'cartographically, Africa certainly exists'.[18] The colonial period modernized Africa, and created cities and infrastructures, shipping and trading lanes, et cetera, which favoured a number of regions over others (coastal over inland, for example). This situation was further complicated by the fact that the artificial boundaries demarcated by the colonial powers provided the framework for the emergence of national consciousness as the driving force behind the struggle for independence, but once this end had been achieved, the very precondition for its continuity depended on its sustained and unified opposition to the colonial powers. This has generated a very complex situation, in that the State (government authorities) has been able to justify the promotion of nationalism as a measure to exclude colonial domination.

The fight against the common oppressor (Western colonists) was indeed sanctified by international law: 'All peoples have the right of self-determination. By virtue of that right they freely determine their political status and freely pursue their economic, social and cultural development'.[19] Somewhat paradoxically, self-determination generated a situation of dependency on the autonomous national State. Initially, however, there was much debate concerning the definition of a 'peoples' and of what 'self-determination' itself signified. The history of decolonization has underlined this, since countries achieved independence at different historical periods, as their associations with the former Western colonizing powers were redefined. The 1950s and 1960s witnessed self-determination by most African countries; for most of francophone sub-Saharan Africa, 1960 proved to be the determining year (Cameroon, Central African Republic, Gabon, Congo, Zaire, and so forth). However, some African countries only achieved independence much later (Zimbabwe in 1980, Mozambique in 1975, Angola in 1975). There is little ambiguity today concerning the significance of 'self-determination' and 'peoples'; they correspond respectively to the autonomous government of a sovereign territory, and to the 'nationals' who reside there. Attention has instead shifted towards the problem of validating and recognizing diversity in these nation states, and to the complex task of constructing identity.

The Right to Violence and the Right to Silence: Human Rights in Africa

Once power has been acquired and concentrated in the hands of a power élite, the concern turns towards maintaining it. African postcolonial governments have promoted a unifying discourse, and opposition and dissent have often become treasonable offences. The government is always greater than the individual, since when violence is perpetrated by them, it is legal and legitimized in its own name.[20] Debate is stifled and alternative discourse is deemed unacceptable. While governments have been eager to promote an official culture, the complex political realities have in turn forced writers and other dissidents to situate themselves in relation to this national paradigm. As Timothy Brennan has demonstrated, 'it is not that people, or the artists who speak for them, can imagine no other applications, but that the solutions to dependency are only collective, and the territorial legacies of the last 200 years provide the collectivity no other basis upon which to fight dependency.'[21]

Political constitutions accord legitimacy to sovereign nations and to their governments. An interesting parallel can be drawn between the foundations of constitutional legislation in the West and in Africa, particularly since African constitutions are usually duplicated according to Western models. As Susan Waltz has explained:

> In the West, the two principal human rights documents—the French Déclaration des droits de l'homme et du citoyen and the U.S. Bill of Rights—were drafted explicitly to limit the arbitrary powers of government. Both documents seek to protect individual liberties against the oppression of those who govern, and both assure due process of law for those accused of wrongdoing.[22]

However, as Waltz goes on to point out, 'so long as authority has control in nondemocratic regimes, it is difficult to imagine that such groups [human rights organizations] will be appreciated.'[23] Recent events in the Republic of the Congo illustrate some of these considerations.

The Congo has a particularly complicated history of ethnic instability. In 1991, the Congolese Government stated that it had 'reaffirmed its faith in the principles of pluralist democracy, to the rights outlined by the International Charter on Human and Peoples' Rights adopted in 1981 by the Organization for African Unity and the African Charter on Human and Peoples' Rights adopted in 1991 by the sovereign National Conference.'[24] Within the framework of this discussion, the following 'articles' in the Congolese Constitution are the most pertinent:

> **Article 7**: The human person is sacred. The state has a duty to respect and protect human life. Every citizen has the right to freely develop her/his personality as long as they respect the rights of others and civil order.

> **Article 8**: The freedom of the human person is inviolable. Any act of torture, any inhumane or degrading treatment are prohibited. No one can be arrested or detained arbitrarily.

> **Article 13**: No citizen may be interned on the national territory, except in those instances provided for by the law. No citizen can be forced for political reasons to reside away from her/his dwelling place or in exile.[25]

The new Constitution thus recognizes that dissent and opposition are lawful, but also the illegality of torture. Since the National Conference was held in 1991 and the Congo became a pluralist democracy, the sociological reality has remained problematic. Political alignment has taken place according to ethnic criteria, and this has in turn exacerbated ethnic animosity, and precluded the possibility of genuine social reform. Furthermore, the previous pattern of military engagement in government has been duplicated. It would seem that the future lies in the irony of the new Constitution and the apparent contradiction that is contained in its wording. The very use of the word 'reaffirm' confirms the previous Constitution's faith in the fundamental principles of human rights, but history has shown that it chose to ignore them. The problem lies once again in the policy of national integration, and the uses that are made of State security to achieve that goal. 'Security' is a broad term, and government's have been able to exercise their constitutional, and therefore legitimate, 'right to violence'. An Amnesty International report entitled 'Torture as Policy' has described this process: 'Torture is usually part of the state-controlled machinery to suppress dissent. Concentrated in the torturer's electrode or syringe is the power and responsibility of the state . . . Torture is most often used as an integral part of a government's security strategy.'[26] The ways in which the abuses of this State 'violence' are exposed are essential to our understanding of the construction of nationalism and national culture.

Dissident Voices

The relationship between politics and literature is especially revealing in the African context. The most important point that we must remember, is that while governments portray texts which are critical of them as anti-national, the works of creative authors are often far from that. Authors subscribe to the construction of the national space within the territorial borders determined by the colonial powers, but attack the State for its failure to recognize diversity and to validate individual identities. The situation is further complicated because a number of government authorities have sponsored an official literature of the State (for example under Ahmed Sékou in Guinea, Agostinho Neto in Angloa, Mobutu in Zaire, as well as in the Congo and Somalia).[27] A number of writers have, however, refused to co-operate with the authorities, and their fictional works have offered an alternative picture which contradicts the official one. Their writings thus undermine the government authorities by exposing them to the scrutiny of the international community. While their critical tone results in governments labelling them anti-national, they in fact participate in broader societal phenomena. As Christopher L. Miller has shown, 'the critique of the postcolonial state can wind-up supporting and creating a national culture. By attacking particular regimes, these publications contribute to an emergent "universe of discourse" that is specific to the nation-state.'[28] In a political environment in which all discussion is perceived as confrontational and hostile, these writers attempt to force discussion upon the authorities. Josaphat Kubayanda has argued that:

> Literary production and criticism actually is an integral part of the process of state formation, for at the heart of the polemic is the search for new political orders for a continent that is viewed by intellectuals as desperately in need of social change. The writer articulates the ideas, words and images that relate to or undercut real power in order to construct powerful alternative utopias or a new sense of nationality.[29]

Indeed, there are often serious consequences to producing anti-governmental literature. These include torture, imprisonment, house arrest and exile. Some of the most well-known victims of government violence since independence include Ngugi wa Thiong'o, Wole Soyinka, Sylvain Bemba, Sony Labou Tansi, Henri Lopes, Emmanuel Dongala, Nuruddin Farah, Jean-Pierre Makouta-Mboukou, Dennis Brutus, and most recently, the execution of Ken Saro-Wiwa, the Nigerian writer and environmental activist, to name but a handful.

The State's legitimate right to violence and to silence, manifests itself in a number of disquieting ways. As Page duBois has demonstrated, political torture is:

> Revealed in narratives depicting appalling cruelty and the most cynical disavowal of the rights of others exemplified by State torturers, the political party torturers, of many parts of the global nation in the present day. A principal motive of torture of this sort is control, the domination of an unpalatable truth. That truth may be communism, nationalism, democracy, any number of threatening political beliefs that disrupt the unity, the unblemished purity and wholeness of the state, or of any entity analogous to the unitary philosophical subject.[30]

Torture thus becomes an effective mechanism with which to impose consent and eliminate dissent, and writers have exposed these activities in their works.

Literature in Africa has consistently responded to the cultural and political environment. The *négritude* movement can be seen as a response to cultural colonialism, while the novels of the Cameroonian writers Mongo Béti and Ferdinand Oyono written during the 1950s opposed economic and political colonialism.[31] Postcolonial writers have explored the complex realities generated by the nation-building process, and have reflected on the difficulties experienced by individuals attempting to situate themselves and to construct identity in these spheres.

In contemporary works, African traditions are portrayed as profoundly different from Western thinking patterns, and the conflict between traditional beliefs and the modern secular world provides the fundamental power struggle that is examined. Under the most repressive regimes, authors have found it necessary to resort to the veil of allegory to conceal their narratives, even if everyone sees through it and knows that the fictional State which is described is in fact the real State. This has been the case for a number of African authors such as Ahmadou Kourouma's imaginary People's Republic of Nikinei (sounds like 'Guinea') in his novel *Les Soleils des indépendances* (*The Suns of Independence*) and Congolese writer Henri Lopes' 'country' in his novel *Le Pleurer-Rire* (*The Laughing-Cry*).[32] In Lopes' novel, the narrator declares: 'To tell the truth, I must say the country concerned is *not on any map*. If you want to find it, it's in time that you must go searching . . .' (my italics; PR, p. 58; LC, p. 40). The recourse to the fictitious 'country' serves of course to throw the censors, but also underlines a more important issue, namely that similar countries do exist in postcolonial francophone sub-Saharan Africa.

Writers reveal the mechanisms employed by the governing authorities in their attempt to eradicate African culture by enforcing a revised history, the imposition of new ideological structures, and the creation of myths which seek to manipulate memory. The novel, *Le feu des origines* (*The Fire of the Origins*) by the Congolese writer Emmanuel Dongala, examines the dangers of such a collective memory.[33] Individual memory serves to construct identity and to empower the individual, and is portrayed as unacceptable to the dominant political order. Government propaganda has sought to demonstrate that the Congolese share a common history, when in fact the creation of a modern, independent nation state only dates back to 1960. Writers thus warn against the discourse of assimilation, suggesting that we look instead beyond this and seek alignment within a framework which encompasses a multitude of identities. In this particular case, Dongala challenges what he sees as the official version of collective memory, so that history itself can be told. In the conclusion to *Le feu des origines*, the character Bunséki attempts to persuade his friend Mandala to write his memoirs; he underlines the importance of such a document for future generations. By association, this serves as an indicator of what Dongala attempted to achieve by writing this work. Dongala's novel constitutes an attempt to depart from the official version of history, employed within the context of nation-building rhetoric, and to inscribe an accurate historical version. For Dongala, alienating government practices have precluded the possibility of transcending the concept of national unity in order to achieve a social environment in which diversity could be validated without fracturing community.

One of the most informative studies on power in postcolonial Africa is Henri Lopes' novel *Le Pleurer-Rire*. Lopes is particularly interesting since between 1967 and 1980 he served as a high-ranking government minister. He has insisted on numerous occasions that one must distinguish between the facts of the author's life and the work itself.[34] However, Lopes is aware that inferences will be made, and as the conclusion to the novel confirms, he has chosen to play upn this ambiguity: 'In fact, I have borrowed nothing from reality, nor yet invented anything' (PR, p. 315; LC, p. 259). We are afforded in this work a unique perspective on the mechanisms of power, how they are acquired, maintained and manipulated. The various attempts to impose national integration and a political model of unity, are exposed for being exclusive and repressive. In the novel, the political leader, Bwakamabé, accords a customary, traditional basis to his power:

> Ever since Africa was Africa, the chief of the village, in our culture, had never been elected. To thirst nowadays for innovation in this domain was to be as uncustomary as asking a man to do the cooking or carry the calabash on his head [PR, pp. 99-100; LC, p. 74].

He simultaneously gives this power base an ethnic dimension, stating that:

> The Nation was saved, because the sun of the shadows, which that night diffused its pale yellow light, had transmitted to us the message of the ancestors: they had chosen Bwakamabé Na Sakkadé to lead all the Djabotama and impose their will upon all the othe' tribes of the new country as defined by the *Uncles* . . . ['Uncles' describes the French colonists. PR, p. 46; LC, p. 30].

The French government is exposed for wanting to maintain economic links, while refusing to officialize relationships. Criticism of Western economic powers for their neo-colonial activities has become a common feature in writings by postcolonial authors, and underlines the need for the imposition of new ethical guidelines. Bwakamabé's repressive political regime is denounced in the French media: 'the regime of Marshal Bwakamabé Na Sakkadé, of which the French Section of Amnesty International has often reported violations of human rights . . .' (PR, p. 272; LC, p. 223). French officials are conscious of the negative effect that news of their involvement with the African leader would have on the French electorate, and so set out to manipulate Bwakamabé by invoking his own arguments for cultural authenticity, and suggesting that he should act independently.

Nationalism and National Literatures

It has become increasingly common for critical approaches to francophone, anglophone and lusophone African literature to be restricted to the 'national' scale; accordingly, the written products that have emerged from independent nation states have come to be described as 'national literatures'.[35] If one considers the radically different sociological realities that have developed during the thirty-year period of 'self-determination', it does not seem unreasonable to suggest that the realities which inform African writers have contributed to a certain specificity that would make it possible for us to circumscribe the text to a given geographical area. However, the fact that is has been impossible to disassociate 'nationalism' from the discourse of the postcolonial State forces us to consider a number of issues prior to engaging in such an inquiry.

One of the main advocates of 'national literatures' is Adrien Huannou, who claims that:

> Since 'all that belongs to a nation is national', and since a literature is made up of all the literary works of a country or region, then all the oral and written works produced by the *nationals* of an African State constitute a national literature. There are therefore as many national literatures as there are States in Africa . . . [My italics].[36]

The discourse on national literatures raises a number of complex issues which go beyond Huannou's tautology. Indeed, it has been argued that some writers have even questioned the colonial borders. Wole Soyinka is one such writer, who in *The Man Died* wrote: 'For the truly independent thinker it is always—and often relevant—to recall the artificiality, the cavalier arrogance, the exploitative motivations which went into the disposal of African peoples into nationalities.'[37] This sentiment has been echoed by Henri Lopes, who has argued that 'beyond any national classification of literature, there are schools and families of writers who form networks that lend value to mankind's common heritage' and that there is a 'need to transcend national contingencies—or rather to enhance identities that are in danger of becoming fossilized in a provincial spirit'.[38] Lopes raises another very important issue, namely the danger of determinism (over-attributing the contents of the written text to a given reality); this denies the role of the author's creative imagination. In the case of writers from the Congo (Emmanuel Dongala, Sylvain Bemba, Sony Labou Tansi, Henri Lopes, et al.) and from Senegal (Sembène Ousmane, Aminata Sow Fall, et al.), to offer only two examples, the respective realities they are surrounded by are similar, but yet these authors have achieved radically different approaches to literature.

The relationship between literature and politics has been further complicated by the active solicitation of writers by the government authorities for the purpose of disseminating official propaganda; national categorizations fail to distinguish between these two types of text.[39] Furthermore, the attempt to reduce a literary work to its national dimension and to align it according to such criteria runs the risk of encouraging a type of comparative discourse, the dangers of which Edward Said warned against in *Culture and Imperialism*:

> As the twentieth century moves to a close, there has been a gathering awareness nearly everywhere of the lines between cultures, the divisions and differences that not only allow us to discriminate one culture from another, but also enable us to see the extent to which cultures are humanly made structures of both authority and dominance . . . There is in all nationally defined cultures, I believe, an aspiration to sovereignty, to sway and to dominance.[40]

Critical inquiries that are forewarned of these dangers will yield interesting findings and contribute to the increasing need for informed readings of the African political and social reality. However, if one considers existing relationships between intellectuals and the government authorities in Africa, an approach which ignores these criteria would be nothing but irresponsible.

From Berlin to the End of the Millennium

Official discourse in postcolonial Africa has called for the elimination of ethnicity, tribalism and regionalism, but yet the State has simultaneously relied on these phenomena to manipulate power. Recent events in African politics have pointed to possible alternative structures as frameworks for transition. One of the most significant efforts has been the staging of National Conferences (Benin 1990, Congo 1991, Togo 1991), prompted by the imperative of seeking new and innovative frameworks for the postcolony, given the failure of existing ones. Governments need to demonstrate a willingness to distance themselves from the political paradigm according to which unity is synonymous with unanimity; they must accept the complexity of the social reality, and validate plurality as a prerequisite to the construction of the national space. The situation is further complicated by the continued exploitation of the African continent by neo-colonial powers, the International Monetary Fund, and other such organizations.[41] Unless this relationship is redefined and Western powers recognize that their activities preclude the possibility of progress, it does not seem likely that the foreseeable future will offer us the spectacle of African leaders joining these superpowers at conference tables or 'summits'. The twentieth century will have ended with such instability and overt violations of the most fundamental basic human rights, that it is impossible to feel that there has been any progress since the 1884–1885 Berlin Conference. Recent events in countries such as Angola, Burundi, the Congo, Nigeria, Rwanda, Somalia, and Zaire confirm this. One can only hope that increased discourse and exposure of these realities will allow us to articulate different observations by the end of twenty-first century.

Notes

1. Henri Lopes, *Le Pleurer-Rire* (Paris: Présence Africaine, 1982) p. 58; *The Laughing Cry*, trans. Gerald Moore (London: Readers international Inc., 1987) p. 40. Quotations from Lopes' work are cited in the text with the abbreviation 'PR'and 'LC', and followed by the page reference.
2. James Smoot Coleman, *Nationalism and Development in Africa: Selected Essays*, ed. Richard L. Skar (Berkeley and Los Angeles: University of California Press, 1994) p. 34.
3. Coleman, p. 122.

4. V. Y. Mudimbe, *The Invention of Africa: Gnosis, Philosophy and the Order of Knowledge* (Bloomington and Indianapolis: Indiana University Press, 1988) p. 83.
5. Mudimbe, p. 83.
6. Coleman, p. 21.
7. Irving Markovitz, *Léopold Sédar Senghor and the Politics of Negritude* (New York: Atheneum, 1969) p. 3.
8. Ali A. Mazrui, 'On Poets-Presidents and Philosopher Kings', *Research in African Literature* 21, no. 2 (Summer 1990) p. 14.
9. Mudimbe, p. 93.
10. Achille Mbembe, 'The Banality of Power and the Aesthetics of Vulgarity in the Postcolony', *Public Culture: Society for Transnational Cultural Studies* 4, no. 2 (Spring 1992) p. 4.
11. Henry Bretton, *Power and Politics in Africa* (Chicago: Aldine Publishing Compant, 1973) p. 8.
12. Max Weber, in Guenther Roth and Claus Wittich (eds), *Economy and Society: An Outline of an Interpretative Sociology*, (Berkeley and Los Angeles: University of California Press, 1978) p. 56.
13. Patrick Chabal, 'Pouvoir et Violence en Afrique postcoloniale' *Politique Africaine* 42 (June 1991) pp. 58–9. My translation.
14. In anglophone African literature, the novels of Ngugi wa Thiong'o, Chinua Achebe and Nuruddin Farah, among others, attest to this.
15. Kwame Anthony Appiah, *My Father's House: Africa in the Philosophy Of Culture* (New York: Oxford University Press, 1992), pp. 161–62.
16. Jean-Loup Amselle, 'Ethnies et Espaces: Pour une anthropologie topologique' in Jean-Loup Amselle and Elikia M'Bokolo (eds), *Au coeur de l'ethnie: Ethnies, tribalisme et état en Afrique*, (Paris: La Découverte, 1985).
17. Crawford Young, 'Evolving modes of consciousness and ideology: nationality and ethnicity' in David E. Apter and Carl G. Rosberg (eds) *Political Development and the New Realism in Sub-Saharan Africa* (Charlottesville: University of Virginia Press, 1994) p. 72.
18. Denis Austin,'Pax Africa' in Simon Baynham (ed) *Military Power in Black Africa* (London: Croom Helm, 1986) p. 166.
19. This is from the United Nations Charter, cited in Richard Pierre and Claude and Burns H. Weston (eds) *Human Rights in the World Community: Issues and Action* (Philadelphia: University of Pennsylvania Press, 1992) p. 424.
20. For an analysis of the processes through which power is accumulated and its use legitimated, see Achille Mbembe, 'Pouvoir, Violence et Accumulation' in Jean-Francois Bayart, Comi Toulabor et Achille Mbembe (eds) *La Politique par la basse en Afrique Noire: Contributions à une problématique de la démocracie* (Paris: Karthala, 1992).
21. Timothy Brennan, 'The national longing for form' in Homi K. Bhabha (ed) *Nation and Narration*, (London and New York: Routledge, 1990) p. 58.

22. Susan E. Waltz, *Human Rights and Reform: Changing the Face of North African Politics* (Berkeley and Los Angeles: University of California Press, 1995) p. 14.
23. Waltz, p. 14.
24. F. Eboussi Boulaga, *Les conférences nationales en Afrique noire: Une affaire à suivre*. (Paris: Karthala, 1993) p. 196. My translation.
25. Eboussi Boulaga, pp. 197–98.
26. Cited in Claude and Weston, *Human Rights and the World Community*, p. 79.
27. I recently discussed this mechanism in a case study of the Republic of the Congo: 'Aesthetics and Ideology: The Performance of Nationalism in Recent Literary Productions from the Republic of the Congo' in Roger Little (ed) *Black Accents: Writing in French from Africa, Mauritius and the Caribbean* (London: Grant and Cutler Limited, 1996).
28. Christopher L. Miller, 'Nationalism and Resistance and Resistance to Nationalism in the Literature of Francophone Africa', *Post/Colonial Conditions: Exiles, Migrations, and Nomadisms. Yale French Studies* 1, no. 82 (1993) p. 95.
29. Josaphat B. Kubayanda 'Dictatorship, Oppression, and New Realism.' *Research in African Literatures* 21, no. 2 (Summer 1990) p. 8.
30. Page duBois, *Torture and Truth.* (London and New York: Routledge, 1991) p. 149. See also Edward Peters, *Torture* (New York: Basil Blackwell, 1985); and Kate Millett, *The Politics of Cruelty: An Essay on the Literature of Political Imprisonment* (New York: W.W. Norton and Company, 1994).
31. The most notable would include Mongo Béti's *Le Pauvre Christ de Bomba* (Paris: Robert Laffort, 1956), *The Poor Christ of Bomba*, trans. Gerald Moore (London: Heinemann, 1971); and Ferdinand Oyono's *Une Vie de Boy* (Paris: Juillard, 1956), *Houseboy*, trans. Clive Wke (London: Heinemann, 1966).
32. Ahmadou Kourouma, *Les soleils des indépendances* (Montréal: Presses de l'Université de Montréal, 1968; Paris: Seuil, 1968/1970); *The Suns of Independence*, trans. Adrian Adams (New York: Africana, 1981). Other examples include Sony Labou Tansi's 'La Katamalanasie' in *La Vie et demie* (Paris: Seuil, 1979); and Tchichelle Tchivela, *Longue est la nuit* (Paris: Hatier, 1980).
33. Emmanuel Dongala, *Le feu des origines.* (Paris: Albin Michel, 1987).
34. See, for example, Henri Lopes, 'My Novels, My Characters and Myself', *Research in African Literatures*, 24, no. 1 (Spring 1993).
35. The most notable is Richard Bjornson's *The African Quest for Freedom and Identity: Cameroonian Writing and the National Experience* (Bloomington and Indianapolis: Indiana University Press, 1991).
36. Adrien Huannou, *La question des littératures nationales en Afrique noire.* (CEDA: 1989) p. 34. My translation.
37. Wole Soyinka, *The Man Died.* (New York: Noonday Press, 1972/1988)

p. 175. Cited in Kubayanda, 'Dictatorship, Oppression and New Realism' p. 8.

38. Henri Lopes, 'My Novels, My Characters and Myself', p. 85.

39. I have discussed this problem at length in 'Aesthetics and Ideology'.

40. Edward W. Said, *Culture and Imperialism* (New York: Alfred A. Knopf, 1993) p. 15.

41. Mongo Beti has addressed this question in his recent *La France contre Afrique: Retour au Cameroon* (Paris: Editions la Découverte, 1993).

Border Crossings: The Internet and the Dislocation of Citizenship

Graham Barwell and Kate Bowles

What is the Internet? History, Use, and Regulation

In a commercial shown on US television in 1993, MCI Communications described the information superhighway as a road connecting all points: 'There will be no more there. We will all only be here.' Even though the nature of this communications phenomenon is such that greater numbers are still experiencing its effects via these discursive speculations rather than by an actual encounter with the network, it is none the less the case that the proposed collapsing of the tyranny of distances (both social and geographical) requires some careful thought. It is our purpose to ask: how will this disruption to the previously distinct hierarchies of here and there, self and Other, centre and margin, West and Orient, impact upon the routines of national self-identification with which Australia and Canada are especially preoccupied? What is the future of cultural nationalism in the age of global storytelling? Can we continue to distinguish between the global and the universal? And if cultural difference is to be erased, whose cultures precisely will be lost?

The Internet is a network or web of computers, in which each is linked to all the others. Just as in the phone system each phone is linked to an exchange which is then linked to a wider national and international network, so is each computer on the Internet linked first to a smaller network, such as AARNet in Australia, then to the world at large. Thus the Internet is really a network of networks. Its origins go back to US Defense Department planning in the 1950s and 1960s in preparation for the

135

maintenance of command and control under nuclear attack. Defense planners argued that the solution lay in decentralizing the communications network, removing the hierarchical organization so there was no fixed centre but a series of nodes which were always in contact with each other, determining the best ways of routing the traffic and checking to see it reached its destination. These policies led to the development of the first group of networked computers in four different sites around the United States, a Defense Department network known as ARPANet (the Advanced Research Projects Agency Network), which came online in 1969 and lasted until 1990.[1]

The possibility of networking computers was soon seen as offering valuable benefits for users in non-military environments. These benefits included not only communications but also access to larger machines than one could otherwise afford and sources of information which had not previously been available. In the 1970s and early 1980s, while some of the leading computer research institutions set up internal networks, or local area networks (LANs) as they came to be known, other networks came into existence as a result of the efforts of groups of individuals or organizations. Some of the early networks were fairly primitive, dependent on the first personal computers, modems and ordinary phone lines, and designed by university students, such as USENet (User's Network)[2] which rapidly became popular for conducting public conversations and computer conferencing. Others were more sophisticated. The US National Science Foundation set up its own network, NSFNet, for a variety of purposes including making access to supercomputers available to researchers outside the military. The NSF funded connections to universities only if the campus planned to make access widely available. Thus the advent of NSFNet brought the Internet to university staff and students. For scholars outside the sciences the network known as BITNet (Because It's Time network)[3] was set up by the NSF and IBM. Through the 1980s people in the various networks wanted to be able to talk to and exchange data with each other. This had been possible for those networks which had been linked to the military network, which, as other networks joined it, became known as the ARPA Internet, and connection soon became feasible in one way or another for those in other networks, like BITNet, through a system of connection points called gateways.

As users in the United States became linked through the Internet, users elsewhere were gaining access to similar groups of networks. In Australia, AARNet, the Australian Academic and Research Network, was established by the Australian Vice Chancellors Committee in 1990 and similar networks sprang up in other countries. As networks linked up within countries, so they linked between countries. Some of the private networks, such as CompuServe and FidoNet, which had come into being in the early 1980s, eventually gained limited connections to the Internet. While the full range of Internet capability is not available from every country, the Internet does stretch to every continent including Antarctica, and e-mail can be sent to most countries.[4] No one knows the number of people currently connected. There are nearly 100,000 host systems in Australia, two million in the United States and some 3.2 million worldwide, which translates into an estimated thiety-six million users.[5] The only certainty is that the Internet has expanded exponentially in recent years.

Along with the expansion of the Internet has gone an expansion of the ways it is used. While it is still used extensively for seeking, exchanging and downloading research information including both sound and images, receiving electronic journals and newsletters, and programmes are operated on other computers through it, some of the most significant activities take advantage of its capacity for interactivity. Electronic mail, which had been an originally minor capability of the ARPA network, is now one of the most widely available features of network access, extending into some of the networks not otherwise connected to the Internet. An offshoot of this capability is the rise of mailing lists, whereby a message sent to one address is automatically sent on to a number of others.[6] Related to mailing lists are public newsgroups of the kind fostered by USENet, where users post messages to be read and responded to by others with similar interests or antagonisms. Other interactive uses of the network include Internet Relay Chat, where typed conversations occur in real time, a facility which proved particularly popular for sex chat—*messageries roses* ('pink chat services')—on the French Minitel network, and MUD (multi-user dungeon) sites, a facility for role-playing involving any number of players which goes back to around 1980.[7] As the Internet has grown so have the devices for finding and manipulating material (such as Telnet, ftp, Gopher, and Mosaic), so that even novice users (newbies) can take advantage of the technology.

Crucially, the Internet is non-hierarchical and not controlled by any one organization. But this does not mean it is not subject to regulation. Access to it was first restricted to those engaged in

US Defense Department research and it was to be used for military purposes only.[8] As the Internet expanded in the United States with the help of Federal Funds through the National Science Foundation and other agencies, regulations were introduced to control the use of the part of the network provided by the NSF, particularly to prevent its exploitation for commercial purposes. Corporations could join but could not use it for advertising since they had not funded it. As personal computers and modems became widely available, individuals who had set up their own mini-networks accessible to anyone with the appropriate equipment and the right phone number became of increasing interest to the US Secret Service, because of fears that they were disseminating illegal information on computer hacking. More recently, attention in Britain and the United States has been focused on reputed online activity by organized groups of paedophiles; and attempts have been made to monitor various channels of communication in order to apply the same restrictions on the electronic exchange of sexually explicit or libellous material as are exerted over the more established technologies of representation: print, video, photography.

The actions of government authorities and the police against these loose coalitions of private individuals and ad hoc online communities, whose ethical bias was towards self-regulation rather than censorship, caused concern. This was the impetus for the foundation of a number of electronic civil liberties groups, the most prominent of which is probably the Electronic Frontier Foundation (EFF), established in the States in 1991 by John Barlow, an ex-lyricist for the rock group The Grateful Dead and now a computer expert, and Mitchell Kapor, the co-founder of Lotus Development Corporation and co-designer of the programme, Lotus 1-2-3. Supported by endowments from other like-minded individuals well-placed in the American computer industry, the foundation aims to develop public awareness of civil liberties and legal issues, to encourage educational activities and support easy access to computing and telecommunications. The EFF has sponsored groups in a number of other countries including both Canada (EFC) and Australia (EFA).[9] The Australian group, established in 1993, is concerned to support, educate, research and advise, especially on legal issues.

The Internet and Nationalism

The origins and history of the Internet are significant both for features of its organization and governance (non-hierarchical and self-governing), and its conceptualization. The range of metaphors used within and about the Internet is particularly instructive. Common tropes include travel—the information superhighway, the infobahn[10]; or places—cyberspace, the ocean[11], the frontier, America[12]—sometimes indicating the purposes for which it is used—a shopping mall[13], a copy machine[14], a sex shop[15]. Other tropes highlight the way in which users view their relationship to it, talking of it as a church[16] or, especially among those who engage in its interactive capabilities, describing it as a virtual community.[17] These metaphors are not mutually exclusive, frequently occurring in significant associations. The concept of the Internet as the frontier, which attracted scorn from some quarters when first proposed[18], is based on the notion that, in the words of the EFF mission statement, the new forms of digital 'communities without a single, fixed geographical location comprise the first settlements on an electronic frontier'. The concept of communities settled along an electronic frontier is extended in the way similar groups which share its aims are termed 'outposts'. It is perhaps not surprising that one of the EFF founders lives on a property in Wyoming.

The American origin of the Internet means that great emphasis is placed on its potential for the promotion of democratic ideals and free trade. A current guidebook notes that in education the availability of access to the network has a 'democratic effect . . . on what is communicated. A student can exchange ideas with a leading authority as a peer.'[19] The NSFNet Acceptable Use Policy, cited by another guidebook as an example of the kinds of regulation applying to some parts of the Internet, specifies that communication with foreign users is acceptable, provided that 'any network . . . the foreign user employs . . . provides reciprocal access to US researchers and educators.'[20] Ironically the American Government also argues that for American users transmission of computer messages overseas is subject to the Department of Commerce's export restrictions. The older civil liberties groups are particularly concerned to see that rights enshrined under US law are not infringed. Thus the EFF declares in its mission statement it will '[s]upport litigation in the public interest to preserve, protect, and extend First Amendment rights within the realm of computing and telecommunications technology' and speaks of ensuring the 'civil liberties guaranteed in the Constitution and the Bill of Rights are applied'. An American commentator notes in connection with network ethics that the two overriding premises are that individualism is honoured and fostered, and that the network is good and must be protected. He adds, '[n]otice these are very close to the frontier ethics of the West, where individualism and preservation of lifestyle were paramount.'[21] The founding ethic could not be more explicitly nationalized.

As the net spread beyond the United States the combination of this original bias with America's reputation for media colonization (the Coca-Colonization effect) caused concern. In Europe, where the Internet protocols for communication between computers were regarded as 'a cultural threat akin to EuroDisney'[22], the French introduced in the early 1980s their own national network, not connected to the Internet, the Minitel system, which was widely used and very successful by the mid-1980s. But the consequence of this success, if the national network is updated and linked internationally, is that it runs the risk of importing into French culture precisely the kinds of influence the *Academie Française* is supposed to resist.

In Japan, participation in the early development of the Internet had been similarly limited by government policies. The use of a modem was illegal until 1985 and Internet accounts were difficult to get. Users were strongly influenced by the America. For example, in the case of TWICS, a conferencing system in Tokyo which joined the Internet in 1986, the co-founders were an American English teacher and a 'Japanese with the sensibilities of an American teenager',[23] and the language used is English. Japanese participation in online culture had also been hampered by a written language based on ideographs rather than an alphabet, as well as certain cultural norms, such as social formalities that can define and limit the terms of argumentative debate. While the telecommunications companies are committed to linking every Japanese home to a fibre-optic network by 2015, the potential for a clash between Japanese and American cultural values is plain. The awkward metaphor for a Japanese virtual community called Beejima reveals the tensions as the national culture tries to accommodate the foreign: 'The image of Beejima was a friendly little island community in the electronic seas of Japan, close to Tokyo but accessible from anywhere, a Japanese system modeled on Japanese context, with an international and multicultural outlook.'[24] In the United States itself some of the dedicatedly non-hierarchical groups have recognised the potential for cultural domination inherent in the notion of the US nation as the centre. Thus in April 1994 EFF offered a defensive clarification of the term 'outpost', to the effect that the 'EFF considers itself as much of an outpost, a pioneer in a new, uncharted territory, as even the smallest local activist'.[25] In other words, the outposts are not to be considered as franchises—but the metaphor remains explicitly American.

The reaction of the Australian government to the Internet suggests that while it recognises, like the French and the Japanese, that the globalization of the Internet may be a form of colonization or at least a manifestation of America's cultural expansionism, it nevertheless is responding with a nationalist discourse which may well be both outdated and unsustainable. Thus, then Prime Minister Paul Keating's 1994 address to the Labour Party National Conference spoke of the information superhighway purely in terms of the necessity of providing Australian content, following the model of the television industry,[26] while the Senate Select Committee on Community Standards Relevant to Telecommunications, which was established in 1991, has looked only at telephone, videotext and Pay-TV services, though it noted in its most recent report that the transmission of 'pornography and violent material from computer bulletin boards and personal computers is a matter of increasing public concern'.[27] A Federal Government task force has recently recommended an amendment to the Commonwealth Crimes Act to ban the transmission of offensive material on computers.[28] While such actions aimed at content, whether Australian or pornographic (the terms are not mutually exclusive), presumably reflect community concerns and are certainly in keeping with the Australian legal system, they fail to recognize that the Internet, developed in the US and deeply encoded with the legal principles and ethics of that country, may pose a more complex problem for Australian culture.

How do we locate this problem within a discussion of postcoloniality? Certainly, the selective global spread of the Internet appears to jeopardize the smooth operation of the nation state at many levels: economic, cultural, legal. Just as certainly, the disembodiment of the Internet citizen complicates our understanding of the everyday performance of nationality, as one factor among a number which are similarly complicated: gender, ethnicity, sexuality, class, all appear to disappear along with the power axis of centre and margin. According to the tenets of terminal connectedness, there *is* no more here or there, or, to reframe the magical effect, 'on the Internet, no one knows you're a dog.'

And yet in one sense it is appropriate to draw attention to the demographics and ethical preferences of the Internet community as American. The purpose of this is not to regress into conspiracy theories of media imperialism, or to agonize over whether or not, as one posting to USENet put it, 'national borders are speed bumps on the information superhighway', but to examine the more complicated challenge to the workings of the nation state that occurs wherever the new community represents itself as supranational or as 'global'. One particular Canadian case, which we have also examined elsewhere,[29] highlights the potential of the Internet for violating the priorities and privileges of non-US national authorities in the control of sensitive information, without necessarily acting in the interests of the United States Government. It is a useful illustration not only of the dislocation of neo-colonization which the medium represents, but also of the perils of uncritical acceptance of such apparent post-nationalism.

The Homolka Case

In June 1993, Justice Francis Kovacs of the Ontario Court of Justice consented to the imposition of a publication ban on the details of the manslaughter trial of Karla Homolka, a young Canadian woman who had been arrested and charged, along with her husband Paul Bernardo, in connection with the kidnapping, sexual assault and murder of two local schoolgirls, Leslie Mahaffy and Kristen French. Excessive public interest in the case was anticipated due to the nature of the crimes, and the rumoured wealth of grisly detail which could emerge. In the interests of preserving a viable trial environment for the second of the defendants, Paul Bernardo, Justice Kovacs deployed the ban mechanism as a means of curbing that potential public and media attention.

In the text of the ban, subsequently made available via the Internet, Justice Kovacs considered the question of the likely American media interest in the trial, particularly given that the murders had occurred in a region close to the Canadian/American border. A Canadian court has no control over media in the United States, obviously, and in his decision therefore to ban foreign reporters from the trial—the only remaining option— Justice Kovacs cited Justice Thorson in the 1984 case of Global Communication Ltd and the Attorney General of Canada, in which it was observed that the 'widest possible latitude' given to media reporting of trials in the United States is offset by a much more rigorously investigative approach to jury selection—which itself of course becomes part of the media narrative, as we saw during 1995 in the infamous O. J. Simpson trial—and by the sequestration of the jury during the trial. In Canada, by contrast, the individual's right to privacy mitigates against such searching personal investigation, and jury sequestration is rare. In that case, Justice Thorson had concluded:

> I offer no comment on the relative merits of the two different approaches, except to say that each shares the common objective of seeking to ensure a fair trial but comes at that objective from a different tradition of legal history.[30]

Accordingly, all foreign media and members of the general public were banned from the courtroom, and only accredited Canadian media, and members of the Mahaffy, French and Homolka families were permitted to attend, bound by the Crown's prohibition on their reporting anything other than the charge and the sentence. Karla Homolka was found guilty of manslaughter, and was sentenced to two concurrent twelve-year terms. In not imposing life sentences, Kovacs acknowledged her co-operation with the police, but concluded:

> No sentence I can impose would adequately reflect the revulsion of the community for the deaths of two innocent young girls who lived their lives without reproach in the eyes of the community.[31]

The Canadian media appealed against the ban but did not violate it, a response which itself caused comment in the US press. The *Washington Post,* for example, subsequently argued that to Canadians, 'censorship at the edges is an acceptable trade-off for social order', and quoted Rowland Lorimer of the Canadian Center for Studies in Publishing as saying that 'If anything, Canada defines itself against the United States by its lack of libertarianism.

We have a positive attitude toward public enterprise. We believe the state can act on behalf of society as a whole.' The article further quoted Stuart Adam, Dean of the Arts Faculty at Carleton University in Ottawa as saying that 'The United States can look anarchic to Canadians. It's impossible to watch the Mike Tyson case, or the Rodney King case, or the William Kennedy Smith case, from the outside and remain confident that they were born in justice.'[32]

There was, however, a significant element of debate in Canada regarding the ban, contextualized within Canada's long history of cultural dispute with the United States. It quickly became clear that the scant details surrounding the case were in themselves so provocative as to generate unprecedented public interest in the trial, on both sides of the border.[33] The few known facts included the bodies having been dismembered before discovery and the charge of 'offering an indignity to the body of the deceased'. After the verdict, the courtroom details were described in the press as 'graphic and shockingly sordid', 'a catalogue of depravity and death', 'gruesome' and 'devastating', family members as 'stunned and shaken' and 'weeping', 'seasoned law enforcement officers and journalists' as 'virtually stumbling' out of the courtroom 'in tears', and Paul Bernardo's lawyer as 'clearly shaken', taking off his glasses and putting his head in his hands while Homolka's twenty-seven-minute statement of her part in the crimes was read to the court. The textual silence at the centre of this hysterical reaction immediately created a blank prescription on which the worst fears of the community, the most graphic of urban legends, could be inscribed. All that was missing was a forum in which these fears could be articulated, collated, and revised.

Rumours had been posted and discussed electronically from the outset, principally in the USENet newsgroups soc.culture.canada and ont.general. In July 1993, two students from the University of Toronto and the University of Western Ontario formed a new USENet newsgroup named alt.fan.karla-homolka to host the discussion, and to provide a location for banned material. This use of alt.fan as a semi-ironic designation is a regular USENet practice, as is the formation of sites for the discussion of information broadcast on television, particularly in court trials. In this case, however, the newsgroup provided an address in cyberspace where information subject to a media ban could collect, immediately challenging the definition of 'publication' on which the ban rested.

Rumours from anonymous respondents with alleged contacts among the sixty journalists who had attended the trial formed the basis of the newsgroup's earliest content. Comments were typically prefigured by 'I'll say right now that this is hearsay but fairly reliable since I am sixth removed . . .' or 'What I'm about to write may be true, and it certainly is sick . . .' By the time media attention was drawn to the Internet itself as a source of information, the group's coalition of editors had assembled these rumours into a Frequently Asked Questions list (or FAQ), in accordance with USENet practice, the contents of which were indisputably grisly but only disputably grounded in fact.

The Internet's role in mediating or fabricating culturally potent indices of 'the unspeakable' is made clear in the original FAQ details regarding the performance of the crimes themselves. Images of stalking, sexual torture, voyeurism, lesbianism, bondage, live dismemberment and, finally, necrophilia combine in this lurid but increasingly coherent paranoid narrative. Inevitably, rumours included the existence of snuff movies, those perverse versions of the funniest home-video genre, which sat alongside the home movies of the victims used by the television news programme *A Current Affair* in its two reports about the crime; a poignant detail added later was the rumour that Paul Bernardo had had the foresight to tape episodes of *The Simpsons* over this incriminating evidence.[34] As the loose collage of speculations cohered into a narrative, these overlaps and interactions with television, video and other mediations or simulacra took on an appearance which could best be described as postmodern.

Sustaining this definition is the fact that the media's appropriation of the principal speculations in the FAQ, in the absence of other hard information, was initially extensive. Indeed, one version of the FAQ claims that the Canadian press suppressed the name of alt.fan.karla-homolka 'for fear their US counterparts would print scoops from it before they did'.[35] The migration of rumour outwards from the FAQ into the media, and thence back into the FAQ, has some significant nodal points. On 19 September 1993, the British tabloid newspaper the *Sunday Mirror* ran a story under the headline 'Killer Ken and Barbie's Video of Horror', filed by their correspondent in New York. Comparing Karla and Paul to British serial killers Ian Brady and Myra Hindley, figures with a high media profile, the article hinted at 'lesbian sex orgies' and videotapes, and plagiarized Canadian reports of the trial, embellishing where necessary.[36] Canadian distributors of the paper were immediately warned by the Ontario Attorney General, Marion Boyd, that they would be subject to a contempt order if copies were distributed to Canadian news-stands, drawing attention to the fact that a ban on publication logically extends from the production to the distribution of information.

This was a problem also being considered in the broadcast media. Canadian cable company Rogers Cablevision was faced with a contempt order if it conveyed Buffalo TV News from across the border, but protested that monitoring its ten US channels eighteen hours per day in case banned details were mentioned, was simply unfeasible. When on 26 October 1993 *A Current Affair* ran a segment on the case, screens across Canada were blacked out by the cable providers. The producers claimed in the segment that their decision to put the story to air had 'almost caused an international incident' and included a quote from Marion Boyd clearly intended to be construed as a Canadian Government threat to an American media provider.

The most significant US media intervention came on 23 November 1993 when the *Washington Post* ran a story from its Toronto correspondent, Anne Swardson, titled 'Unspeakable Crimes: This Story Can't be Told in Canada. And So All Canada is Talking About It', including most of the banned information, and appearing to be sourced in the FAQ. This encouraged other American newspapers in the border region, who had previously observed at least the spirit of the ban. Newspapers in Buffalo and Detroit reprinted the *Post* story, and although the *Buffalo News* substituted a 'story about dolphins' in its overseas edition, Canadians living near the border simply drove across to bring back copies of the US version. Newspaper stands sprang up near border crossings, and customs officers were left with the somewhat ludicrous option of limiting each returning Canadian to one copy, confiscating the rest, in a move reminiscent of the distinction between personal use and intent to sell in anti-drugs legislation. American magazines and periodicals covering the emerging story, in which the ban had replaced the crime as the centre of the controversy, offered special editions to Canada, and US television programmes were blacked out from Canadian screens. Despite this apparent sensitivity, however, the US media increasingly tended to represent itself as a kind of resistance movement servicing news-starved Canadian citizens, in an almost parodic reversal of the refuge Canada had offered to US draft dodgers during the Vietnam war.

While media attention intensified, and the intervenors (now including Rogers Cablevision) returned unsuccessfully to the Appeal Court to protest that the ban was unenforceable, journals dealing specifically with new information technologies began to debate the role the Internet had played in making the banned information available. The situation regarding production and distribution of information was no clearer there, and both Internet providers and their consumers had attracted the hostile attention of the Ontario police. In its April 1994 edition, US publication *Wired* magazine included a story containing a number of factual errors regarding the creation of alt.fan.karla-homolka, but including one item of banned information, the details of Karla Homolka's plea.[37] The hard-copy was therefore banned in Canada, prompting a *Wired* press release titled 'Cyberspace Cannot Be Censored', denying that the ban had even been breached, and taking the opportunity to advertise *Wired*'s online availability in the guise of a defence of freedom of speech. In addition, the magazine's publisher Louis Rossetto was quoted as saying 'Banning of publications is behaviour we normally associate with Third World dictatorships.'[38]

This comment was then seized upon by Toronto free newspaper *eye WEEKLY*, also available online. *eye* called *Wired* to confirm that they had equated Canada with a Third World dictatorship, to query their description of the banning of *Wired* as 'utterly chilling', and to confirm their suspicion that *Wired* had not acquainted itself with the details of the ban, including the fact that the plea itself was banned material. When this turned out to be the case, *eye* concluded scathingly that all that was chilling was 'what a terrible time an American publication is having understanding this story'.[39] Anyone who has seen a hard copy of *Wired* will have no trouble at all understanding the David and Goliath aspect of this encounter between a free street-newspaper and the giant of the cyberspace magazine trade.

A strange twist then occurred in April 1994 with the production of a press release from the so-called 'Citizens Coalition for Responsible Government' based in Buffalo. Attacking the 'socialist' Ontario Government, extensively plagiarizing the *Washington Post* article and using absolutely unsubstantiated material from the FAQ, the Coalition offered a 'detailed info pack' for the sum of US$20, the money to contribute to a mass mailing campaign.[40] This finally prompted some Canadian journalists to break their silence, at least to the extent that they denied that the evidence at Homolka's trial had included information on snuff movies. 'Most of it is fabrication—99 per cent untrue', said one television reporter who had attended the trial. 'None of what we heard was grisly, or what I would describe as grisly.' Another agreed: 'What I heard in court was certainly nothing like that.'[41]

Internet Citizens and National Government

In part, the case of Karla Homolka and the Internet hinges on questions of the authority which we attribute to printed material. It is this authority which supports the application of a ban on publication, even as the definitions of publication begin to unravel. The mode of production of electronic texts operates to erase the differences in status between types of information: transcripts of television shows, private correspondence, conversational expletives, unsubstantiated rumours and explorations of the sadistic imagination, all sit alongside electronically scanned articles from the print media, and legal texts which argue against the publication of all the other texts. No one appears to profit.

In addition, with the unravelling of socio-geographic notions of distance, coalitions of concerned citizens of one country can appear to be located in another simply by logging in to an overseas mailserver: one of the FAQ's original authors has been electronically located in Finland and Texas, all the while remaining corporeally in Toronto. It is precisely this seeming dislocation of citizenship which complicates any notion of legal 'rights' in such cases. While the office of the Ontario Attorney General, the Ontario Police Department, and other agencies whose conceptualization of national borders is obliged to remain concrete, have made strenuous efforts to limit the transnational spread of electronic transmissions of banned information, it is clear that the Internet gives its citizens both the means and the inclination to resist nationalist efforts at censorship.

The fact that those citizens are also congregating *across* national boundaries in what we may call moral clusters (those for or against gun control, those who oppose the availability of unrestricted sexually explicit material, homosexual lobby groups and far-right militia organizations, to name but a few), many of whom are united in their opposition to governments of any national hue attempting to control the technology, undermines any reading of Internet history as a history of simple imperialism. If no one profits from its valueless circulation of information, then that economic motive for classical imperialism, which extends to other contemporary media such as film and television, is removed, leaving a kind of disembodied but undeniably moral imperative: the mode of colonial discourse without the motive. Ironically, this creates the impression that what has been effected is precisely that model of cultural diversity, on a global scale, to which the Australian Government has committed itself at the national level.

Has the Internet redistributed the means of power and cultural production sufficiently that it becomes appropriate to talk of postcolonialism in this context? How clear is the connection between diversity and hybridity, and how significant is that aura of the postmodern that surrounds its eclectic and egalitarian patterns of information gathering? Without resorting to the neo-imperialist thesis, we would none the less argue that the Internet is far from attaining that utopian status where the politics of class, gender and national identities have become redundant. A survey conducted and published on USENet recently commented that among its respondents 80 per cent were male, 80 per cent were white, and the median age was 31 years; 85 per cent claimed post-secondary education, and 29 per cent had completed a postgraduate programme of studies; 82 per cent described their location as urban or suburban. Although the authors acknowledge that 32 per cent of their respondents were non-American, the untranslatable specificities within this group regarding the significance of, say, urban versus rural locations, are smoothed into the demographics for the sample as a whole. This manoeuvre appears as evidence of the global dislocation of the Internet community precisely as it subsumes the particular identities of the minority groups into that of the largest population, the white American college-educated male.[42]

The cultural presumption behind this elision of difference is a characteristic of the Internet which we cannot afford to ignore. Although the net defence against accusations of imperialism is that if there is no more 'here', there can be no more colonizing of 'there', the risk is that the American-dominated English-speaking communications revolution is merely absorbing 'there' into 'here' in a classic faux pluralist manoeuvre. The equal and opposite risk is that second-world Governments of settler colonies such as Australia and Canada, who have often found themselves to be neither unequivocally here nor there along the moral continuum of colonial to postcolonial discourse, will resort to an unsustainable and outdated model of cultural nationalism in order to manage the new medium. If there is no here or there, then to steer a course between the two we need a new metaphor: to say that 'we will all only be here' remains in the same metaphorical territory, mistaking those of us who *are* here for all of us ('Who's "we", paleface?'), and thus losing the inadequate but useful accounts of identity on which theories of postcolonial subjectivity rest.

Until such a metaphor is devised, the most practical descriptive recourse is the embrace of contradiction, acknowledging that borders, and thus nations, are in a transitional phase, both existing and not existing, and that the political significance of both conditions to the Internet and its citizens must be taken into account. This relationship of this paradigmatic instance of dual but simultaneous identity—not quite hybridity—to either post-modernism or to postcolonialism is yet to be fully developed.

Notes

1. Howard Rheingold, *The Virtual Community: Finding Connection in a Computerized World* (London: Secker and Warburg, 1994) p. 84.
2. Richard J. Smith and Mark Gibbs, *Navigating the Internet* (Carmel, Ind.: SAMS-Prentice Hall, 1993) p. 7.
3. Smith and Gibbs, p. 7.
4. See the map in Ed Krol, *The Whole Internet: User's Guide and Catalog,* second edition, Nutshell Handbooks (Sebastapol, Cal.: OUReilly, 1994) p. 490.
5. Bruce Juddery, 'AARNet Users to Pay from Next Year', *Campus Review* 14–20 (April 1994): 1, and 'Internet Explodes', *Sydney Morning Herald,* 29 August 1994, p. 49.
6. This too had happened with ARPANet with the setting up of a list for discussions about science fiction, SF-Lovers, and it was found to have the effect of fostering a sense of shared culture (Rheingold p. 77).
7. Rheingold, chapters 5 and 8 cover MUD sites and the French network in some detail.
8. The SF-Lovers list on ARPANet ran into trouble because it was considered an inappropriate use (Rheingold p. 77).
9. Information about the EFF, including its mission statement, is readily available from its ftp site at eff.org. Information about its offshoots is held at the same site under/pub/groups/[Canada, Australia, etc.]. A listing of all (not just EFF-affiliated) groups supporting the online community is available under /pub/groups/outposts.faq.
10. The latter is much favoured by *Wired* magazine.

11. As in the Merit Network's computer-based tutorial, *A Cruise of the Internet*, version 2.2 (April 1993), introduced with a drawing of a 30s ocean liner. This is available by ftp from nic.merit.edu under/ internet/resources/cruise.
12. Seen in a posting to a USENet newsgroup, alt.binaries.pictures.tasteless, under the title 'Can't We End These Porno Newsgroups?' earlier in 1994.
13. 'Open Letter', a posting from Doctress Neutopia, to the USENet newsgroups, alt.pagan, alt.activism, alt.censorship, 18 May 1994.
14. Kevin Kelly, 'The Hypeway: A Wired Worker Provides a Guide to the Digital Realm', *Guardian*, reprinted in *Gazette* (Montreal) 25 June 1994: B1-2.
15. Seen in 1994 in a posting signed with a woman's name to a USENet newsgroup, alt.binaries.pictures.tasteless, along the general lines that the Internet provides an opportunity for women to visit a virtual sex shop anonymously and safely, rather than having to expose themselves to physical danger in the frequently unsafe urban locations of actual sex shops.
16. Krol uses this simile in discussing the governance of the Internet, p.16.
17. This is the metaphorical foundation of Rheingold's book.
18. John Schwartz, 'Cyber Citizens are Bringing in the New World Order,' *Washington Post*, reprinted in *Sydney Morning Herald* 18 July 1994, p. 46.
19. Smith and Gibbs, p. 17.
20. Krol, pp. 495–96. Krol discusses export restrictions on page 37. The NSF policy is available by ftp from nic.merit.edu under/nsfnet/ acceptable.use.policies/nsfnet.txt.
21. Krol, p. 40.
22. Krol, p. 18.
23. Rheingold, p. 215. Our account of developments in France and Japan derives from chapters 7–8 of Rheingold's valuable book.
24. Rheingold, p. 216.
25. Electronic Frontier Foundation and Stanton McCandlish, 'International, National, Regional and Local Groups Supporting the Online Community', version 3.13 (8 April 1994). Available by ftp from eff.org under pub/groups/outposts.faq.
26. An edited text of the speech appeared under the title 'PM: We Need to be there to Lead Australia into the Next Century' in the *Sydney Morning Herald* 27 September 1994, p. 11.
27. Senate Select Committee on Community Standards Relevant to the Supply of Services Utilizing Telecommunications Technologies, *Report* (Canberra: Parliament House, May 1993) p. 30.
28. Paul Conroy, 'Call to Restrict Access to Computer Porn,' *Age*, reprinted in *Sydney Morning Herald* 18 July 1994, p. 2.
29. 'A Case of Violation: Karla Homolka, the Internet and the Presentation of the Unspeakable,' paper presented at the Law and Literature of

Australia Annual Conference, Queensland University of Technology, 30 September–2 October 1994. There is a full discussion of the case by Frank Davey in *Karla's Web: A Cultural Investigation of the Mahaffy-French Murders* (Toronto: Viking-Penguin, 1994).

30. Quoted. in R. v. Bernardo, (1993) O. J. no. 2047, Action no. 125/93, Media Ban, paragraph 117. The text of the ban, divided into numbered paragraphs, is available through the Internet from a web server in Indiana at URL http://www.cs.indiana.edu/canada/karla.html. This site also has other material relating to the case.

31. Quoted in D'Arcy Jenish, 'Unspeakable Crimes', *Maclean's* 19 July 1993, p. 4.

32. Charles Trueheart, 'Canadians Debate New Curbs on Speech, Press', *Washington Post* 31 January 1994.

33. As at least one American news editor commented, the geographical proximity of his readership to the region patrolled by Homolka and her husband required that he publish the banned information (whatever the quality of his sources); if details leaked into Canada, this would be regrettable but could not be a primary consideration.

34. The 'Paul Teale/Karla Homolka Frequently Asked Questions List (FAQ)', version 3.0 (10 June 1994), a transcript of the *A Current Affair* segment and the *Sunday Mirror* article (mentioned below) are all available from the Indiana web server.

35. 'The Paul Teale/Karla Homolka Frequently Asked Questions List (FAQ)', 3. c.iv.

36. Tim Miles, 'Killer Ken and Barbie's Video of Horror', *Sunday Mirror* 19 September 1993.

37. Anita Susan Brenner and B. Metson, 'Paul and Karla Hit the Net', *Wired* April 1994, p. 28–9.

38. Taara Eden Hoffman, 'Cyberspace Cannot Be Censored', 23 March 1994. Available online from *Wired* at URL http://www.wired.com/Info/Homolka/canada.ban.pr.html.

39. K. K. Campbell, 'A Walk on the Wired Side: U.S. Mag Fails to Grasp Finer points of Homolka Press Ban', *eye WEEKLY* 31 March 1994. Available online via gopher from ee.mcgill.ca/11/community/efc/events/wired.

40. The author in this case is believed to be Dr. Joe Baptista.

41. Tom Buckham, 'Canadian Journalists Say Document Detailing Homolka Trial, Murders is Hoax', *Buffalo News* 12 April 1994. Available online from the Indiana web site.

42. Internet/Usenet Survey Report, presented at the annual meeting of the American Political Science Association in New York City, 1–4 Sept. 1994, and posted by co-author Michael Margolis to eff.org.

Voice, Space, Form:
Roja (Maniratnam, 1992), Indian
Film and National Identity[1]

Ravi S. Vasudevan

An introduction to the Indian cinema as a site for a postcolonial imagining of identity could begin with some of its 'national accomplishments'. It could dwell on the way in which, since the dawn of the talkies in 1931, the Indian cinema was able to withstand the competition of Hollywood cinema[2] and develop into what is currently the largest film industry in the world. This commercial cinema has generated a number of distinctive genres, such as the devotional film, which sought to reproduce traditional forms of worship with democratizing implications. It also exhibited identifiable stylistic peculiarities and choices.[3] Outside the mainstream, India's art and avant-garde practices carved out a niche in international exhibition as a vehicle of an authentic national expression which at the same time could satisfy international canons of good cinema.

As with all such enumeration of 'national' virtues, such a gestural listing would cover over more than it reveals. It would skirt the problem of the way in which subjectivity was constructed in interactions with the narrational peculiarities of other (international) cinemas, and with indigenous art forms. To take an example, the 1951 International Film Festival of India exhibited work of the Italian neo-realist cinema, and this event had resonances of a very different sort in commercial films, the emergent art cinema, and, for want of a better term, a kind of intermediate practice. Appropriate examples of these three streams would be *Boot Polish* (Prakash Arora, Bombay, 1954), produced by the key Indian film-maker, Raj Kapoor, *Pather Panchali/Song of the Road* (Satyajit Ray, Calcutta, 1955) and *Do Bigha Zamin/Two Measures of Land* (Bimal Roy, Bombay, 1953), a Bombay film which employed realist *mise-en-scène* and narrative strategies within the larger melodramatic conventions of the commercial cinema. These different types of cinema were all self-conscious of the neo-realist movement, and sought to absorb it into the familiar tropes, narrative and performative resources and aesthetic ambitions of an Indian cinema, multiply conceived.[4] However, in a certain tradition of Indian film criticism these different practices were then hierarchically organized into a regime of cultural distinction. Ray's film was deemed superior to the others in the canons of international and national criticism, and within the national field, the director claimed his vision of cinema generated more authentic representations of India than the popular cinema.[5] The plurality of the dialogue with the international was therefore subjected to a nationally hierarchized exclusivism. Of course, it was more than that as well. The art cinema discourse also attempts to figure, programmatically and perhaps narcissistically, a spectator better suited to the perceived goals of an independent and socially dynamic India, virtues not only of authenticity, but also of a realist disposition and, more fundamentally, of a reality orientation. Thus what was set in motion was a politics and sociology of the spectator of popular cinema, one which subtly denigrated his or her capacities as a *citizen*.[6]

The idea of a single Indian cinema is also complicated by the fact of its multi-regional nature, something which the notion of the world's largest film industry obscures. This image is often identified with the Hindi commercial film produced in Bombay, now often referred to as Bollywood, as if in derision of its ineffectual mimicry of north American commercial cinema. In fact, the Hindi film market has been supplied by a number of industrial centres across the country. In the 1930s and 1940s, in studios in Calcutta and Pune as well as Bombay, films were produced in both a Hindi version and in the languages of the 'regions' which, after independence became the federal states of West Bengal and Mahrashtra. Subsequently, the equivalence of national cinema with Bombay has become even more tenuous with the development of powerful industries in Tamilnadu, Andhra Pradesh and Kerala producing films in Tamil, Telugu and Malayalam. Although these linguistic markets have never outstripped the geographical reach of the Hindi cinema within India, and, indeed, have sought to cash in on that market as well, the volume of production of each of these industries is often more than that of the Bombay industry.[7] It is also notable that these other cinemas have often been at the cutting edge of the popular cinema, both in terms of technological change and narrative innovation.

Apart from the questions of regionality, another set of identities important in understanding the Indian cinema are those of community and caste. Whereas the question of caste hierarchy, and especially the questions of untouchability, have not had a significant representation in the Indian popular cinema since the end of the 1930s, the question of socio-religious community certainly has, and has been the object of radical concern. The overwhelming majority of the populace is of the Hindu religion, and the traumatic partition of India in 1947, which was accompanied by large-scale rioting and genocide amongst Hindus, Muslims and Sikhs, had a long-term effect on the relationship between religious and national identity. The Indian State officially denies any such identification, claiming a secular distance from all religions. At the level of political practice, this has increasingly involved the shoring up of the conservative dimensions of community identity amongst minorities for fear that any critique of these features would reinforce their sense of historical marginalization. In more recent times, the State has proven ineffectual against, and sometimes covertly supportive of, a fascistic current which seeks to assert the Hindu identity of India against its multi-ethnic, multi-cultural features. One charge from the Hindu right has been that the State's minority strategy had a purely opportunistic rationale in the search for 'vote-banks' organized around the endorsement of reified identities. But vote-banks are also communities of interest, highly variable in their function, and have never been the monopoly of minority communities, or of any particular party. The Hindu right's mobilization of a 'Hindu vote' is a case in point, and has taken the minority Muslim community as its primary target. This threat has been particularly marked in recent developments centred around the destruction of a mosque at Ayodhya in Uttar Pradesh under the aegis of Hindu chauvinists.

In this essay I try to identify the significant elements of a national hegemony as it is worked out through the cinema, but also as they are held in tension with other currents which subtly pressurize the overall framework of that hegemony. I will do this by drawing upon a film which has excited considerable debate in left-wing circles recently. This is *Roja* (Maniratnam, 1992), a Tamil film dubbed into Telugu and subsequently into Hindi, which has been a great financial success at the pan-Indian level. The existence of the film in a number of language versions and the story's focus on Tamil and Kashmiri identity conjure up various issues of regionality and nationhood. This focus necessitates a certain preliminary filling in of the history of these states.

Very briefly, the Muslim dominated border state of Kashmir has been at the centre of the Indo-Pakistan conflict, both sides laying claim to this strategic territory. In recent times, there has been an escalation of militant and separatist sentiment within the state, leading to the marginalization and emigration of a significant number of Kashmiri Hindus. These developments fed into the majoritarian Hindu chauvinism I have described, its protagonists seeing the separatist movement as Pakistan-instigated, as based on a 'fanatical' Muslim nature, and as more generally emblematic of the marginality of Hindus in India because of the alleged 'appeasement' of minorities. It is argued that Hindu 'tolerance' and the weak-kneed secularism of the postcolonial State have encouraged Muslim conservatism and political aggression. Apart from the quite fascistic nature of the argument, it fails to take into account a particular problem, that of the brutality of the Indian army in its dealings with the Kashmiri populace. This in turn has caused a popular resistance to the Indian State in Kashmir which has distinguished the present political phase from previous currents of separatist sentiment.[8]

As regards Tamil identity, from the 1920s, a movement espousing a rationalist, anti-hierarchical ideology, the Self-Respect movement, had developed a critique of high Hinduism and the caste system. In its subsequent incarnations as the Dravida Kazhagam and the Dravida Munnetra Kazhagam, it assumed a militant stance against the domination of the Hindi-speaking north over the local language and identity.[9] This movement settled into the political establishment by the end of the 1960s, the parties it generated forming State governments ever since. The linguistic tension between Tamilnadu and the Hindi-speaking northern states has varied in intensity. At the turn of the 1990s, the importance of a distinct Tamil identity was complicated by the emergence of an extremist and separatist movement from within the Tamil minority of the neighbouring island State of Sri Lanka. The ruling party of Tamilnadu at that time, the DMK, was supportive of the movement and averse to undertaking any action against Sri Lankan Tamil separatists working out of Tamilnadu;

and the Indian Government, led by Rajiv Gandhi, conciliated this sentiment. However, it was subsequently involved in a pact with the Sri Lankan government by which an Indian Peace Keeping Force was deployed in an unsuccessful bid to curb the violence. This alienated the Sri Lankan Tamil extremists from the Indian State and led to an extremist group assassinating Rajiv Gandhi in 1990. Subsequent Tamilnadu regimes have distanced themselves from Tamil extremism in Sri Lanka.

These two regional backdrops are central to our understanding of how nationhood is imagined in *Roja*. In the prologue, Wasim Khan, a militant leader is captured by Indian forces in Kashmir. The main body of the film opens with the song *Chhoti si aasha* ('Simple desires'), sung by the heroine, Roja, against the backdrop of what is the Tamil countryside.[10] The story then introduces Rishi Kumar, the urbane, Madras-based cryptographer (decoder) working for Indian military intelligence. He wishes to marry a simple village girl and arrives to inspect Roja's elder sister, Lakshmi, as a prospective bride. Lakshmi tells him she wishes to marry another, but is prevented by a family feud. Rishi chooses Roja instead, to save her family from embarrassment. Roja's resentment on behalf of the sister dissolves at Rishi's home in Madras, when he explains his behaviour and Lakshmi confirms his version over the telephone. The reconciled couple leave for Kashmir, where Rishi has to do a job of decoding for the military. In the film Kashmir is composed of locations from hill resorts in the northern state of Himachal Pradesh and from Tamilnadu. The couple's idyll is interrupted when the militants abduct Rishi to demand an exchange with Wasim Khan. A distraught Roja, incapacitated by her knowing no language except Tamil, takes the help of a palmist and wandering holy man, Chachchu Maharaj, to plead with police, army, and even Wasim Khan himself, for the return of her husband. The one army officer, Royappa, she can talk with, is strongly against such a deal. The forces of the Indian State will not at first accept the exchange, but seem to finally succumb to Roja's emotional pressure. In the meanwhile, Rishi expresses a staunch nationalist determination in the face of extreme militant brutality, but also a desire to convince the militant leader, Liaquat, of the inhumanity of his enterprise. Coincidentally, Liaquat can speak Tamil because he studied in Coimbatore, a dynamic industrial centre of Tamilnadu. Liaquat's sister is a silent, anxious presence, clearly disturbed by Rishi's suffering. She and Liaquat are both grief stricken when their younger brother, sent to Pakistan for training, is killed by Pakistani soldiers. Subsequently, the sister releases Rishi. Rishi's only obstacle now in his headlong rush to freedom is Liaquat. But the earlier exchanges between the men, and the death of Liaquat's brother are meant to have 'humanized' the militant, and he lets Rishi go. The hero is reunited with Roja who, emotionally overwhelmed, falls at his feet, caressing his wounds, as the military officer, Royappa, and the holy man, Chachchu, look on with relief.

From this summary, we may observe the way in which the film elaborates a series of differences defined by identities of region, language, gender, community and nation. It is the film's work to neutralize the range of differences which it posits through an investment in ideologies of nationhood, humanism and modernity. The power-laden implications of this exercise have been outlined by Tejaswini Niranajana,[11] and Rustam Bharucha.[12] They argue that *Roja* demonizes the Kashmiri militant as a Muslim fundamentalist, that it idealizes the modern middle-class Hindu male as the fount of a committed and developmentally dynamic nationalism, and that it neutralizes or at best appropriates the woman into this larger project. I consider this analysis persuasive but will argue that it glosses over the points at which such ideological orientations stumble and falter in the process of story-telling.

We can think of the space of the fiction as being composed of four areas, the Indian side of Kashmir, the mobile militant space, the Tamil countryside and the city of Madras. What happens in the film is that Roja's desire to touch the sky, to bind the cosmos within herself (images from the song, *Chhoti si aasha*), is refashioned, and a boundary placed around it as she comes to understand that she inhabits the political space called India. Her objective is to recover her husband, to bring him back into this (for her) newly identified space. Earlier spaces are still pictured and coalesce through the narrative function of communication media, telephone and television, into a new, national simultaneity.

If nuclear patriarchy and the nation state provide the coordinates within which Roja functions, the figures of the militant and the woman endanger their stability. In the introductory song sequence Roja is presented as an energetic character unburdened by household or occupational responsibility, a pre-adult figure, but with definite attributes of desire of an excessive, undefined nature. Her investment in Rishi's marrying Lakshmi is akin to a projection of her own undefined desires, and it would appear marriage provides her with definition. This marriage is not a conventional arrangement, and the tenor of conjugal relations quickly shifts into a romantic, companionate one. However, the crucial narrative development of Rishi's capture is set up because Roja leaves the conjugal precincts for the innocent enough activity of seeking out a *mandir*, a Hindu temple. Her unannounced departure panics her husband, who rushes out with scant security and is thus made vulnerable to the militants. Roja threatens to exceed the boundaries delimiting nuclear patriarchy/nation state, first as adolescent, subsequently as transgressive married woman. This appears to jeopardize the narrative goal of the film, in so far as it rests on an investment in the definition of national boundaries. However, the discourse embedded in Roja's narratively influential move to the temple is not that of an acknowledgement of limits but rather an implicit drive for their transcendence. The 'innocent' religiosity of the devout Hindu girl, expressing a 'rustic' belief that the god of Kashmir is not different from the god of Tamilnadu, offers the Hindu religion as a framework transcendent of regional difference. Even more significantly, the movement is a function of spatial excess, resonant with the desire that the national space is not governed by points of danger or threat. In short, to use Kum Kum Sangari's phrase to describe the function of women whose agency is circumscribed by patriarchal authority and must gain their ends through men, there are the traces here of a rhetoric of incitement.[13] Roja's movement outwards is akin to an incitement of the hero to move beyond the limits set to civilian national life. She affords a way for the hero to enter dangerous spaces to enable a vision of reconciliation with the Kashmiri/Muslim extremist, the basis for a future emotional reintegration.

The symbolic significance of the temple indicates that the terms of a future reintegration are figured as Hindu. Of course, the logic of narrative incitement is not worked out as an aggressive reintegration, in the manner of reconquering lost space, but, inevitable in the strategy of a consensual hegemony, as a humane resolution achieved through persuasion. Also, it is not my point that these are the only terms on which identification is activated. Indeed, the woman in the film becomes a kind of tabula rasa traversed by a variety of fragmentary identities, and the stage for a series of incommensurable positions.

Roja cannot do anything except plead with the police and the military. At one level, it is symbolically important that she stay on 'this' side, within the national boundary. Hereafter, whenever she moves in the direction of the militant camp, she is accompanied by the army. The latent discourse is the highly conventional one of the virtuous woman, the linchpin of familial and national rectitude, who must not move outside the precincts of the home/the nation state. However, this constraint is transcended in the organization of images. Roja's incapacitation is succeeded by shots of a television news broadcast informing the original village community and Rishi's mother in Madras of the kidnapping. The binding into a national simultaneity[14] of a community composed of the anxious images of village and mother presents the narrative context for a transformation of the State into an institution that nurtures and cares rather than one driven solely by a mechanical efficiency. The incapacitated community delegates its function to Liaquat's sister 'on the other side', who is introduced immediately after these images. This delegation is reiterated more physically and locally as Roja, now accompanied by Royappa and his men, glimpses the sister, and there is a significant exchange of looks between them. It is the sister, of course, who achieves the goals inaugurated by this narrative move when she releases Rishi, thus questioning the terms of the hostage exchange, and indicating her estrangement from the militant method. The displacement and doubling of Roja protects the Indian woman from the contamination of transgressed boundaries, but it also provides the crucial function of female nurture. This duplicitous scenario of 'female doubling' is a fairly typical maneouvre of the commercial cinema in India when it has to circumvent the moral boundaries it places around its ideal women characters.

The functions of female care are not simply aligned, in a subordinate fashion, to the ideal of a nationalist-humanist rationality as represented in the figure of the husband, and the spectacular dynamism of the Indian army. If the Kashmiri woman, Roja's double, refuses the terms of the militant method, Roja, despite her alignment with the symbols of a latent Hindu nationalism and her voicing of its common sense majoritarian rhetoric at one point, is also the vehicle for quite another figuration of identity. This is to do with a politics of identity grounded in the film's symbolic use of language.

In their concern with *Roja*'s identification with a Hindu middle-class led dynamic of modernity, the film's critics highlight the hero's use of English in both language versions.[15] Such analysis fits with the crystallizing image of Maniratnam as a film-maker who attends to the modern 'Westernised' components of the middle-class.[16] This is a problematic position, for *Roja*'s success has been substantial, far beyond this restricted social domain. Clearly the film's use of English has not alienated this spectatorship. While certain phrases used by the hero indicate a conversational idiom, others are hardly indicative of a great familiarity with the language. Finally there are a string of words which conjure up the mystique of State and public order, terms which are also the focus of public knowledge and anxiety. 'Security' and 'curfew', tersely invoked by the technocrat hero do not require a 'Westernized' viewer for their deciphering.[17]

The image of the modernizing middle-class is foregrounded as the fulcrum of narrative resolution, and therefore of national identity. But there is a wider *address* in the film. The English language as the mark of Rishi Kumar's urbanity is both a focus for 'style' identification, but also potentially for the suggestion of a cultural alienation. In a scene in which Rishi Kumar introduces his wife for 'security clearance' he is brushed off by his elderly boss who welcomes Roja through references to a shared village culture. In regard to the question of identification, we then need to think of an interlocking chain here rather than a solitary point in the position of the hero.

In the politics of the film's use of language, the heroine occupies a crucial position. When Madhoo, the actress who plays Roja, was asked why she had not made many films she reacted quite strongly, emphasizing that she had a substantial career in south Indian films,[18] though she only started her Bombay career with *Phool aur Kante/Flowers and Thorns* (Kuku Kohli, 1992).[19] The suppression of information about another space, the south, provides us with an appropriate framework to assess *Roja*. Most of the critics have referred to the original Tamil version as essentially equivalent to the dubbed Hindi one. But in the original version, language functions to highlight differences of identity which are entirely suppressed in the Hindi version: the protagonists come from Uttar Pradesh, not Tamilnadu. Uttar Pradesh, the populous north Indian state, has been at the centre of national politics since the 1920s, and has produced all but two of India's prime ministers. As I have pointed out, in contrast Tamil identity has often been self-consciously marginal, even oppositional to the pan-Indian one, and so this dubbing constitutes a very significant elision indeed. The logic of the national market here is one of linguistic and political levelling. This is not to suggest that the original *Roja* encodes an 'authentic' Tamil culture, something which only Tamil speakers and scholars can evaluate. Indeed, there is already a process of 'hegemonization' in the social narrative of the marriage, suggesting to some commentators the matching of an urban élite non-Brahmin with a woman from a socially lower rank.[20] What I want to draw attention to is the act of appropriation involved both in the dubbing and in the restriction of the analytical focus to the Hindi version.[21]

In the original film, language is not expressive of a restricted geography, of a communication predicated on the particularity of place, but is the function of a space of a supra-local intelligibility. By having Liaquat graduate from Coimbatore the hero can communicate with him in Tamil, and can thereby claim the cultural space of the nation for the language. On the other hand, for Roja, placed within the confines of a domestic and instinctual discourse, the Tamil language works to exclude her from the larger nationalist outlook. This pattern of exclusion may be productively linked with the heroine's difficulties in communicating with the representatives of the Indian State. The anxiety attached to this inability brings an imperative of everyday emotions and desires to bear in the narrative. Thus, when the colonel, Royappa, speaks with her, there is no language block, but there is a difference in discourse, that between the nation's interest and the individual's. In contrast, when Roja pleads with a central minister to save her husband, he signals his interpreter to be quiet at a crucial point because the language of emotion has broken through. Narratively, this proves decisive in shifting the axis of the State towards the human needs of the domestic and the everyday.[22]

But if on the one hand the woman deepens the imaginary of the nation state, there is a point at which her placement and expression reiterate another quite contrary trajectory. There are stereotypical invocations of a popular nationalist discourse in Roja's outlook,[23] but the overall subordination of State to the intimate emotions of conjugal loss and recovery in her coincide with regional identity. The plotting of a logic different from that of the nation state is thus coloured with a resistance echoing with earlier definitions of the Tamil relationship to India. This is where the film bears the residual traces of a still contentious outlook on the nature of the Indian State, if as an inertial presence, rather than as an active element in the narrative. The film can at one level be seen as a kind of sublimation of the Tamil identity into the Indian one, as 'an exorcism of the collective guilt felt by Tamilians over Rajiv Gandhi's assassination'.[24] But ironically the

162

identity which the narrative seeks to sublimate comes across as incommensurable with the rationality of the nationalist self. This is not to argue that Maniratnam has intentionally created this ambivalence, but that in labouring to transform the text of Tamil identity into that of an Indian one, the film came up against a symbolically intractable edifice.

Roja then demonstrates contradictory features at the level of representation which provide us with an understanding of the difficulties involved in the construction of a national identity. These difficulties are reflected in the way in which spaces are put together, and the way subjectivities are narrated in the filmic text. As I have noted, certain places referred to in the film as 'Kashmir' or 'the Tamil countryside', are actually composed of other places, making the pro-filmic a compound of displacements. However, these displacements can also put different types of desire into play. Kashmir was formerly the favoured setting for romantic escapade in the popular Bombay cinema. The political impossibility of shooting there now remaps the romantic imaginary as a fabrication. The gap between the physical and narrative referent exposes the crevasse between the desired emotional fullness—of romance, of the nation-state in its ideal form—and its realization. For Roja this is the romance of new identity, in so far as she enters new and unthought of spaces which 'fill' her and redefine her. But, in actual fact, there is a suggestive split in the physical referent. In the scene where Rishi introduces Roja to Kashmir, the film invests in vision, Rishi covering Roja's eyes, the camera tilting up the snowscape, in an exultant, revelatory way. But Kashmir here is Kulu Manali, the untroubled hill resort of Himachal Pradesh. Implicitly there is an equivalence and redundancy of such resorts in the film-goer/tourist imagination. If this aspect of the representation of contested space is not predicated on knowledge or recognition and the film-goer can still participate in the fiction of Kashmir, there is another location which is not so easily skirted. Certain key military scenes of 'Kashmir' were staged in Wellington, in the Nilgiri hills of Tamilnadu. The Tamil, and more broadly 'south Indian' tourist is likely to recognise this place, the Madras Regimental Centre and Staff College, located as it is *en route* to the major tourist resort of Ootacamund. This recognizability serves to relocate the drama of national integration in Tamilnadu, thereby echoing the larger set of drives, of Tamil identification with the pan-Indian nation, within which the narrative operates. This recognition underlines that in crucial respects the characters have not moved very far. In contrast to the locational absences and equivalences that elsewhere mark the representation of Kashmir in the film, in the employment of Tamil locales to represent this absent place, there is a certain over-representation of Tamil identity and place, making it the latent subject of the film. Of course, these features are elided in the dubbed Hindi version, as the non-Tamil audience is asked to see Tamilnadu as Uttar Pradesh!

Formally, *Roja* has been identified as reflecting a 'realist' disposition that addresses recent developments in the orientations of middle-class culture. In the 1970s the Indian Government's National Film Development Corporation supported social-realist films, as in the work of Shyam Benegal, Mrinal Sen, Govind Nihalani and others, that explored various topical issues of social exploitation, political and moral corruption. The realism of Maniratnam, in contrast, is privately financed and very much of the mainstream rather than the parallel cinema. Moreover, as Tejaswini Niranjana points out, its realism is oriented to celebrate middle-class modernity rather than develop a stance of social criticism. In its mobilization of certain devices of identification, a linearization of dispersed and disparate information into a character-centred, goal-oriented frame, the film echoes the methods of the classical Hollywood cinema. This form of spectatorial coherence contrasts both with the critical orientations of the State-supported parallel cinema, and with the particular omnibus, attraction-based elements of popular Indian cinema. In the latter instance, the main narrative line tends to be highly circular in its orientations, even if a 'secular' rearrangement of elements is achieved. Further, this line tends to be interrupted and dispersed by musical and performative instances that provide us with different locii to understand 'character', based not only on oppositions of the melodramatic kind, but on a series of con-trasting capacities and dispositions.[25]

In a sense then, we might assess *Roja*'s structural features as emblematic of the drive to orient Indian society to the psychic and perceptual needs of a dynamic national formation. In terms of these formal dimensions, however, there are certain elements which must give pause to the formulation that *Roja* represents a straightforward departure from earlier currents. The particular way this formal reorganization is used to express nationalism, as well as its distinct aesthetics of spectacular framing, undercuts a straight-forward linearization. Maniratnam clearly works with certain realist concerns, at the level of restrained acting styles, and a classicism of formal and narrative construction. At the same time however, he focuses on spectacular and performative dimensions which externalise thematics from their smooth anchoring within the flow of character actions and subjectivities. This is evident at a series of points in *Roja*: in the representation of the army, the might of the State; in the representation of certain aspects of the real, especially the narrative positioning of technology; and finally, in the expression and positioning of character within the formally and referentially overdetermined framework of the song sequence.

In the representation of the army, the film invests in a mode of display which is not always related to narrative causality. The investment is in the movement and display of the military institution, of the travelling camera, of the techniques of the stunt. While these features are yoked to the narrative of the hunt in the film's prologue, where the army track down and capture Wasim Khan, subsequent episodes of display have no such narrative pay-off. These scenes recall the type of motivations of spectacle associated with the ritualized staging of State power, as in Independence and Republic Day parades, except that the tableau form characteristic of pageants is here played out in narrative time. The realist citational aspect of the film, in which verisimilitude is sketched in by the background detail, also enables the highlighting of the State as a visual form, composed of the soldiers undergoing regimentation in a scene shot at the Madras Regimental Centre, Wellington.

Another narratively unassimilated feature is both the discourse and the narrative sequence relating to the hero's professional activity. A mystique attaches to Rishi Kumar's work, both as impenetarable verbal sign, as the village women stand bewildered when he informs them of his work, and as activity. Avowedly undertaking decoding for the military, his work is given no narrative context. We are not provided information about it that would make his activity goal-oriented and subject to deadlines, locking the activity into a hermeneutic unravelling of the narrative. Further, any expectations that his abduction is related to the militants' need for information only he can provide are swiftly belied. It would seem that any Indian national would have done, or at least any State functionary. Performing a negligible narrative function then, Rishi's work is primarily presented for our *view*. Posed before his monitor, and looking at a series of mathematical figures incomprehensible to us, this sequence fits into a larger tendency to figure the scientific as a compendium of mysterious signs, the preserve of a narrative agent whose specialist skills makes him into an élite figure remote from common or everyday knowledge and identity.

These alienations from narrative flow stand metonymically for a larger framing of the relations between State and subject, and the domain of science and the subject as they are relayed in the wider extra-cinematic universe of signs rather than within the film text. Inflected in the film by notations of propaganda and of mystique centred on an image of professionalized modernity, these scenes invite us to think of a different architecture of the film text, in which blocks of time hover in the space of the text, secure in their exemplary authority, but requiring other agents to mobilize affect on their behalf.

This particular regime of spectacle is much more complicatedly organized around the person and the body of the woman. In the song sequence *Chhoti si aasha*, the montage constructs Roja as body through choreography and interplay with natural textures, especially water. But she is also positioned as person when she is pictured in a number of social situations, especially of family life, but also in her assumption of public roles, driving a tractor, graduating from college, even taking on the garb of the patriarch. As some critics have suggested, the rhythms of body construction tend to fetishize both the woman and the countryside in the manner of the adfilm. However, the vivacity of the actress Madhoo's performance combines with the wider features of her social articulation in the montage to generate a highly condensed and dynamic narrative of the woman. This narrative is not so much an interplay between family life and a professional future; rather, it plays out the idyll of a tension-free negotiation of many roles. Structurally speaking, this sequence is as impacted as the foregoing instances which I have discussed, but it is fuller in its work of narrative condensation and it is, if only implicitly, in contradiction with the main narrative line of the film. This subsequent narrative constantly blocks dreams of a future for women that the idyll generated around Roja conjures up. Despite protests by the girl, her education is derailed by the parents' decision that she must marry Rishi to save the family honour. Subsequently, the high mobility that the girl exhibits has to be constrained by the dictates of territoriality, as I have shown.

Maniratnam has then modified the terms of popular cinema, sharpening its somewhat disjointed and disparate form of address

166

into regimes of spectacle, performance and narrative fragment that have a more articulate relationship, of development, antagonism and reversal, than is conventional. One of the features which might be said to distinguish its narrative form from the conventions of the popular is the way a certain didactic element, encompassing structures of rhetoric, dialogue and visual figurations such as the tableau, have been displaced from the expression of moral imperatives centred on the logic of family identity into that of political imperatives, representing the interests of the nation state. As I have suggested, this process of displacement and refiguration seeks out a number of spatial nodes, in the images of State and modernity, alongside the more conventional sites of articulation.

The drive for a certain type of integrity has been enabled by the honing of form through its articulation with the methods of classical Hollywood cinema, its regimes of subjectivity, linearity and its norms of balance in composition and editing. This interaction derives from a longer engagement, stretching from the 1930s,[26] and is part of the story of the Indian cinema as a key institution in the imaginary negotiation of modernity. I have tried to suggest how that story, rather than being an unravelling of a drive towards a coherent, formally integrated modern subjectivity, bears the imprint of other traditions and different forms of identity. Finally, and almost inevitable perhaps for a popular political project of this order, it generates space for a directive, hortatory function, a didactics of address which speaks as much of the need to cohere meaning as the difficulty of doing so.

Notes

1. This is a substantially revised version of an article entitled 'Other Voices: *Roja* against the grain', *Seminar* 423, (New Delhi, November 1994, pp 43–47). I would like to thank Radhika Singha for her comments.
2. The standard reference work is still E. Barnouw and S. Krishnaswamy, *Indian Film*, (London and New York: Oxford University Press, 1963; 1980)
3. Amongst others cf. Ashish Rajadhyaksha, 'The Phalke Era', *Journal of Arts and Ideas*, 14–15 (1987); 'Neo-traditionalism: Film as popular art in India', *Framework*, 32–33, (1986); Ravi S. Vasudevan, 'Shifting codes, dissolving identities: The Hindi social film of the 1950s as popular culture', *Journal of Arts and Ideas*, nos 23–24, (1993); and 'Addressing the spectator of a third world "national" cinema: The Bombay social film of the 1940s and 1950s', *Screen*, vol. 36, 4 (December 1995).

4. I have analyzed an area of common thematics for these films in 'Dislocations: The cinematic imagining of a new society in 1950s India', *Oxford Literary Review*, volume 16, (1994) pp. 93–124

5. Cf. Satyajit Ray, 'What is wrong with Indian films', *Our Films, Their Films*, (Calcutta: Orient Longman, 1976).

6. See my 'Shifting codes, dissolving identities', pp. 60–65, for a preliminary attempt to analyse this discourse and its political resonances.

7. For a recent survey, see Manjunath Pendakur, 'India', John A. Lent, *The Asian Film Industry* (London: Croom Helm, 1989).

8. For an account of recent developments, see Balraj Puri, *Kashmir: Towards Insurgency*, (Delhi: Orient Longman, 1992).

9. For the early phase of the modern Dravidian movement, cf. Eugene F. Irschik, *Politics and Social Conflict in South India: The non-Brahmin movement and Tamil Separatism, 1916–1929*, (Berkeley and Los Angeles: University of California Press, 1969); for a stimulating theorization of the overall thrust of these developments in Tamil politics see the work of M.S.S. Pandian, 'Notes on the Transformation of "Dravidian" Ideology: Tamilnadu, *c.* 1900–1940', *Social Scientist*, vol. 22 nos. 5–6, (May-June, 1994); and ' "Denationalizing" the Past: "Nation" in E.V. Ramaswamy's Political Discourse', *Economic and Political Weekly*, (16 October 1993).

10. It would seem the locations used are not always from Tamilnadu, but I have not been able to establish from where exactly they are drawn .

11. Tejaswini Niranjana, 'Integrating whose Nation? Tourists and Terorists in *Roja*', *Economic and Political Weekly* (4 June 1994) pp. 79–82.

12. Rustam Bharucha, 'On the Border of Fascism: Manufacture of Consent in *Roja*', *Economic and Political Weekly* (4 June 1994) pp. 1390–95.

13. Cf. Kumkum Sangari, 'Consent, Agency and the Rhetorics of Incitement', *Occasional Papers on History and Society*, no. LIX, (Nehru Memorial Museum and Library, 1992).

14. For a now classic statement on the temporal and communicative framework of the imagined national community, see Benedict Anderson's *Imagined Communities: Reflections on the Origins and Spread of Nationalism*, (London: Verso, 1983).

15. Bharucha raises the question of the linguistic politics involved in dubbing but does not expand on it. 'The real politics of language in the film has been determined by its dubbing from Tamil into Hindi . . . the other political dimension of language in *Roja* is its uncritical, even "positive" use of the English language (which, of course, remains the same in both the Hindi and Tamil versions of the film). From the sweet banalities of "I love you" to the more professional use of the word "cryptologist", *Roja* reveals its openness to "westernization" which is part of its project of "development" in India.' Bharucha, p. 1395.

16. 'In quite a few of his films . . . Maniratnam has cultivated an audience primarily composed of the newly articulate, assertive and self-confident middle class . . .', Niranjana, p. 79.

17. For an interesting argument on the phenomenon of bilingualism in different contexts of Indian writing and speech, see Harish Trivedi, 'Literary bilingualism and the linguistic hegemony in modern Indian culture', seminar on *Modern India: Terms of Discourse*, Indian Institute of Advanced Study, Shimla, May 23–27, 1994.

18. I use this umbrella term simply because of the easy circulation of films between Kerala, Tamilnadu, Andra and Karnataka through dubbing.

19. Interview on Times FM Channel, (21 August 1994).

20. Venkatesh Chakravarthy and M.S.S. Pandian, 'More on *Roja*', *Economic and Political Weekly*, (March 12, 1994) pp. 642–44, and discussion with M.S.S. Pandian.

21. Again, the Telugu version would presumably not have the same resonances as the Tamil one.

22. This is analogous with Helen Foley's comments on the place of the affective in ancient Greece: 'The emotional, domestic sphere cannot be allowed direct political power and the wife must subordinate herself to her husband in marriage; but the maternal or domestic claims are nevertheless central and inviolable, a crucial check on the bellicose male dominated democracy.' 'Sex and State in Ancient Greece', *Diacritics*, quoted by Laura Mulvey, 'Notes on Sirk and Melodrama', in Christine Gledhill (ed.) *Home is where the Heart is: Studies in Melodrama and the Woman's Film* (London: British Film Institute, 1987) p. 76. Of course the Indian State in *Roja* is not depicted in such excessive terms, and cannot be, for ideological reasons argued below; but the affective is shown to be a necessary element in the constitution of the nation state.

23. As when she asks Wasim Khan why he doesn't leave India if he doesn't like it.

24. Niranjana, p. 82.

25. See my 'The Melodramatic mode and the Commercial Hindi Cinema: Film History, Narrative and Performance in the 1950s', (*Screen*, vol. 30: 3, 1989), pp. 29–50; and 'Addressing the Spectator'.

26. See my 'Shifting Codes, Dissolving Identities' for an analysis of the combination of codes from Hollywood and indigenous visual culture in Hindi film around independence.

Tribes or Nations? Post or Fence? What's the Matter with Self-Definition?

Powhiri Rika-Heke

When I read about or hear about the collective groups of indigenous peoples who occupy various places throughout the world they are often, though not always, referred to as tribes. For example, the Indian tribes of the United States and Canada, the Aboriginal tribes of Australia, the Maori tribes of New Zealand. It seems that only those who are particularly sensitive to, in this instance, the power of the English language, use the term nation to describe these various groups of people.

According to the New Zealand Pocket Oxford Dictionary, 1990, a tribe is defined as the following: 'group of (esp. primitive) families under recognized chief and usu. claiming common ancestor; any similar natural or political division; (usu. *derog.*) set or number of persons esp. of one profession etc. or family (*the whole tribe of actors*)'. And nation is defined thus: 'community of people of mainly common descent, language, history, or political institutions and usu. sharing one territory and government.' As a matter of interest the same source definition of primitive is: 'ancient, at an early stage of civilization (primitive man) undeveloped, crude, simple (primitive methods).' I wonder why various power cultures tend to use such a seemingly, it appears to me, derogatory term such as tribe, to define peoples who are no longer the powered movers and shakers in their own lands?

Perhaps my reference for definition of these terms is not the most academic or even comprehensive, and may indeed be considered overly simplistic and naïve, but I would hazard to guess

170

that the majority of English speaking peoples who have access to dictionaries have access to one such as that which I have also used. It is also my contention that the definitions I have quoted here would fit the general understanding of most English-speaking peoples. My experience of the written word, and even the spoken word, in most Western cultures, is that it is more powerful than the fallout from a nuclear explosion the magnitude of those experienced on the Pacific Ocean atolls of Bikini or Moruroa.

In New Zealand, or Aotearoa as I prefer to call these islands and which I will continue to do for the rest of this article, communities of indigenous peoples who share common descent, language, history, political institutions and one territory are, more often than not, called tribes. Even members of these groups themselves sometimes use the term 'tribe' to describe their descent groupings. However, it is not surprising that the term 'tribe' has been adopted to describe large units of indigenous peoples because it is the word most commonly used by the powered institutions, not only in Aotearoa, but right around the world, and the indigenous peoples, in the main, have not thought about dictionary definitions of the word. I must confess that, before I began to really think about the power of words and the damage some can do to undermine people's self-esteem, their confidence, how they view themselves and even how they are perceived by outsiders, I also used the term 'tribe' with reference to myself and my people and to the other groups of indigenous peoples of Polynesian extraction, groups from which I am not directly descended but to whom I can make past *whakapapa* (genealogical), political, or historical links. At present, if I don't use the word *iwi* to describe our community and *whakapapa* groupings, I prefer to use the term nation which is, I think, a more accurate description as well as being a less judgemental and paternalistic one.

I will use, however, the post-contact term 'Maori', as a general definition to describe the various nations which are indigenous to the islands of Aotearoa. To most outsiders, the indigenous people of Aotearoa are Maori. But to use such an all-embracing term would be as accurate a description as describing all indigenous peoples of Africa as Africans, or all peoples of Europe as Europeans. The situation in Aotearoa is that we, as indigenous peoples, are only Maori to outsiders or to ourselves when we can't be bothered to differentiate and explain our differences. Amongst ourselves we talk of Ngapuhi, Ngati Hine, Te Aupouri, Te Rarawa, Ngati

171

Kahu, Whakatohea, Ngati Porou, Kai Tahu or whatever other nation group is being referred to. As you can see it would be inconvenient to individually list the many different nations which make up the indigenous population of Aotearoa, and there are many more than those I have named. So, for that reason as well as others which will be discussed later, I will, as stated earlier, use the post-contact popularized term 'Maori' to describe myself and my peoples.

As I use this term, I am also aware that my use of the category 'Maori' reflects the contradictions and struggles I and other Maori have about the words we use to describe who we are. The contradictions and struggles I experience with the term 'Maori' are created because it has been used conveniently and arrogantly by Pakeha (a New Zealander of European descent) to collectivize 'the Maori',[1] to somehow deal with our differences from them in the simplistic manner of constructed dualisms of savage and civilised, heathen and Christian, immoral and moral. John Rangihau, a renown scholar from Tuhoe articulated his suspicion 'that Maoritanga is a term coined by the Pakeha to bring tribes together because if you cannot divide and rule then, for the tribal people, all you can do is unite them and rule. Because they then lose everything by losing their own tribal histories and traditions that give them their identity.'[2]

Where once the term 'Maori' was used by Pakeha to denigrate and ridicule, the classic codification of colonial discourse, it has now been claimed as a title of honour in the same way that 'black' became a symbol of strength and pride for African Americans during the civil rights movements of the 1960s and 1970s. The term 'Maori' has also been utilized by its group members to affirm and enhance a Maori sense of separate identity from Pakeha, and some Maori have talked about our distinctiveness and our separateness in the most positive terms. For example, the Maori Bishop of Aotearoa, Whakahuihui Vercoe, when commenting about a Maori member of parliament, Apirana Ngata (Ngata, of Ngati Porou, was the first Maori to attend a New Zealand University, gaining an arts degree in 1893 and then a second degree in law in 1897, before being elected as a liberal MP for Eastern Maori in 1905 and becoming Native Minister in the United Government of 1928), said, 'He wasn't a politician. He was this wise Maori, talking knowledgeably . . . I never placed *him* in a Pakeha society.'[3] Eddie Durie, the Chairperson of the Waitangi Tribunal and Chief Judge of the Maori Land Court, writes 'there is definitely a separate

Maori ethos from a New Zealand ethos, a whole different world view. It's one we can be very proud of.'[4]

In Aotearoa I am seen, by the power culture, as Maori. But, while I acknowledge the move by some Maori to claim 'Maori' as a powered identity marker, I have my own difficulties in doing the same. My self-identity is positioned in relation to other *tangata whenua*, which literally means the 'people of the land', the other indigenous people of Aotearoa. To them and to myself I am not Maori. I am Ngati Hine, Ngapuhi, Te Rarawa, Te Aupouri and Ngati Kahu. I can also trace my *whakapapa* to Tuhourangi, Kati Mamoe, Ngati Kahungunu and Ngati Porou, though these links are much more tenuous because I was not born and raised in those *rohe* or districts. While I also acknowledge the white sheep in my closet and will never deny their existence, those connections are of less significance to me in Aotearoa because I am seen, not as either Irish or Scottish or English, or even German, but rather as Maori.

However, as an *Ausländerin* studying in Germany, as I am at present, I am identified, firstly, as a New Zealander and then as Maori. Strangely, I do not define myself as a New Zealander except when the New Zealand national teams are playing the British Lions in rugby, or the Australians in netball or the Pakistanis in cricket. At times such as those I am fiercely a New Zealander. But as a general rule the term has no significance for me primarily because it denies my Maoriness and that of my peoples. It ignores the fact that Maori people lived in Aotearoa long before it was 'discovered and claimed' for the Dutch by Abel Tasman or the English by James Cook. It denies the colonial history of betrayal and theft and the resultant establishment of a permanent underclass in our society which is too populated by Maori dispossessed of their cultural heritage, their language, their history, their land. No, New Zealander is not a label which has any real significance to me or my life except in the international arena. I mean, for example, I probably couldn't move through passport controls with a passport issued by Ngati Hine, which is the main nation with which I identify.

Before venturing into the arena of postcolonialism and cultural nationalism I'd like to tell you a story or three. You already know that the word 'Maori' is a convenient term which has been adopted to describe the indigenous people of Aotearoa. Did you also know that Maori people had occupied the islands of Aotearoa for aeons before the mainly British colonists started arriving and that, while some of my peoples trace our origins to Hawaiki, our Polynesian ancestral homeland, many others of us claim our beginnings from the very land of Aotearoa itself? For these nations and also, for the first 'boat people' of a thousand or so years ago, because of intermarriage and other interdependent alliances, we are all *tangata whenua*/the people of the land. We are of the land. It is our mother, *Papatuanuku*, our life sustainer. We need her. She doesn't need us though she was part of the plan which created our human-ness so that we could take care of her. She is the primary source of our cultural identity and our spiritual being.

While we, as Maori, can identify ourselves as particular nations according to the pieces of land we occupy we are, rather than nations as such, people who belong to the land in which we live and who are responsible for looking after her. Other people, other nations who occupy adjoining lands, do not 'own' their lands either. They are also the people who belong to the land, who have the responsibility of looking after her. Across the mutual borders, in times past, there were sometimes cultural exchanges, political marriages, reciprocal hunting and food gathering rights which were carried out according to the protocols which ensured the maintenance of harmony. We also had, and still have, laws, which came from the land, which were handed down through the generations in our story-tellings. Many of these laws which have survived to this day, have done so despite efforts by the colonials to make the people forget them. That's another story.

Around the end of the eighteenth century some people, mainly from Europe, but particularly Britain, as well as some of the British cousins from the United States of America, started treading the shores of Aotearoa. They didn't know our laws or even try to find out about them. They established their own laws which reflected different values and a different relationship to the land. They used words and concepts which we do not have in relation to the land. Words like 'legal title', 'ownership', 'trespass'. Their laws talked about one person owning the land. Their laws denied the existence of our laws which did not allow for individuals to own land but rather for individuals to be responsible for the land for the greater benefit of all the people. Their laws allowed them to 'buy' and 'sell' that which was not theirs to 'buy' and 'sell'. Some of the people who bought the land never even saw it. They didn't want the land for what it was but for what it represented on pieces of paper. They, and others like them, some who arrived to claim 'their' land, had pieces of paper which said the land was theirs and so they tried to make it so. And we, who lived on the land, who looked after the land so that she could look after us, we didn't have those pieces of paper and so the land was, according to the strangers, not ours any more.

In order for some Pakeha to feel that the land they claimed to own was theirs, they erected buildings, fenced things and people in or out, built roads all over the place. Signs declaring the land 'private property', 'trespassers will be prosecuted or shot' sprang up all over the land. But these outward trappings of ownership didn't make the land any more theirs, except on pieces of paper. It didn't change Maori spiritual or emotional ties to the land, it didn't stop us feeling obligated to the land, nor did it make us feel that the land would disappear simply because land title was not ours. The land remains, as does our connection to it which was formed in the aeons before the Pakeha and their systems tried to wrench it from us.

Even though many of us now live on the ancestral lands of nations to which we do not have direct *whakapapa* links, and even though other peoples, not of our own nation live on our ancestral lands, we are still responsible for that land which was gifted to us from our ancestors. Just because Pakeha papers say that the lands we occupy, outside of our nation borders, through Pakeha purchase is ours, doesn't mean that it is ours spiritually. It will always, no matter how long we occupy those places, 'belong' to the *tangata whenua*, the people who have a spiritual obligation to look after it.

At the moment, in Aotearoa, there are legal battles in progress about the Pakeha Government returning tracts of land which were stolen from the original inhabitants of the land. There are also negotiations in progress regarding the compensation Maori should receive for resources, such as, for example, fishing rights, which were also stolen.

Late in 1994, nearly 155 years after the signing of the 1840 Treaty of Waitangi—the international contract made between the *iwi* Maori and the British Crown which granted, among other things, peaceful settler entry to Aotearoa as well as the establishment of government, but also reaffirmed that Maori were guaranteed 'full exclusive and undisturbed possession of their Lands and Estates, Forests, Fisheries and other properties which they may collectively or individually possess'[5]—the chief negotiator for the Maori nation of Tainui signed a preliminary agreement to settle Tainui's land claim. This claim stemmed from the Crown's 'confiscation', though I would call it theft, of 1.2 million acres after British troops invaded Tainui territory in 1863. The agreement included, as well as an apology from the Crown, an acknowledgement of thanks to Tainui for their contribution to the development of the country, and the provision of a NZ$170 million cash settlement to enable the Tainui to buy further land. It also returned some 35,000 acres to Tainui. The fact that the lands confiscated and subject to claims have a current market of around NZ$12 billion is one of the many contentious factors which has some members of Tainui not only speaking out against this agreement, but even taking legal action to have it overturned.

While some Maori, as evidenced in the Tainui case, have become fiercely embroiled in the machinations of State policy making and also in the formation of State legislation, and are also endeavouring to put a price on the land so that the Pakeha Government can pay compensation for Maori lands alienated through past and present legalized thefts of one sort or another, it doesn't mean that all Maori agree with this way of settling past grievances. It doesn't even mean that all Maori, or even the majority of Maori necessarily recognize Pakeha sovereignty, or Pakeha notions of nation, or Pakeha law or any other Pakeha institutions, or even Pakeha title to the land or resources in dispute. It doesn't mean that we agree that land or other resources only have monetary value even though some of us decide to enter into debates about cash-measured compensations. It doesn't mean that all the rules invented by Pakeha power structures are rules that Maori will follow or that we will even play their games. It drives power cultures crazy when their adversaries don't play the games they invented, to the rules they designed to advantage themselves. And it makes power cultures even crazier when their opponents agree to play the game and then ignore all the rules, and, in doing so, win the games. There's a story in all this somewhere, but that will have to wait for another time.

It's interesting how words such as 'sovereignty', 'nation', 'ownership' can mean different things according to who is using the words and who has the power, and the situation in which they are being used. Power cultures tend to define and redefine words according to their whim. A Murri woman, a member of one of the Aboriginal nations of Australia, reminded me of some of the postulations of the British Government during the Falklands war, and again during the Gulf war. At the time of the Falklands war, Margaret Thatcher was Prime Minister. During one press interview she declared British determination to show the Argentinians that 'sovereignty cannot be changed by invasion'. Funny that. She also said, during the Gulf war, after she had been succeeded as Prime Minister by John Major, that she rejected the idea of negotiation with Saddam Hussein because 'there can be no discussion with someone who just goes and takes someone else's land. He has to get out. No matter how long he stays there, we will never recognize his right to be there.' I seem to recall that many Maori, as well as other First Nations people around the world have been saying the same thing about Britain and her colonists who invaded our lands.

And what about these ideas of postcolonialism, ideas of the hybrid, the syncretic and the ambivalent, ideas of a strategic or oppositional nationalism? Do they apply to Maori? Do they apply to Aboriginal Australians? Do they apply to the First Nations people of North America? I think not. I shall, nevertheless, proffer my layperson's understanding of what the term means to me. If the term 'post' means after, then 'post' colonialism must therefore mean after colonialism has ended. But for Maori, and I might venture to add, for many peoples throughout the world, there has been no end to colonialism. It is not part of our recent past and nor does it simply inform our present. Colonialism is happening now. It is our reality. No, colonialism is not a finite process which has now ended. We continue to live with the direct consequences of colonization. We, as Maori, have all been colonized to some degree, whether we like to believe it or not. We have been and, to some extent, we always will be. This isn't to be pessimistic, morbid or defeatist, rather it is to accept this reality and to see it and confront it. As L.Whiu puts it:

> And in meeting our realities *kanohi ki te kanohi*, face-to-face, we can construct processes which address the negative impacts of our colonization, rather than deny or euphemize the invidious impact of the colonizing process. Part of our constructive processes has been to try and safeguard some of our cultural treasures, to protect and nurture who we are as Maori, as *iwi*, as *hapu* or various clan groups within our respective nations. We have endeavoured to stand in our own space, as defined by us, and based on our ancient ways and philosophies, in order to centre *kaupapa* Maori, our Maori ways of operating.[6]

Linda Smith, writing of the necessity and strength of this cultural location, says 'kaupapa Maori upholds the validity of Maori views of the world and the potential of those world-views to add insight to the lives of Maori people and indeed to the lives of others who are engaged in similar struggles.'[7]

In the mid-1990s, amid international debates centred around postcolonialism and cultural nationalism, is Maori concern with questions of cultural identity our foray into the living out of cultural nationalism? Does it really matter who we say we are? Why do we want to protect or even foster our identity as Maori? Why must we nurture our Maori selves? Why, in fact, is our culture or our Maoriness, however we define it, under threat of extinction?

In validating ourselves us Maori, we do subsequently distinguish ourselves from Pakeha New Zealand. However, this is a necessary part of the creative process of reconstructing our selves whole. Our challenge is to weave the fragments of our colonized realities into an integral and dynamic whole, which reflects who we are as Maori, iwi, hapu; and not merely prescribing who or what we should be. This is not simple. How could it be? We operate within and with a Pakeha world view based on the destruction of our own. 'As such we must simultaneously uncover the external impact of colonization as it continues to invalidate Maori world views, while also exposing the contradictory perpetuation of colonization by these apparently Maori world views.'[8]

It is beyond dispute that our culture has and continues to be threatened by the enveloping waves of Pakeha-centred rhetoric reflected in the claims that 'we are all one people' or 'we are all New Zealanders'. As Moana Jackson asserts with regard to the imposition of Pakeha law, 'in effect . . . the notion of one law for all has simply come to mean one Pakeha law for all.'[9] Similarly, the claim that we are all one people or all New Zealanders in effect simultaneously ensures Pakeha hegemony while denying Maori identity. This rhetoric 'expresses our country's deeply rooted commitment to assimilation as a solution to complex relations in a heterogeneous society'.[10] That these claims to homogeneity continue to be issued reflects the entrenched nature of Pakeha cultural arrogance. This arrogance ensures that 'the descendants of the colonists continue to be utterly confident that their experience is real and simply commonsense. So much so that many say that there is no Pakeha "culture". It is taken for granted as normal.'[11]

Having realized the first two prerequisites of the process of settler colonization, that is, firstly by changing the population balance between colonizer and colonized, and secondly by imposing the institutions, laws and values of the colonizer, too many Pakeha colonists are now intent upon the need to attack, unrelentingly, any Maori initiatives or responses to both past and present, unfair and immoral Pakeha practices. Thus the 'we are one people, we are all New Zealanders' myth-making acts as a cover for the deliberate and concerted violence perpetuated in a cultural assault.

This continued cultural assault has also meant that current Maori protest over land and land rights, as in the instance of the 1994 Maori occupation of the Moutoa Gardens in Wanganui, has 'provoked' Pakeha impatience to turn to anger and retribution. Some of this retribution was evidenced in the torching of a Maori cultural centre, which was seen as an indication that some Pakeha may meet inflammatory Maori acts with equally fiery reprisals. The old hatreds, and I mean Pakeha hatreds, are resurfacing in 1997 and are seen as justifiable because Maori are refusing to recognize Pakeha law and seem to be getting away with it.

The extent of this action by Maori, and reaction by Pakeha, exposes the sinister reality of those ideologies which motivate and delineate colonization processes, processes which continue to be actively promoted in the insatiable quest by Pakeha to retain power and control over, not only themselves, but others they have contact with. Commentators have described this reality as eurocentric, white supremacy, cultural myopia, cultural denigration, cultural imperialism and neo-colonialism. Whatever we call it, our reality as Maori, as indigenous people of Aotearoa, is that our cultural survival continues to be threatened by the perpetuation of philosophies, policies and processes based on these ideologies. That threat will remain for as long as these philosophies exist in the minds, hearts, and ways of being, lived out by both Pakeha and Maori. Until we all grasp hold of who we are, proclaiming that to ourselves, to each other and to the rest of the world, we will always be susceptible to these attacks on our soul.

So what has all this to do with postcolonialism and cultural nationalism? Not much, but it will give you some idea about where I place myself as an indigenous person from Aotearoa who happens to write—poetry, short stories, the occasional journal article, 'academic' essays—but doesn't consider herself a writer, though that's one of the reasons I was invited to contribute to this collection of essays. It may also help you to understand that if I had talked about cultural nationalism as it is understood in a common academic context I would not have talked about patriotic feelings with reference to the New Zealand of the international community.

The cultural nationalism I would have referred to would have been that which the different Maori nations celebrate through all our initiatives, through our protests about Pakeha processes which continue to rape our souls and shred our hearts, through our comings together to sing and dance and laugh and cry, and through our pride in artists and writers from any of our nations. And I would have talked about the everyday struggles too many Maori have to meet in order to preserve our mana, our dignity and our sense of pride in who we are as *tangata whenua* in the face of a colonialism which has, whether consciously or unconsciously, more often than not worked toward our assimilation into Pakeha culture and our eventual demise and disappearance. Perhaps I'm being too harsh. Maybe we would have been wanted, and maybe are still wanted, to add the grotesque and exotic touch to museum displays. Perhaps we're still wanted to dance and smile for overseas dignitaries because Pakeha culture is so featureless that the Pakeha themselves really do believe that it is not worth sharing with powerful and important visitors from over the seas. Perhaps?

And postcolonialism? Well, whatever that particular theory is about, it has very little to do with me as an indigenous person, as a First Nation woman from Aotearoa who was born into a colonial society, has lived with both the positive and negative consequences of a colonial society, and who will die in a society which will go on colonizing me and my people and other disempowered peoples who choose to make Aotearoa their home because that is simply the nature of the beast. And that's another story.

Notes

1. See R.R. Pere, *Concepts and Learning in Maori Tradition*, (Hamilton: University of Waikato Press, 1983) p. 5.
2. J. Rangihau, 'Being Maori', in Michael King (ed) *Te Ao Hurihuri* (Auckland: Hicks Smith, 1975) p. 175.
3. W. Vercoe, 'A self-sufficient Maoridom', in Witi Ihimaera (ed)*Kaupapa New Zealand/Vision Aotearoa* (Wellington: Bridget Williams Books, 1994) p. 113.

4. E. Durie, 'Not Standing Apart', in Ihimaera, p. 18.
5. Article the Second, Treaty of Waitangi (English translation) quoted in Claudia Orange, *The Treaty of Waitangi* (Wellington: Bridget Williams Books, 1992) p. 258.
6. L. Whiu, 'Cultural Identity' (unpublished University of Waikato Law School Honours Research Seminar paper, 1994) p. 16.
7. L.T. Smith, *Mana Wakine–Mana Maori. A Case Study*, (Auckland: Maori Education Research and Development Unit, Education Department, University of Auckland, 1990) p. 2.
8. Whiu, p. 16.
9. M. Jackson, *The Maori and the Criminal Justice System–A New Perspective: He Whaipaanga Hou Part 2* (Wellington: Department of Justice, 1988) p. 265.
10. Ranganui Walker, *Nga Tau Tohetohe/Years of Anger* (Auckland: Penguin, 1987) p. 134.
11. I. Ramsden, 'Doing it for the Mokopuna', in Ihimaera, pp. 256–57.

Work-in-progress, from *Jonestown*. Draft 1994

Wilson Harris

This extract is taken from fiction-in-progress provisionally entitled *Jonestown*. The Longman *Chronicle of America* tells of the 'tragedy of Jonestown' and of the scene of 'indescriable horror' that greeted the eyes of reporters when they arrived in Jonestown in a remote forest in Guyana in late November 1978.

Questions are raised about the charismatic power of a cult leader to induce such self-inflicted holocaust.

This fiction possesses its trigger in such events but it is in no way a historical portrait. Jonah Jones, Deacon, Francisco Bone, Mr Mageye, Marie, the Medicine Man—who appear in this excerpt—are archetypal and fictional characters. They bear no resemblance whatever to living and dead persons.

Francisco creates a book of Dreams in order to break the severe trauma he suffers across the years in surviving the holocaust. He sees Jonestown as a recent manifestation of the enigma of vanished populations, abandoned cities, lost cultures in the Central and South Americas.

Francisco is affected by a strand in the ancient Maya civilization in which the linearity of time is breached in favour of a twinning of pasts and futures. As a consequence, Francisco's 'self-confessional, self-judgemental' book acquires what he calls 'past futures, future pasts'. These affect 'tenses' in his original narrative. Different generations and ages come into immediate juxtaposition in his *re-visionary text*. At the heart of the fiction runs an uncanny conviction, born of the labours of humanity, the apparently meaningless sacrifices and brutalizations that cultures have endured, that a numinous necessity exists to diverge from incorrigible unities of plot and place and character. Such a divergence brings into play subtle but far-reaching changes in the structure of time and, as a consequence, potential for an accumulation of archetypal motifs that may signify a hidden capacity in the Imagination to anticipate and by-pass 'inevitable' catastrophe, biased orders, or frames, or literalities that have been enshrined as the logic of fact and fiction.

Wilson Harris
26 September, 1994

The tragedy of Jonestown—or Jonah City (as I found myself calling it)—lay heavy on my conscience when the magical child Marie returned to Port Mourant hospital. She was naked, wet, dripping with the sea of rain in the Guyana savannahs through which she had run from Deacon. She had risen, it seemed, from the belly of the elements, land and river and sea. She was a pointer—within the trauma of conscience and Dream I suffered —into Jonah's whale of eternity, Jonah's shroud and sky and sun, Jonah's Jonestown in which I had lain on the Day of the Dead when the holocaust occurred.

I knew I had to weigh, with profoundest imagination, the foundations of cities, riverain foundations, falling or rising oceanic foundations, foundations in Plato's cave, in the cave of the Moon, light/space/earth-cradle foundations, in assessing the Day of the Dead under Jonah's whale of a sky. That sky dripped now its tears upon the Virgin body. Marie was a magical child, a wild runner of grace. That sky dripped through the leaking roof of the poor people's hospital upon the apparition of the Wheel of civilizations that she had brought with her. Hospitals and Ships are symbols of the globe. The sky dripped around the globe through the ceiling of many bombed villages and churches and homes.

I had joined Jonah Jones and Deacon in the 1970s in attempting to build a City of Eternity. A new Rome perhaps for South America. JONESTOWN. Jonah saw himself in the belly of the White Whale of American legend as a new Aeneas afloat upon coffin and cradle. I was one of Jones's carnival lieutenants. I played music on a Maya drum. I possessed five fingers then—when I played in 1978 in Jonestown—but in my resurrection backwards in time into Port Mourant and Crabwood Creek and Albuoystown in 1939 I was to find myself with three. For Deacon's random gunfire had blown two fingers away on the day he saved my life and shot Jones in the nick of time in 1978. I had given up all hope of survival when Jones pointed his gun at me.

Deacon occupied a privileged station—when we first began the construction of Jonestown—as the great evangelist's right hand peasant angel. No one knew but he nursed a fear of the loss of his soul after the death of his son Lazarus, the child Marie bore him in 1954. Marie was but a slip of a child in 1939 but Deacon, not much older than she then, had set his eyes upon her in the peasant world in which they were born.

I was not Utopian I knew in contemplating a new Rome at the heart of the rainforests since I believed the oceans would rise within generations and shake Guyana to its coastal foundations cemented by imperial adventure, plunder and piracy. The virgin Ship on which I sailed within chasms of creation would need to rise and sail inland . . . I was not Utopian I dreamt in contemplating a modest beginning in 1978, a modest settlement, an experimental nucleus of humanity numbering thousands at most . . . How many I wondered had inhabited the ancient ruins of Chichén Itzá and Tula when their walls first arose? Records had vanished. Population censuses in ancient America were problematical. Hieroglyphs remained which were untranslatable but a source of potency to empower every archetypal, fictional re-construction of the past in the present.

Whatever the others thought, my place—on Jonah's left hand in Jonestown—possessed the instinctive logic of the collective unconscious, collective ages secreted in the soil of psyche.

Every new foundation in the Americas, however small, however apparently diminutive, was cradle for giants of chaos, redemptive chaos, redemptive tapestry of Soul in which to rehearse capacities of unpredictable architectures of the future-in-the-present.

How does one build a new architecture out of the rubble of traditions and out of diasporas across millennia? I mentioned Chichén Itzá and Tula a moment ago. Another of the most ancient—now long abandoned—ancient cities in the Americas is Teotihuacan (which translated into English may mean *the place where the gods stowed away to sail into 'Moby Dick'* or (in my translation which is less indebted to hieroglyphs on ruined temples that blend into Ahab's doomed voyagers in space) *cradle and grave, stone-age epitaphs beneath which lie the bones of Marie's child Lazarus seeded into future ships and diasporas and resurrections.*

184

I cling to my translation, transgressive text though it is. It subsists upon holes in ruined Christian navies and fortresses erected against pre-Christian ages. I dream of an arch to the Beloved Virgin Ship through and beyond every Christian navy into the seed of pagan Soul, a numinous paganism available to us now—available to me—as I mourn the dead of the City of Jonah Jones crushed under the Wheel of Charisma within a one-sided, exclusive pact; I mourn with every magical child and every Sorrowing Virgin.

I had broken that exclusive pact—it was true—but so late I achieved virtually nothing, it seemed, except to save my own skin, when Deacon shot Jones, and to write this self-confessional, self-judgemental fiction with pen and lip covered, I feel, in the soil of the grave and the salt of the sea.

Marie's tears of rain (which covered her hair and her eyes) formed a pool that settled at her feet in the Port Mourant hospital.

A thirsty, panting dog arose from a dying man's bedside and dipped his tongue into the pool. He lapped the water as if it were blessed milk. He returned to the side of his master, a dying man whom the Doctor or magus Medicine Man—Marie's putative father—humoured in his last hour. I glimpsed his longing to depart with his dog at his heels through a hole in the Virgin's Wheel.

Diaspora signifies an exodus of peoples, a dispersal of peoples, even the flight of peoples. They swim pools of the Virgin, and lakes and rivers of God, they cross the Behring Straits, they mass against the Mediterranean, they scale mountains and cannibal horizons, they drown in oceans, they cross from Cuba and Haiti . . .

The conversion of *diaspora* into an experimental, sacramental witness of peoples drawn up from oceans, rivers and precipices, runs in parallel with the genius of an unfinished resurrection and with Marie's multi-form, multi-pigmented child Lazarus stained with all soils and places and ages: not only Palestine but Mexico and Teotihuacan.

I have no illusions. Jonestown caved in in 1978 under the weight of the holocaust, persuasive holocaust, mass-suicide that Jones advocated rather than surrender to the Roman/American Police, self-inflicted holocaust, age-old proclivity to reach for eternity's closure of time, end-of-time syndrome that the Reverend Jonah Jones preached to his flock. But I retained the thread of time when time seemed finished. Within the severity of trauma I retained a forward/backward thread or twinship of futures and pasts that was native to my Maya spiritual forebears. I sailed back upon a Virgin Ship from Jonestown in 1978 to Port Mourant in 1939 and further back still to ancient El Dorado.

I sailed into a poor people's hospital to re-visit, it seemed, the dying and the dead that I knew in Jonah Jones's doomed Mission!

Dying and dead who mirrored the living and the hopeful at the outset of the Jonestown Mission in 1978. The past arouses itself in Maya fictionality of truth when the uncanny terrifying future arrives on a twinship. Yes, fiction may breach linearity, transgress against linearity, to achieve an incredible counterpoint in the medium of time . . . What is time? Does time colonize the Imagination or is time an adventure forwards and backwards simultaneously in space?

Within such an adventure one has no illusions of superiority for one's pre-possessions and misconceptions tend to break into painful self-discovery, painful humility yet re-constitutive passion, insight, genius for re-entering the womb of plural generations . . . Resurrection is native to the womb.

The patients in the Port Mourant hospital in 1939 (when World War Two lit up flares across the Atlantic Ocean) may have seemed wholly divorced from Jonah's flock in 1978. They were different but they were a relationship of Carnival mirroring blood in feature and mask. They shared cherries of blood in hopeful mask or upon bitter despairing lip. They shared cherries of hope *in the apparition of the year 1978 when Jonestown was being built.* They shared cherries of despair *in apparitional hospital and grave in 1939* when they lay on their sick beds as if they had drunk the very poison that Jones's followers had consumed . . . Or received the self-same rain of bullets.

Each cherry—within the chasm of a generation, a century, a millenium—was a rounded thread I unravelled and inserted into a transgression of literal texts that Christ understood only too well, a transgression of absolutes, absolute individualism, absolute polarization of cultures, absolute individual glory, absolute imprisonment in tragedy, in favour of a re-visionary extensive architecture that begins to embrace all humanity or humanities in their arousal from passivity of text, hypocrisy of text, and the hollow grandeur of entombed libraries and establishments.

Was Jonestown (the doomed city of Jonah Jones as it looms for me now in telescopic yet cycling backwards Carnival Nemesis through Marie's Wheel in the poor people's Port Mourant hospital in 1939) a pointer after all into the misconceived foundations of cities, inner cities, Rio de Janeiro, flood-prone Georgetown,

Washington? Was it a slumbering Nemesis, did it call to us to rehearse a resurrectionary play as one sailed from the future into the rubble of the past? Was it subconsciously active in minuscule proportions of dust drifting to the stars in every bomb blast and from the rubble of traditions as these bore upon the future? I had sailed upon the Virgin Ship from Jonestown to Port Mourant. But something I did not understand yet, something inimitably peculiar, was involved in bridging again the chasm of a generation. I needed to take a weightless measure of *uncrushed* Spirit through the Virgin Wheel and unravel its levitation and its fall, its ascent and descent, into an experimental nucleus of humanity beset by hazards I had overlooked in 1978.

Such an experimental nucleus—such immersion in hazards that civilization needs to re-imagine—seems to me wholly necessary in the 1990s as one millenium draws to a close and another begins to open. I have been immersed in this self-confessional, self-judgemental Dream-book throughout the 1980s and into the 1990s and it is still incomplete. I know I shall not have finished it even when I dream I have finished it . . . Such is one's despair. Such is one's ecstasy.

'The unfinished Wheel is my father's gift to you,' said Marie. 'Even as the futuristic Camera is Mr Mageye's. The Wheel is God's gift to civilizations. And Carnival Lord Death has had to tolerate the mystery of the revolution, the resurrection, implicit in it.'

An astonishing utterance to come from the lips of a mere child. Had she spoken or had I dreamt it? She was still naked, trembling, water still dripped from her hair and eyes and skin, and I wanted to reach out and embrace her.

I had come from the Day of the Dead in Jonestown. I had arrived in a hospital for the living. I cross frontiers as the twentieth century draws to a close and another door opens in time.

Because of this—because if a peculiar, gravity/anti-gravity sensation inserted into tenses, past futures, future pasts, in every diminutive survivor—catastrophe possesses a *re-visionary* momentum in the Womb of space and I am sensitive to a prospective seed in Marie's peasant body, Deacon's prospective child Lazarus. He used to boast of such a seed in San Francisco even before he returned to Guyana to wed her in 1954. He used to boast and project the desire for such a son upon me! I was a surrogate Lazarus!

'I am not your precious Lazarus,' I would cry. 'I am Francisco Bone from Albuoystown in *La Penitence*, Guyana.' But he laughed.

'I challenge you to compose a cradle of fiction such as no one has written.' I shrank from him but he poked me in the ribs as if I were a Bone upon Jacob's ladder, a skeleton familiar with cradles and graves in heaven and upon earth.

I recall his boast and how he played at being my fictional father in San Francisco College when he and I—the recipients of scholarships that brought us to the United States from Guyana —met the American Jonah Jones for the first time in the 1940s.

'I am your bloody father,' he would say playfully and tauntingly. But I recalled the ghost of the Frenchman, the eighteenth-century slave-owner, who owned the estate *La Penitence*, and was also my father!

He shook his friendly fist in my face. 'I am a peasant angel Francisco Bone. I am the obscure but true folkloric father of the New World. Not your damned Frenchman.'

Deacon would laugh but Jonah Jones would knit his brow and strike the frame of the College in rage and annoyance.

'Nonsense Deacon,' he would say. 'You are not a true-blooded Puritan. I am the father of you and every other fucking bastard.' His rage would melt and he would laugh in Deacon's smiling teeth. It was a joke, a good joke—I would reflect—for a prospective evangelist and minister of religion.

'You Francisco, you Deacon—are my sons. Together in the Americas we will forge a strong pact and build a new Rome that's unlike the Pope's Rome. Troy, believe me, has been sacked and Rome or Berlin or Paris or London is addicted to racism and fascism. Fascism is the death of the Imagination. Imagination dead Imagine.'

I wanted to shout now to Jonah Jones 'Have *you* succeeded now in ridding yourself of the disease?'

I wanted to shout the question to him across a chasm of generations but my tongue froze and his ear for all I knew, was sealed. I wanted to shout within my own grave of memory—as though I too had died in Jonestown—as though I too lay on the sick bed of civilization in Port Mourant hospital—but I was a diminutive survivor and my voice was weak and small. I was jolted all at once within the shadows of time by the Medicine Man's voice. He was crying to his daughter as if he were close to me yet a far way off—'Marie, where have you been? Running in the savannahs again with invisible companions?' He was smiling wryly. 'I do not know their names but perhaps Mageye and Francisco are as good a guess as any. What shall I do with you Marie? You

188

will catch your death of cold.' He flung a towel around her and massaged her head and arms and limbs.

She seemed an astonishingly frail, beautiful child who would have been a princess had she been born in a palace in the kingdom of El Dorado.

Then the Medicine Man—who sometimes acted as a king—pulled a nurse's uniform from a cupboard and drew it over her head as if it were a cinematic, therapeutic screen or game, as if it were all happening in Mr Mageye's futuristic Camera.

The Voice on the lips of a child that I had heard before rang again in my ears—'The Wheel is God's gift to civilizations'.

I stood still as everything moved. Was I at the very centre of Fiction's Wheel as a diminutive survivor of holocausts, pageants, kingships, priestcraft, deceptions, promises, heart-breaking, back-breaking labour of common/uncommon peoples since the dawn of civilisation? The Wheel was God's gift to civilizations.

How then, I wondered, was it that the ancient Maya civilization and the ancient kingdom of El Dorado did not possess the Wheel?

'But they did, in a manner of playing gods and charioteers,' said the Virgin-princess of El Dorado. 'They possessed wheeled playthings and toys to run not only in the common people's hospital but in a princess's cradle. Toy chariots ran on wheels. Each chariot was loaded with a cherry that represented the promise of bountiful harvests and grain. My father, the king, used to stand on a platform and promise wonderful bread and circuses, chariot races and cherries sweet as cake. Taxes were reduced on the eve of every election.'

'Were there elections in the kingdom of El Dorado? That's good news!'

Good news always took one by surprise. And my heart was buoyed by the El Doradonne cherry. El Dorado had been a magnet for numerous Hollywood films, soap operas, alchemies to turn rich mud into poverty's gold. So easy to misconceive uncrushed Spirit that the Virgin-princess dangled before my eyes; and in such misconception to be tempted to seize it! No wonder she spoke in parables of ominous shape and pattern. No wonder she had appointed a knotted thread of blood in her cradle that runs into stocks and shares and golden lies of prosperity entertained by all races, all classes, all peoples. As much as to say 'you need to break the literality of a frame that you associate with my Virgin lips in order to see your own profoundest, creative, re-creative responsibility. Alas we educate ourselves to feel, to think, through frames

189

of language *that we have enshrined into absolutes, the absolute seizure of truth.'*

What is truth?

It is true that the cherry tree is a sacred tree in the kingdom of El Dorado.

It is true that the tree resembles gnarled, ornamental branches in a Japanese garden.

It is true that the sacred tree of ancient El Dorado may secrete itself now in mutilations of wood that we associate with Christmas trees.

It is true that the golden man or king of El Dorado broke the sacred tree and sculpted from it the retinue of his court, his civil servants, and labourers in the field who pulled blocks and stones with their bare hands to build his palaces and pyramids.

As such the tree was framed and ordained into a cult of unreflective humanity, a fixture and plaything of dynasties.

I could bear it no longer. I shrank from the Virgin's eyes, from the Virgin princess of a long vanished kingdom into which I had sailed within the Cinema of the Wheel.

'Doctor,' I cried. He turned to me from one of his patients in the hospital.

'Doctor,' I repeated. 'You are Marie's father. You are a magus. You are a king. You are a Medicine Man as the Arawaks and the Macusis put it. I do not really know who you are. I won't frame you I promise. I won't frame you into another biased God. Can truth be true or free when it becomes the servant of ruling misconception, ignorance and bias?

'Tell me please! I need to know of my own *numb* state, my own *benumbed* senses, my own trauma, my own ignorance.'

I held up my left hand.

'Mr Mageye had eyes to see in his class in Albuoystown. Do you *see* in this hospital? I am one of Marie's companions! Do you see with the eyes of science? Science has x-ray eyes.

'I lost two fingers when Deacon fired a random shot. The funny thing is I felt nothing at all. I was in a state of great shock at the sight of the dead bodies in Jonestown. Piled everywhere.

'It was not until I sailed back into the past that I knew I was different. A wound in my hand! I had lost two fingers. I knew when I touched a Carnival drum and sought to play! I knew in Albuoystown.

'Now I know again in Port Mourant. I know of my wound because I can relate this to the common people of a vanished kingdom who were broken on the sacred tree into labourers in the field. They did not know how broken they were, how manipulated, how wounded.

'They carried the trauma of a civilization. They were rendered numb by apparently meaningless death and sacrifice all around them. What is the difference between me and them?'

It was a prayer steeped in pathos—perhaps hopelessness—but the Doctor (from within a series of Carnival masks of deity so that he became a sick God, a healing God, a terrible God, a wise God, a loving God, a hating God, a dismembered God, a whole God) was able to respond. 'I am the mystery of space within all literal texts, all literal Gods, in this hospital. Space transgresses literality.' He was smiling or I would have been filled with dismay at such apparent hubris. There was no hubris however in the magus-Medicine Man or Carnival Doctor. Doctors were Gods in poor men's hospitals. And the Medicine Man's smile made me feel that I was known and accepted for the broken creature I was long before I knew of my own illness of Spirit.

'All wounds, all stigmata,' the Doctor said, 'carry a counterpoint in the orchestra of the ages. One knows yet does not know one's wound, so to speak, in some private mystery or theatre of music that animates oneself and one's unfathomable creator. One comes to know one's wound sometimes through the veiled or unveiled eyes of others, sometimes when one voyages back into the past and finds one is the same yet not the same person. One strikes an exquisite chord or lament in the orchestra of ages with a wounded hand. Then one knows one has returned to the past from the future! Strangest paradox of inimitable being and non-being, person and apparitional presence.

'You returned to Mr Mageye's classroom in Albuoystown and discovered you were the same yet not the same child he taught a couple of generations earlier. And, as a consequence, the parameters of time changed subtly. In the same token of fictionality's embrace of truth the gnarled labourers in every field—who are so benumbed they are unconscious of dismemberments they endure —will come abreast of these in some extraordinary recess of memory. The plot of civilizations—the apparently *unredeemable* structure of character and plot—is broken . . .'

Index